BAPTISMAL AND MARRIAGE RECORDS,
REV. JOHN WALDSCHMIDT,
COCALICO, MODEN KRICK, WEISSE-ICHEN LAND AND SELTENREICH.
GEMEINDE.
LANCASTER COUNTY, PENNA.

1752-1786.

TRANSLATED BY
LUTHER R. KELKER,
HARRISBURG, PENNA.

CLEARFIELD

Originally published in *Pennsylvania Archives*
Sixth Series, Vol. VI (1906–07).

Reprinted for
Clearfield Company, Inc. by
Genealogical Publishing Co., Inc.
Baltimore, Maryland
1996

International Standard Book Number: 0-8063-4659-0

Made in the United States of America

BAPTISMAL AND MARRIAGE RECORDS.
REV. JOHN WALDSCHMIDT, 1752-1786.

REV. JOHN WALDSCHMID.

1724-1789.

From Fathers of the Reformed Church, Volume 11, pps. 88-92, Rev. Henry Harbaugh, D. D., Lancaster, 1857.

John Waldschmid was a native of the province of Nassau, in Western Germany. He was born August 6th, 1724, and educated for the ministry, in his native land. When, in 1751-2, Mr. Schlatter visited that country, with a view of securing ministers for the destitute American vineyard, he was one of the six young men who volunteered to accompany him to the New World. With the rest, he was examined and ordained, at the Hague; soon after which solemn occasion, they sailed for America, arriving at New York in the night preceding July 28th, 1752; and thence went to Pennsylvania.

Soon after their arrival in Pennsylvania, Mr. Schlatter accompanied him to Lancaster county, and installed him as pastor over the congregations of Cocalico (since called Swamp), Weiseichenland (then called Sebastian Reicher's church), Modecreek, and Zeltenreich. From a notice in the Record-Book of the Cocalico church, we learn that he was installed in his charge October 22d, 1752. He administered the Holy Supper in that congregation, for the first time, November 19th, 1752, to seventy-two communicants; "after having, on the previous day, preached a preparatory sermon, and inquired in regard to evidence of their fitness for the reception of that ordinance." On the 26th of the same month, he administered the Holy Supper to sixty communicants, in the congregation of Weiseichenland; and, January 28th, 1753, at Mode-creek.

On the 14th of May, 1754, he was married, by the Rev. William Otterbein, to Mary Elizabeth, daughter of Christian Grub.

After Dr. Stoy ceased preaching at Tulpehocken, Mr. Waldschmid supplied that congregation two years, in connection with his charge, from 1756 to 1758. Some years later, he also preached, for a time, in the congregation of Heidelberg. His ministry in that church ceased in 1770, when they complained to Cotus that he was "a litle inactive, and neglectful of them;" after which, that congregation was joined with Reading. Whether there was just ground for this complaint, it is not easy to decide; we are inclined to think, that the distance he lived from the congregation, and their desire to be more conveniently connected with Reading, may explain it, at least in part. If this be so, it was neither the first nor the last time when persons saw faults in a minister, on which to build a justification of their own schemes. The long time during which this man of God labored successfully in the same charge, it seems to us, presents an argument, in favor of his efficiency, that far outweighs this incidental complaint.

Still, there was, at one time, also some dissatisfaction expressed by some in his own charge. In the Cotal proceedings of the year 1760, it is said: "In regard to the Rev. Mr. Waldschmid, it appears that his congregations are satisfied with his preaching; only they desire that he might be more diligent in family visitations, and more prudent in his general conduct." Tradition remembers him as a remarkably good-natured, mild, and easy man. With all his goodness, and devotion to the Church—of which there is no doubt—he may have needed, at times, the impulse of a special stimulus, to keep him moving with freshness, ministerial dignity, and pastoral earnestness.

As already intimated, he continued in the same charge to the end of his life. In the Record-Book, already referred to, we find the following touching entry, made by the hand of filial affection: "God, the Almighty, took our dear father out of the world to Himself, into a blissful eternity, on the 14th of September, 1786, between nine and ten o'clock in the forenoon. On the 15th, in the afternoon, at two o'clock, we committed his remains to the grave. The Rev. Mr. Boos preached his funeral sermon, from Psalm lxxiii, 23, 24. God grant that we may all come to where he is! Amen. The tombstone was erected October 6th, 1787; costs £7 and 2 shillings."

A circumstance, in connection with his tombstone, happened, about six years later, which was thought very singular; and which is not only traditionally remembered in the neighborhood, but we find a record of it in the Church-Book. On a Sunday, June 2d, 1793, while a large congregation was assembled in the church, listening to the Word of God, and when the winds were quiet, the tombstone of the Rev. Mr. Waldschmid suddenly broke off at the top of the ground, and fell flat upon the tomb. "Many saw it," says the Record, "and all heard it fall." The wonder, in connection with this event, was vastly increased, in the minds of the people, by the fact that Mrs. Waldschmid, who was demented, long before, and had not spoken a word for years, began to speak again with others, on that same day!

Mr. Waldschmid is buried in the graveyard connected with the church now called Swamp (in early times Cocalico), in Lancaster county, Pa. His widow survived him many years,

REV. JOHN WALDSCHMIDT—1752-1786.   151

and died July 12th, 1803. Besides daughters, he had two sons to perpetuate his name: one of them moved to the west; another, whose name was John, lived and died in the Swamp, on the farm where his father had resided, several miles northeast of the church. One of Mr. Waldschmid's daughters was the mother of the two Revds. Gring, who are still laboring in the ministry, in the German Reformed Church. On his tombstone is written:

"Hier ruhet in Gott
der
Ehrw. Johannes Waldschmidt,
Geb den 6 August, 1724.
Ins Predigtamt verordnet 1752.
Starb den 14 September, 1786,
Alt 62 Jahre, 5 wochen, 4 Tage."

BAPTISMAL AND MARRIAGE RECORDS,

REV. JOHN WALDSCHMIDT,

COCALICO, MODEN KRICK, WEISSE-
ICHEN LAND AND SELTENREICH.
GEMEINDE.

LANCASTER COUNTY, PENNA.

1752-1786.

TRANSLATED BY
LUTHER R. KELKER,
HARRISBURG, PENNA.

IN NAHMEN GOTTES. AMEN.

Dieses Buch ist Verchret worden von den Herrn Hollandern, damit darin die Junge Kinder, getauff auch gezeuchret wurden, von 4 gemeinden, Cocalico Moden Krick, Weisseichenland or Seb. Reyger's Kirch, und Seltenreich, mir Johannes Waldschmidt als Pfarrer der 4 gemeinde von Hr. Schlatters ubergeben zu Langaister der 25, 8 bris 1752, nach deme den 22 8 bris, 1752, ein gesetzet word von ihm.

AACHE—Sophia Loisa, d. Gorg; b. ———; bap. Feb. 10, 1755; sp. Sophia Loisa Amweg.

AACHE—Catharina, d. Johannes & Anna Maria; b. Mch. 2, 1773; bap. Apr. 4, 1773; sp. the Parents.

AACHE—Peter, s. Johannes & w. Maria; b. Sept. 14, 1783; bap. Oct. 12, 1783; sp. Peter Zimmerman & w. Anna.

ACHE—Christina, d. Heinrich & w. Catharina; b. Nov. 5, 1765; bap. Dec. 1, 1765; sp. Casper Faddeicher & Christina; d. Samuel Verber. Gorg, s. of above; b. June 16, 1767; bap. July 12, 1767; sp. Gorg Ache.

ACHEBACH—Snna Regina, d. Johannes; b. ———; bap. Feb. 5, 1758; sp. Peter Sander and w.. Anna Eva, d. of above; b. ———; bap. June 22, 1760; sp. Martin Burgholder & a.

ACHEBACH—Anna Margreth, d. Mathias; b. ———; bap. Nov. 28, 1755; sp. Thomas Scherb &a. Anna Maria, d. of above; b. ———; bap. Feb. 18, 1762; sp. Abraham Hassler & w. Anna. Maria Elisabeth, d. of above; b. ———; bap. Jan. 8, 1772; sp. Maria Elisabeth, d. Gorg Schneider. Anna Catharina, d. Matthais & w. Anna Margreth; b. Apr. 11, 1764; bap. May 27, 1764; sp. Heinrich Munche & w. Anna Catharina.

ACKERMANN—Maria Barbara, d. Balser & w. Elisabeth; b. July 30, 1779; bap. Oct. 6, 1779; sp. the Parents.

ADAM—Maria Margaretha, d. Bernhart & w. Anna Margaretha; b. June 14, 1760; bap. Sept. 4, 1760; sp. the Parents.

ALBRECHT—J. Michel, s. Christian & w. Elisabeth; b. Feby. 7, 1765; bap. Mch. 17, 1765; sp. Michel Grauel & w. Anna Maria.

ALLEEN—Gorg, s. John & w. Susanna; b. Jany. 16, 1778; bap. Jany. 5, 1779; sp. Martin Eifer & Dorrothea Wolff.

ALTHAUS—Susanna, d. Conrath & w. Maria Barbara; b. Dec. 10, 1781; bap. Jany. 20, 1782; sp. Michael Weinhold & w. Sussanna.

AMWEG—Elisabeth, d. Jacob; b. ———; bap. Mch. 13, 1763; sp. Martin Burgholder & w. Johan Michel, s. of above; b. ———; bap. Oct. 17; 1768; sp. Joh. Michael Amweg & Susanna Degenhart.

AMWEG—Heinrich, s. Jacob & w. Anna Elisabeth; b. Jany. 19, 1766; bap. Feby. 9 1766; sp. Christof Heinrich Reinhold & w. Sophia Loisa.

AMWEG—Maria Magdalena, d. Jacob & w. Anna; b. Nov. 2, 1780; bap. Dec. 24, 1780; sp. Peter Benss & w. Maria Magdalena.

AMWEG—Catharina, d. Jacob & w. Catharina; b. Sept. 11, 1778; bap. Nov. 15, 1778; sp. Heinrich Burgholder & w. Cath-

158   BAPTISMAL AND MARRIAGE RECORDS.

arina. Michael, s. of above; b. Dec. 4, 1781; bap. May 5, 1782; sp. Johannes Gerhard & w. Susanna.
AMWEG—Wilhelm, s. Jacob & w. Catharina; b. Nov. 18, 1783; bap. Apr. 11, 1784; sp. Heinrich Farnssler & Regina Reinhold, both single. Anna Margretha, d. of above; b. Dec. 14, 1785; bap. May 14, 1786; sp. Gorg Brunner & w. Anna Maria.
ANDREAS—Johann Jacob, s. Johannes & w .Barbara; b. Mch. 27, 1753; bap. Apr. 1, 1753; sp. Johann Jacob Waggener & Anna Ursula Egly.
APPEL—Maria Catharina, d. Johannes & w. Maria Elisabeth; b. May 30, 1781; bap. Feb. 10, 1781; sp. Johann Gorg Weber, Jr. & w. Anna Margretha.
ARMJOEM—Isaac Jacobus, s. Peter & w. Magdalena; b. Mch. 15, 1755; bap. May 4, 1755; sp. Isaac Berry & w. Rahel.

BACHER—Johann Adam, s. Gorg & w. Margaretha; b. May 24, 1753; bap. June 10, 1753; sp. Johann Adam Fackler & w. Barbara.
BAHMER—Anna Margretha, d. Michael & w. Barbara; b. Sept. 6, 1782; bap. Oct. 29, 1782; sp. Anna Margretha, widow of Adam Bahmer & mother of Michael.
BARRY—Johannes, s. Isaac & w. Rahee; b. Dec. 5, 1753; bap. Dec. 23, 1753; sp. Johannes Bonnet & Catharina, d. of Jacob Enck.
BARRY—Magdalena, d. Ludwig; b. ———; bap. Jan. 11, 1759; sp. Casepr Theel & w.
BART—Eva, d. Stefy & w. Catharina; b. Aug. 10, 1762; bap. Oct. 12, 1762; sp. Eva Salate.
BASSLER—Johann Heinrich, Johannes, ch. Heinrich & w.; b. Mch. 3, 1757; bap. Apr. 9, 1757; sp. Heinrich Zeller & w. Maria Margretha; Peter Johannes Lein & w. Dorothea.
BAUER—Johan Wilhelm, s. Heinrich & Maria Margretha; eine concunbine; b. Feb. 7, 1779; bap. Apr. 18, 1779; sp. Wilhelm Schneider & Sophia Brunner.
BAUER—Johannes, s. Jacob; b. ———; bap. June 9, 1763; sp. Johannes Wenger & Gerthraut Schweitzer.
BECHTEL—Anna Maria, d. Adam &. Catharina; b. Oct. 13, 1779; bap. Apr. 30, 1780; sp. Burckhart Bechtel & w. Anna Maria. Sara, d. of above; b. Apr. 1, 1783; bap. Oct. 26, 1783; sp. Thomas Zell & w. Catharina.
BECK—Fillippus, s. Jacob & w. Anna Maria; b. Jan. 26, 1754; bap. Feb. 24, 1754; sp. Filip Grunewald & Margaretha Beck.
BECKER—Christina, d. Peter & w. Elisabeth; b. Apr. 24, 1780; bap. June 11, 1780; sp. Johannes Serbe & w. Catharina.

REV. JOHN WALDSCHMIDT—1752-1786.   159

BECKER—Johann Jacob, s. Peter & w. Susanna; b .July 13, 1753; bap. July 16, 1753; sp. Felix Schutz & w. Fronica (Child died July 20th).
BEER—Susanna, d. Rudolf & w. Anna Eva; b. Mch. 7, 1781; bap. May 3, 1781; sp. Susanna, wife of Peter Schmeid.
BEHMER—Filipp, s. Michael & Barbara; b. Apr. 15, 1786; bap. May 7, 1786; sp. Filipp Behmer.
BENCKLE—Joh Peter, s. Michael; b. ———; bap. Aug. 1, 1750; sp. Joh. Peter Klein & Anna Eva Amweg.
BENDER—Eva, d. Heinrich & w. Catharina; b. Nov. 1, 1761; bap. Apr. 11, 1762; sp. Conrath Reicher & w.
BENNER—Margretha, d. Peter & w. Margretha; b. Apr. 16, 1760; bap. June 10, 1760; sp. Johannes Schmeid & w. Barbara.
BENSS—Susanna, d. Weyerle & w. Anna Maria; b. Oct. 9, 1751; bap. Mch, 1753; sp. the Father.
BERGER—Johann Henrick, s. Johann Christian & w. Maria Elisabeth; b. Apr. 3, 1765; bap. Apr. 27, 1765; sp. Henrich Freymann & w. Catharine.
BERLET—Christina, d. Bastian & w. Maria; b. Apr. 20, 1782; bap. Aug. 11, 1782; sp. Freidrich Fromm & w. Catharina.
BERNHART—Johann Peter, s. Christian & w. Catharina; b. Feb. 12, 1753; bap. Mch. 4, 1753; sp. Peter Burckener & Catharina Elisabeth Kohl. Elisabeth, d. of above; b. Dec. 20, 1754; bap. Jan. 19, 1755; sp. Ulrich Mishler & w. Elisabeth. Barbara, d. of above; b. Feb. 5, 1757; bap. Mch. 6, 1757; sp. Martin Beier & w. Anna Barbara.
BES—Johan Christian, s. Christian & w. Barbara; b. Apr. 9, 1756; bap. Aug. 2, 1756; sp. Ludwig Heinrich Schuy & w. Elisabeth.
BIEGEL—Johann Heinrich, s. Wilhelm Heinrich & Margretha; b. Sept. 3, 1780; bap. Dec. 2, 1781; sp. Valentine Epler & w. Margretha.
BILLING—Anna Christina, d. Johann; b. Mch. 1, 1757; bap. June 5, 1757; sp. Abraham Hassler & w.
BILLING—Anna Ursula, d. Johannes; b. ———; bap. Sept. 27, 1758; sp. Michael Amweg & w. Johannes, s. of above; b. ———; bap. Nov. 7, 1761; sp. Bartholemay Zibach & w. Margretha, d. of above; b. ———; bap. Feb. 25, 1763; sp. Heinrich Walter & w. Margreth.
BILLING—Anna Maria, d. Joh. Siegfried; b. ———; Jan. 30, 1756; sp. Jacob Hassler & w.
BILLINGER—Joh. Ludwig, s. Joh. Seigfried; b. ———; bap. Dec. 17, 1759; sp. Ludwig Schweitzer & w.
BILLMAN—Anna Maria, d. Hanss; b. ———; bap. Jan. 4, 1761; sp. Anna Maria Ury.

160 BAPTISMAL AND MARRIAGE RECORDS.

BILLMAN—Catharina, d. Johannes; b. ———; bap. Mch. 12, 1759; sp. Ulrich Mischler & w.

BILLMAN—Johan Jacob, s. Johannes & w. Elisabeth; b. Apr. 20, 1764; bap. May 20, 1764; sp. Joh. Jacob Amweg & w. Elisabeth.

BILLMAN—Johannes, Joh. Peter, Christian, Anna Barbara, Elisabeth, ch. Hanns Billman; b. ———; bap. Oct. 19, 1755; sp. ————— (Some of them well grown).

BILLMANN—Anna Christina; d. Johannes; b. ———; bap. Nov. 19, 1757; sp. Anna Maria Graber. David, s. ob above; b. ———; bap. Sept. 28, 1768; sp. Wilhelm Walter & Anna Susanna Wust.

BINCKLE—Maria Catharina, d. Heinrich; b. ———; bap. June 20, 1772; sp. Ludwig Shweitzer & w.

BINCKLE—Johannes, s. Heinrich & w. Anna Maria; b. Dec. 26, 1781; bap. Jan. 20, 1782; sp. Ludwig Schweitzer, Jr. & Catharina, d. of Johannes Kuntz.

BINCKLE—Phillipina, d. Heinrich & w. Barbara; b. Feb. 22, 1778; bap. Mch. 15, 1778; sp. Filip Spohn & w. Catharina.

BINCKLEY—Catharina, d. Marx & w. Magdalena; b. Aug. 22, 1779; bap. Oct. 24, 1779; sp. Martin Kissinger & Barbara Schweitzer.

BINCKY—Johannes, s. Marx & w. Magdalena; b. Jan. 14, 1777; bap. May 19, 1777; sp. Johannes Brunner & Sophia (name blotted).

BLAHSER—Wilhelm, s. Peter & w. Elisabeth; b. Mch. 15, 1783; bap. June 15, 1783; sp. Christophel Hefft & w. Catharina.

BLASSER—J—ohannes, s. Peter and w. Elisabeth; b. Oct. 25, 1780; bap. Feb. 18, 1781; sp. Johannes Hemminger & Barbara Schleybach, both single.

BLOSSER—Peter, s. Peter & w. Elisabeth; b. Mch. 10, 1785; bap. Oct. 22, 1785; sp. Heinrich Weith & w. Catharina.

BOHL—Johannes, s. Heinrich & w. Catharina; b. May 14, 1760; bap. Aug. 17, 1760; sp. Peter Brininger & w. Elisabeth; near Jeremia's Miller's.

BOHMER—Gorg Friederah, s. Friedrich; b. ———; bap. July 3, 1757; sp. Gorg Ache & w. Catharina.

BOHMER—Elisabeth, d. Michael & w. Elisabeth; b. July 20, 1781; bap. July 22, 1781; sp. Michael Roth & w. Elisabeth.

BOHMER—Anna Maria, d. Michael & w. Maria Barbara; b. Dec. 20, 1784; bap. Jan. 1, 1785; sp. Michael Hasting & w. Anna Maria.

BOLLANDER—Maria Juliane, d. Peter; b. ———; bap. June 22, 1755; sp Michael Binckle & w.

BOLLANDER—Catharina, d. Stefy & w. Margreth; b. July

REV. JOHN WALDSCHMIDT—1752-1786. 161

11, 1786; bap. Aug. 6, 1786; sp. Joh. Jacob Walter & Elisabeth Bollender.
BOLLENDER—Stefan, s. Peter; b. Oct. 10, 1756; bap. Oct. 30, 1756; sp. Stefy Bollender & w.
BOLLENDER—Catharina, d. Peter & w. Fronica; b. June 2, 1765; bap. June 16, 1765; sp. Gorg Ache & w. Catharina.
BOLLENDER—Elisabeth, d. Stefain & w. Margretha; b. Nov. 20, 1784; bap. Jan. 2, 178^r; sp. Abraham Hassler & Elisabeth Bollender, both single.
BOLLINGER—Maria Eva, d. Jacob and w. Anna Maria; b. Sept. 16, 1753; bap. Sept. 30, 1753; sp. Abraham Rohland & w. Maria Eva.
BOLLINGER—Catharina, d. Rudolf & w. Margretha; b. Sept. 11, 1753; bap. Sept. 30, 1753; sp. Conrad Heyburger & w. Catharina.
BONNET—Johannes, s. Johannes & Margretha Dorrothea; b. Feb. 9, 1761; bap. Feb. 10, 1761; sp. Adam Steger & w.
BOSSER—Johannes, s. Casper; b. ———; bap. Mch. 12, 1772; sp. Johannes Brunner & Susanna Kissinger.
BOSSER—Sofia, Jacob, ch. Casper & w. Catharina; b. Feb. 4, 1779; bap. Oct. 21, 1783; b. Feb. 9, 1781; bap. Oct. 21, 1783; sp. Joh. Gorg Holtzinger & w. Magdalena; sp. Peter Kessler & Catharina, d. Johannes Kuntz. (The children were baptized in their father's house on the same day that their Grandmother m. J. Gorg Holtzinger, Oct. 21, 1783.)
BOSSHAAR—Catharina, d. Johannes & Anna Maria; b. Nov. 19, 1753; bap. Dec. 30, 1753; sp. Daniel Bosshaar & Catharina, d. of Peter Becker.
BRAUNINGER—Johann Martin, s. Johann Martin & w. Maria Magdalena; b. Apr. 30, 1776; bap. Apr. 2, 1766; sp. Dietrich Fernssler & w. Elisabeth Margretha.
BRENDEL—Johann Marx, s. Johann Marx & w. Anna Elisabetha; b. Jan. 31, 1755; bap. Mch. 31, 1755; sp. Samuel Wolff & w. Magdalena.
BRENDEL—Anna Maria, d. Wilhelm & w. Anna Maria; b. Mch. 29, 1777; bap. Apr. 27, 1777; sp. Andreas Sober & w. Christina.
BRUBACHER—Anna Maria, d. Isaac & w. Anna Maria; b. Apr. 14, 1754; bap. May 12, 1754; sp. Johannes Brubacher & Anna Christina Diefendorffer.
BRUNNER—Sophia Loisa, d. Gorg; b. ———; bap. July 14, 1754; sp. Sophia Loisa Amweg. Johan Peter, s. of above; b. ———; bap. July 29, 1758; sp. Peter Wolferberger & w.
BRUNNER—Elisabeth, d. Gorg & w. Anna Maria; b. Dec. 19, 1782; bap. Feb. 1783; sp. Peter Brunner & Eva Achebach.

11—Vol. VI—6th Ser.

BRUNNER—Anna Maria, d. Gorg & w. Anna Maria; b. Feb. 3, 1783; bap. Apr. 30, 1786; sp. Matthias Achibach & w. Margreth.

BRUNNER—Barbara, d. Gorg, Jr. & w. Anna Maria; b. May 10, 1784; bap. May 31, 1784; sp. Johannes Schweicker & Sophia Brunner.

BRUNNER—Anna Catharina, d. Gorg Michael; b. ———; bap. Apr. 12, 1752; sp. Fillip Kissinger & w. Anna Catharina. Johannes, s. of above; b. ———; bap. May 17, 1752; sp. Johannes Templemann & Margretha Brunner. Anna Maria, d. of above; b. ———; bap. Apr. 17, 1764; sp. Anna Maria, d. Martin Keller.

BRUNNER—Margretha, d. Gorg Michael & w.; b. ———; 1749; bap. Nov. 4, 1749; sp. Ludwig Entzmenger & Margretha Brunner.

BRUNNER—Johannes, s. Johannes & w. Sophia; b. June 7, 1783; bap. Aug. 21, 1783; sp. the Parents. Catharina, d. of above; b. Feb. 26, 1779; bap. Apr. 18, 1779; sp. Gorg Brunner, Jr. & Catharina, d. of Peter Fusser. Sophia, d. of above; b. Feb. 8, 1871; bap. Apr. 8, 1781; sp. Martin Kissinger & Sophia Brunner. Anna Maria, d. of above; b. Mch 23, 1785; bap. Sept. 18, 1785; sp. Phillip Schweicker & Anna Maria Brunner, both single.

BRUNNER—Sophia Loisa, d. Johann Gorg & w. Barbara; b. June 2, 1754 bap. July 14, 1754; sp. Michael Amweg & his unmarried d. Sofia Luisa.

BRUNNER—Catharina, d. Peter & w. Eva; b. Feb. 6, 1784; bap. Apr. 11, 1784; sp. Gorg Brunner, Jr. & w. Catharina. Eva, d. of above; b. Dec. 1, 1785; bap. Mch. 19, 1786; sp. Gorg Achebach & Eva Brunner, both single.

BRUNNER—Maria Thorodea, d. Ulrich; b. ———; bap. Dec. 1, 1751; sp. Maria Thorodea Eder.

BRUNNER—Christian, s. Ulrich & w. Fronica; b. May 17, 1764; bap. May 27, 1764; sp. Christopel Bickle & w.

BRUNNER—Margretha; d. Wolf Heinrich Brunner & w.; b. ———; bap. ———, 1749; sp. Ludwig Ensmenger & Margretha Brunner.

BUCHER—Joh. Heinrich, s. Heinrich; b. ———; bap. Oct. 7, 1759; sp. Jacob Amweg & Anna Maria Schweitzer.

BUCHER—Johannes, s. Heinrich & w. Susanna Catharina; b. June 26, 1784; bap. Sept. 12, 1784; sp. Christofel Kern & w. Margretha.

BUCHLER—Johannes Simon, s. Heinrich & w. Eva; b. Mch. 18, 1784; bap. Nov. 14, 1784; sp. Johan Simon Blanckebichler & Maria Eva Wagner, both single.

BULLINDER—Maria Barbara, d. Stepany & w. Margretha;

b. Mch. 7, 1781; bap. 8, 1781; sp. Filip Jacob Schenkel & w. Juliane.

BULLINGER—Christian, s. Jacob & w. Anna Maria; b. Feb. 28, 1761; bap. Apr. 15, 1761; sp. Gorg Michael Weiss & w. Christina.

BULLINGER—Emanuel, s. Jacob & w. Barbara; b. Feb. 15, 1754; bap. Feb. 24, 1754; sp. Emanuel Suss & Elisabeth Kohl.

BULLINGER—Peter, s. Stephany & w. Margaretha; b. Nov. 10, 1782; bap. Dec. 22, 1782; sp. Johann Filipp Schenkel & w. Barbara.

BULLMAN—Johann Michael, s. Abraham & w. Elisabeth; b. Nov. 10, 1780; bap. Dec. 12, 1780; sp. Michael Fischer.

BULMANN—Maria Catharina, d. Johannes & w. Barbara; b. June 7, 1760; bap. June 22, 1760; sp. Simon Riegel & Maria Catharina, d. of Peter Ruth, both single. (In the Congregation on the Cacusa by Hains.)

BURCKERT—Jeremias, s. Andreas & w. Anna Barbara; b. Aug. 13, 1777; bap. Sept. 9, 1777; sp. Jeremias Simmer & w. Anna Barbara. Johann Nicolaus, s. of above; b. May 8, 1780; bap. June 11, 1780; sp. Johann Nicolaus Haller & w. Christina. Gorg, s. of above; b. Jan. 11, 1783; bap. Mch. 23, 1783; sp. Jeremias Simmer & w. Anna Barbara. Andreas, s. of above; b. Sept. 23, 1785; bap. Nov. 6, 1785; sp. Gorg Gebhart & w. Margretha.

BURCKHOLDER—Johannes, s. Heinrich & w. Catharina; b. Oct. 24, 1778; bap. Nov. 15, 1778; sp. Jacob Amweg w. Catharina.

BURCKHOLDER—Anna Catharina, d. Heinrich & w. Rosina; b. Feb. 9, 1783; bap. Mch. 16, 1783; sp. Ludwig Schweitzer, Jr. & Catharina Gerhart.

BURGHOLDER—Johann Gorg, s. Martin; b. ———; bap. June 8, 1753; sp. Gorg Brunner & w.; Christof Heinrich, s. of above; b. Dec. 3, 1754; bap. Feb. 9, 1755; sp. Christof Reinhold & Sophia Loisa Amweg.

BURCKNER—Christian, s. Christian & w. Barbara; b. Sept. ———, 1750; bap. May 25, 1755; sp. Peter Burckner. (Father of the child died before it was baptized.)

BURGHOLDER—Anna Eva, d. Martin; b. ———; bap. July 1, 1758; sp. Michael Amweg & w. Johann Peter, s. of above; b. ———; bap. Apr. 28, 1769; sp. Michael Amweg & w. Johann Michael, s. of above; b. ———; bap. Aug. 20, 1771; sp. Michael Amweg & w. Elisabeth.

BURGHOLDER—Gorg, s. Martin & w. Anna Eva; b. ———; bap. Apr. 24, 1765; sp. Mr. Heinrich Walter & w. Margretha.

164 BAPTISMAL AND MARRIAGE RECORDS.

CAPES—Judith, d. Gorg & w. Catharina; b. Apr. 4, 1783; bap. Oct. 26, 1783; sp. Elisabeth Eschelman.
CHILYAN—Johannes, s. Abraham & Elisabeth; b. Oct. 27, 1778; bap. Nov. 22, 1778; sp. Gottlieb Mack & w. Anna.
CHILYAN—(Killian) Jacob s. Abraham & Anna Elisabeth; b. May. 8, 1777; bap. Sept. 15, 1777; sp. Jacob Chiljan, for whom the child was named.
CHOX—(Jacques) Maria,, Sophia, ch. Samuel & w. Catharina; b. May 30, 1780; bap. Dec. 24, 1780; sp. Jacob Hassler, Maria Hassler, Sophia Hassler, all three ch. of Bastian Hassler.
CONRAD—Catharina, d. Daniel & w. Barbara; b. July 7, 1760; bap. Aug. 17, 1760; sp. Rosina Schanck.

DANNER—Elisabeth, d. Alexander; b. ———; bap. July 12, 1752; sp. Marx Egly & w.
DANNER—Johannes, s. Michael & w. Elisabeth; b. Dec. 23, 1782; bap. Mch. 14, 1783; sp. Heinrich Kafroth & w. Margretha.
DEATO—Johannes, s. Michael & w. Anna Barbara; b. June 25, 1753; bap. Sept. 16, 1753; sp. Simon Duy & Elisabeth Kohl.
DECKER—Peter (bro't by Stephen Bollinger), Heinrich; b. ———; bap. ———, 1757; sp. Peter Boll & w.
DEFY—Elisabeth, d. Wilhelm & w. Elisabeth; b Feb. 1, 1754; bap. Mch. 3, 1754; sp. Fillippus Ranck, Jr. & w. Magdalena.
DIEFFENDORFER—Anna Maria, d. Johann Adam & w. Anna Margaretha; b. May 29, 1754; bap. June 30, 1754; sp. Gottfried Bickle & Anna Maria Rabb.
DIEFFENDORFFER—Johannes, s. Michael & w. Elisabeth; b. Feb. 11, 1754; bap. Mch. 3, 1754; sp. Johannes Dieffendorffer, Jr. & Anna Maria Rapp.
DEITERICH—Johann Balser, s. Johann Nicolaus & w. Anna Margretha; b. Dec. 23, 1754; bap. Jan. 26, 1755; sp. Halsar Bosshaar & w. Anna Maria.
DOCK—Jacob, s. Jacob & w. Phillipina; b. Dec. 22, 1776; bap. May 8, 1779; sp. Jacob Schwartz Walter & w. Maria. Julianna —d. of above; b. Sept. 8, 1781; bap. July 13, 1782; sp. Filip Dock, Jr. & Barbara, d. Johannes Ruhm, both single
DOCK—Jacob s. Johann Nicolaus & w. Anna Maria; b. Mar. 22, 1778; bap. May 8, 1779; sp. Jacob Schwartz Walter & w. Maria. Johannes, s. of above; b. Jan. 6, 1781; bap. July 13, 1782; sp. Andrew Riehm & w. Barbara.
DOCK—Johannes "nun zwar ehelent", s. Johannes & w. Elisabeth; b. Apr. 26, 1782; bap. Apr. 29, 1782; sp. Johannes Aumuller & w. Catharina.

DOCK—Salome, d. Matthias & w. Dorrothea; b. Apr. 15, 1780; bap. June 23, 1780; sp. Johannes Serbe, Jr. & w. Margaretha Bunsch.

DOCK—Wilhelm, s. Philip & w. Margaretha; b. Aug. 2 (cir.) 1767; bap. July 13, 1782; sp. The Parents.

DOMMEN—Johann Jacob, s. Johann Jacob & w. Susanna; b. Mch. 6, 1754; bap. Apr. 7, 1754; sp. Johann Jacob Bullinger & w. Anna Maria.

DORR—Jacob, s. Abraham & w. Magdalena; b. Mch. 21, 1762; bap. Apr. 9, 1762; sp. Rudolf Bullinger & w. Margaretha.

DORR—Abraham, s. Conrad & w. Barbara; b. July 25, 1779; bap. Nov. 1779; sp. Abraham Huber & w. Magdalena.

DOST—Anna Maria, s. Josef & w. Sara; b. Dec. 16, 1783; bap. Apr. 11, 1784; sp. Thomas Bunsch & w. Anna Maria.

DREISBACH—Catharina Elisabeth, d. Martin; b. ———; bap. May 3, 1759; sp. Georg Schneider & w. Johannes, s. of above; b. ———; bap. Sept. 24, 1762; sp. Jost Walter & w. Elisabeth.

DUBS—Fronica, d. Johannes & w. Barbara; b. Jan. 15, 1760; bap. June 10, 1760; sp. Heinrich Lohmuller & w. Fronica (Foot note states, 9th. June, 1760, I preached on the Schwadera (Swatara) at the Dubs Church after many requests, and baptized the child.)

DUMMY—Anna Christina, d. Johann Jacob & w. Susanna; b. June 20, 1755; bap. July 13, 1755; sp. Fillip Schaffer & &. Anna Christina.

DUTZ—Lehnhard, s. Jacob & w. Rebecca; b. July 22, 1759; bap. Oct. 6, 1760; sp. Lehnhart Umberger & w. Maria Barbara.

DUY—Emanuel, s. Simon & w. Catharina; b. Jan. 17, 1755; bap. Jan. 30, 1755; sp. Emanuel Suss & Anna Margaretha Schutz, both single.

EBERHARD—Anna Maria, d. Johannes & w. Anna Maria; b. Dec. 29, 1781; bap. Apr. 1, 1782; sp. The Parents.

EBERHART—Johann Gorg, s. Gorg & w.; b. ———; bap. May 13, 1750; sp. Hanss Zwally & w.

EHHALT—Magdalena, d. Matthias & w. Elisabeth; b. Oct 27, 1759; bap. Nov. 25, 1759; sp. Andreas Beck & Anna Weber, both single.

EICHHOLTZ—Johannes, s. Heinrich & w. Margaretha; b. Nov. 15, 1782; bap. Feb. 11, 1783; sp Johannes Heldry & w. Eva.

EISSEMANN—Elisabeth Eva, ds. Christian & w. Catharina Margaretha; b. Jan. 14, 1784; bap. Apr. 12, 1784; sp. Johanne Zerbe, Jr., Elisabeth Blanckebill and Gorg Rufner, Catharina Leininger. Christian—s. of above; b. Feb. 14, 1786;· bap. May 7, 1786; sp. Peter Geiger & w. Anna Maria.
ELI—Elisabeth, d. Christian & w. Regina; b. Oct. 15, 1782; bap. Apr. 6, 1783; sp. Abraham Hassler & Elisabeth, d. of Michael Walter.
EMBICK—Joh. Justus, s. Christoferus & w. Maria Elisabeth; b. Oct. 12, 1754; bap. Oct. 27, 1754; sp. Jacob Hoessinger & Maria Barbara Ruder.
ENCK—Catharina, d. Jacob & w. Anna Maria; b. Oct. 12, 1756; bap. Nov. 13, 1756; sp. Johannes Enck & Catharina Laber, both single. Johannes, s. of above, b. Mch. 2, 1758; bap. Mch. 27, 1758; sp. Johannes Enck & Barbara Luber. Anna Maria, d. of above, b. Mch. 7, 1760; bap. Apr. 4, 1760; sp. Stophel Weitmann & w. Anna Maria.
EPLER—Johannes, s. Johannes & w. Elisabeth; b. Mch. 21, 1782; bap. Apr. 28, 1782; sp. The Parents.
EPLER—Daniel, s. Peter & w. Catharina; b. Nov. 28, 1781; bap. Dec. 25, 1781; sp. Johannes Hahn & w. Magdalena.

FACKLER—Michael, s. Johann Adam & w. Barbara; b. Feb. 24, 1754; bap. Mch. 3, 1754; sp. Michael Weiss & w. Barbara.
FAUST—Johan Heinrich, s. Heinrich & w. Magdalena; b. Sept. 29, 1784; bap. Oct. 31, 1784; sp. Peter Diehl & w. Anna Maria.
FEDER—Anna Maria, d. Gorg, b. ———; bap. Feb. 5, 1758; sp. Heinrich Ache & w. Anna Maria.
FEHL—Johan Philip, s. Valentine & w. Elisabeth; b. July 18, 1777; bap. Aug. 3, 1777; sp. Michael Bohmer. Anna Margaretha, d. of above; b. Mch. 7, 1780; bap. Apr. 29, 1780; sp. Anna Margaretha Bohmer. Johann Adam, s. of above; b. July 1, 1781; bap. Sept. 27, 1781; sp. Adam Bohmer & Margretha, d. of Michael Roth.
FERLING—Jacobus, s. Jacob & w. Catharina; b. Dec. 24, 1752; bap. Jan. 1, 1753; sp. Samuel Reyger & w. Juliana.
FERNSSLER—Maria Elisabeth, d. Dietrich & w. Elisa Margareth; b. Dec. 4, 1768; bap. Dec. 26, 1768; sp. Peter Gauer & Magdalena, d. of Abrabam Stien.
FIEDELING—Magdalena, d. Gorg & w. Susanna; b. Oct. 5, 1781; bap. Mch. 30, 1782; sp. Lehnhart Keppling & w. Magdalena.

FISCHER—Catharina, d. Johannes & w. Catharina; b. Sept. 29, 1778; bap. Oct. 18, 1778; sp. Conrad Kirschner & w. Catharina.

FISCHER—Johannes, s. Johann Gorg & w. Catharina; b. Mch. 12, 1782; bap. Apr. 1, 1782; sp. Johannes Fischer & w. Catharina.

FOLTZ—Julianne, d. Gorg Michael; b. ———; bap. Sept. 20, 1767; sp. Friedrich Hassler, Juliane Bollander and the mother of the child. Johan Friedrich, s. of above; b. ———; bap. Sept. 16, 1700; sp. Friedrich Hassler & Barbara Ulrich.

FOLTZ—Margretha, d. Gorg Michael & w. Barbara; b. Aug. 31, 1783; bap. Nov. 2, 1783; sp. Heinrich Sander & w. Margaretha.

FRANCK—Catharina, d. Nicolaus & w. Christina; b. Oct. 9 1774; bap. Mch. 5, 1775; sp. The Parents.

FRANCKHAUSER—Peter, s. Michael, Jr. & w. Dorrothea; b. May 27, 1782; bap. July 14, 1782; sp. Peter Funck & w. Catharina, sister of Michael Franckhauset, Jr.

FREY—Dorrothea, d. Jacob & w. Catharina; b. Sept. 24, 1773; bap. Nov. 16, 1773; sp. Friedrick Horn & w. Susanna.

FREY—Elisabeth, d. Johannes & w. Anna Elisabeth; b. Mch. 9, 1757; bap. Mch. 27, 1757; sp. Conrad Felte & w. Catharina.

FREY—Catharina, d. Matthias & w. Elisabeth; b. Oct. 31, 1785; bap. Feb. 12, 1786; sp. Johann Nicolaus Schuck & Barbara Kepplinger, both single.

FREYBERGER—Magdalena, d. Jacob & w. Magdalena; b. ———; bap. Mch. 17, 1765; sp. Magdalena, w. of Wilhelm Hedricks.

FROMM—Magdalena, d. Friedrick & w. Christina; b. Apr. 19, 1782; bap. Aug. 11, 1782; sp. Bastian Berlet & w. Maria.

FROSCHAUER—Catharina, d. Gorg & w. Magdalena; b. July 28, 1762; bap. Oct. 12, 1762; sp. Jacob Froschauer & Catharina Krebs.

FUHRMANN—Elisabeth, d. Paul & w. Barbara; b. Jan. 1, 1754; bap. Jan. 27, 1754; sp. Andreas Hollsbaum & w. Fronica.

FUNCK—Michael, s. Filipp & w. Christina; b. Nov. 15, 1783; bap. May 2, 1784; sp. Michael Funck & w. Magdalena. Phillipus, s. of above; b. May 20, 1786; bap. June 25, 1786; sp. Melchoir Segler & w. Catharina.

FUNCK—Johannes, s. Johannes & w. Elisabeth; b. Oct. 7, 1778; bap. Apr. 11, 1779; sp. Michael Fanckhauser & w. Dorothea. Susanna, d. of above; b. Feb. 1, 1783; bap. June 15, 1783; sp. Peter Bohm & w. Susanna.

FUNCK—Elisabeth, d. Peter & w. Catharina; b. Oct. 11, 1779; bap. July 14, 1782; sp. The Parents. Johan Gorg, s. of above; b. Apr. 8, 1782; bap. July 14, 1782; sp. Michael Fanckhauer & w. Dorothea.

FUNCKHAUS—Anna Barbara, d. Michael & w. Dorothea; b. Nov. 27, 1784; bap. Apr. 16, 1785; sp. Peter Funck & w. Catharina.

GACK (JACK)—Anna Maria Anna, ds. Samuel & w. Catharina; b. Nov. 3, 1769; b. Dec. 11, 1774; bap. Jan. 19, 1775; sp. The Parents. Catharina, d. of above; b. June 27, 1778; bap. Nov. 15, 1778; sp. Christofel Hassler & w. Catharina.

GEBEL—Johannes, s. Henrich & w. Maria Elisabeth; b. Mch. 20, 1780; bap. Apr. 30, 1780; sp. Conrath Gebel & w. Elisabeth.

GEBHARD—Maria Magdalena, d. Gorg & w. Anna Margaretha; b. Nov. 18, 1778; bap. May 23, 1779; sp. Peter Benss & w. Magdalena. Johannes, s. of above; b. Nov. 25, 1780; bap. June 3, 1781; sp. Johannes Mumma & w. Barbara.

GEIGER—Maria Catharina; d. Peter & w. Anna Maria; b. Dec. 11, 1778; bap. Dec. 25, 1778; sp. Jacob Hoffer & Catharina Grammeler. Anna Maria, d. of above; b. Oct. 16, 1780; bap. Nov. 26, 1780; sp. Gorg Blanckebiller & w. Anna Maria.

GERHARD—Susanna, d. Johannes & w. Susanna; b. Sept. 22, 1781; bap. Oct. 6, 1782; sp. Friedrick Gerhard & w. Susanna.

GERHART—Catharina, d. Johannes; b. Sept. 26, 1779; bap. Nov. 7, 1779; sp. Catharina Gerhart.

GERHART—Johann Heinrich, s. Johann Heinrich & w. Anna Catharina; b. Dec. 1, 1753; bap. Dec. 16, 1753; sp. Johann Heinrich Schramm.

GEYER (GEIGER) (?)—Peter, s. Peter & w. Maria; b. Aug. 3, 1782; bap. Sept. 29, 1782; sp. Andreas Kreiner & w. Elisabeth.

GRUNEWALD—Anna Maria, d. Peter & w. Elisabeth; B. Feb. 5, 1781; bap. June 3, 1781; sp. Widow Ursula Kachel.

GICKER—Johannes, s. Johannes & w. Catharina; b. Dec. 7, 1782; bap. Mch. 30, 1783; sp. Henrich Gicker & w. Maria Margretha.

GILSINGER—Johann Phillipino, s. Johannes & w. Rosina; b. Jan. 15, 1768; bap. Feb. 14, 1768; sp. Johann Filip Krick & Eva, d. of Martin Brauninger.
GIPRE—Jacob, s. Jacob & w. Elisabeth; b. Dec. 22, 1781; bap. Apr. 28, 1782; sp. Jacob Albrecht.
GRAMLING—Elisabeth, d. Adam & w. Elisabeth; b. Dec. 9, 1784; bap. Mch. 27, 1785; sp. Friedrick Richmeschneider & w. Margretha.
GRAMLY—Adam, s. Adam & w. Elisabeth; b. May 20, 1782; bap. June 3, 1781; sp. Jacob Hoffer & Elisabeth Kohl.
GRING—Johannes, s. David & w. Anna Maria; b. Jan. 27, 1793; bap. Mch. 10, 1793; sp. Johannes Waldschmidt & w. Susanna.
GROH—Catharina Elisabeth, d. Gottfried & w. Elisabeth; b. Nov. 17, 1764; bap. Apr. 27, 1765; sp. Georg Gernand & w. Catharina Elisabeth.

HAASS—Maria, d. Lorenss & w. Catharina; b. Feb. 21, 1781; bap. ———; sp. Maria Fehl.
HACH—Joh. Christian, s. Christian & w. Catharina; b. Apr. 30, 1759; bap. May 27, 1759; sp. Martin & Anna Spittler.
HAGER—Anna Maria Fronica, d. Wernert & w. Anna Maria; b. Sept. 24, 1752; bap. Sept. 31, (sic) 1752; sp. Jacob Holssinger & w. Anna Maria Fronica.
HAHN—Anna Maria, d. Daniel & w. Hanna; b. Aug. 8, 1782; bap. Sept. 22, 1782; sp. Anna Maria, d. of Heinrich Hahn & Sister of Daniel, still single. Isaac, s. of above; b. Mch. 22, 1785; bap. May 29, 1735; sp. The Brother, Josef Hahn.
HAHN—Eva, d. Johannes & w. Magdalena; b. Mch. 23, 1782; bap. Apr. 7, 1782; sp. Jacob Epler & w. Magdalena. Elisabeth, d. of above; b. May 9, 1784; bap. May 24, 1784; sp. The Brother-in-law, and Sister, viz: Conrad Eckert & w. Elisabeth.
HAHN—Johann Jacob, Johnn Gorg, Anna Elisabeth; b. Jan. 13, 1778; b. May 3, 1783; b. Dec. 20, 1780; bap. Dec. 5, 1784; ch. Johannes & w. Salome; sp. Johann Hoffer & w. Elisabeth, Jacob Hoffer & w. Anna & Anna Elisabeth, widow of Peter Sabel.
HAIN—Anna Catharina, d. Gorg & w. Maria Eisabeth; b. June 14, 1760; bap. June 22, 1760; sp. Casper Hain & w. Anna Catharina.
HALLER—Maria Barbara, d. Johannes Nicolaus & w. Christina; b. Mch. 4, 1780; bap. June 11, 1780; sp. Andreas Burckert & w. Anna Barbara. Samuel, s. of above; b. Mch.

19, 1783; bap. May 25, 1783; sp. Heinrich Simmer & w. Catharina.

HAMAN—Johan Jacob, s. Jacob; b. ———; bap. Sept. 13, 1750; sp. Jacob & Eva. Amweg.

HARD—Johann Filipp, s. Conrad & w. Juliana; b. Jan. 24, 1773; bap. Feb. 21, 1773; sp. Phillipus Hard & Margretha Frey, both single.

HARNISCH—Abraham, s. Christian & w. Catharina; b. Feb. 28, 1784; bap. May 1, 1784; sp. Abraham Hassler & Magdalena Diehl. Christian (The Father) is the son of Samuel Harnisch, and although twenty years old and married, had never been baptized until now, May 1, 1784, when he was baptized with his son, Abraham. He answered for himself. Maria Catharina, d. of above; b. July 13, 1785; bap. Oct. 16, 1785; sp. Gorg Neumann & w. Catharina.

HARNISCH—Catharina, d. Johannes & w. Eva; b. Feb. 15, 1782; bap. May 26, 1782; sp. Friedrich Walck & Maria Diehl. Johannes, s. of above; b. Feb. 16, 1783; bap. June 1, 1783; sp. Martin Burckholder & w. Eva.

HARNISCH—Heinrich, s. Johannes & w. Anna Eva; b. Feb. 19, 1785; bap. May 15, 1785; sp. Heinrich Reinhold & Barbara Barriss, both single.

HARNISCH—Johannes, s. Samuel & ———; b. Feb. 15, 1754; bap. Dec. 12, 1783; sp. ———; sp. name not stated; wife's name not stated.

HARNISCH—Anna Margretha, d. Samuel, Jr. & w. Elisabeth; b. Oct. 14, 1765; bap. Mch. 23, 1766; sp. Mr. Heinrich Walter & w. Anna Margretha.

HARNISH—Maria Elisabeth, d. Samuel, Jr.; b. Aug. 20, 1767; bap. Oct. 4, 1767; sp. Engel Becker & w.

HARTING—Fillippus, s. Christian & w. Barbara; b. Sept. 26, 1783; bap. Dec. 7, 1783; sp. Philip Eckel & Juliana Harting, both single.

HARTING—Joh. Michael, s. Johannes Michael & w. Anna Maria; b. July 30, 1782; bap. Sept. 29, 1782; sp. Valentine Bahmer & Magdalena, sister of Michael, both single.

HARTMANN—Johan Peter, s. Filipp & w. Christina; b. Oct. 27, 1783; bap. Dec. 7, 1783; sp. Peter Schweitzer & Barbara Siegenthaler, both single.

HARTMANN—Johannes, s. Philip & w. Christina; b. Mch. 24, 1780; bap. Apr. 29, 1780; sp. Jacob Tritsh & w. Catharina.

HARTUNG—Johan Valentine, s. Michael & w. Anna Maria; b. July 20, 1779; bap. Aug. 15, 1779; sp. Valentine Bohmer & Barbara, d. of Nicolaus Weinhold.

HASSLER—Johan Casper, s. Abraham; b. ———; bap. Sept. 25, 1757; sp. Casper Kabel & w.
HASSLER—Abraham, s. Abraham; b. ———; bap. Jan. 29, 1759; sp. Casper Theel. Anna Catharina, d. of above; b. ———; bap. Mch. 10, 1761; sp. Philip Jacob & w. Elisabeth. Anna Barbara, d. of above; b. ———; bap. May 12, 1763; sp. Gorg Siegethaler & w.
HASSLER—Anna Susanna, d. Abraham & w. Anna; b. Oct. 17, 1765; bap. Feb. 9, 1766; sp. Gorg Brunner & w. Anna Barbara. (The father died before the child's baptism.)
HASSLER—Johannes, s. Abraham & w. Catharina; b. Aug. 26, 1787; bap. Sept. 30, 1787; sp. John Waldschmidt, Jr. & w. Susanna. (Performed by Rev. Boos.) Wilhelm, s. of above; b. Oct. 9, 1791; bap. Nov. 6, 1791; sp. Wilhelm Waldschmidt & w. Barbara. (The child died, no date.)
HASSLER—Jacob, s. Bastian; b. ———; bap. July 18, 1758; sp. Jacob Amweg & Magdalena Harnish.
HASSLER—Magdalena, d. Bastian, Jr.; b. Nov. 6, 1779; bap. May 3, 1780; sp. Magdalena, widow of Christian Schlichty.
HASSLER—Friedrich, s. Bastian, Jr. & w. Anna; b. May 19, 1783; bap. July 20, 1783; sp. Heinrich Reinhold & Barbara, d. of the decd. Christian Schlechty.
HASSLER—Catharina, d. Casper & w. Elisabeth; b. Sept. 30, 1779; bap. Nov. 7, 1779; sp. The Mother of the child.
HASSLER—Anna Barbara, d. Casper & w. Elisabeth; b. Dec. 20, 1780; bap. Mch. 18, 1781; sp. Barbara Hassler. Anna Elisabeth, d. of above; b. Dec. 1, 1782; bap. Mch. 16, 1783; sp. Abraham Hassler & Anna Elisabeth Schlechty. Johannes, s. of above; b. Jan. 20, 1785; bap. May 1, 1785; sp. Stefain Bollender & w. Margaretha. Anna Maria, d. of above; b. Mch. 24, 1786; bap. Apr. 18, 1786; sp. The Parents.
HASLER—Elisabeth, d. Christofel & w. Catharina; b. July 18, 1781; bap. Aug. 5, 1781; sp. Ludwig Schweitzer, Jr. & Elisabeth, d. of Bastian Hasler.
HASSLER—Johannes, s. Jacob & w. Barbara; b. July 23, 1783; bap. Aug. 10, 1783; sp. Johannes Hassler & Christina, d. of Johannes Dauterich. Adam, s. of above; b. Feb. 10, 1786; bap. Mch. 7, 1786; sp. Christofel Hassler & w. Catharina. (The child died Mch. 8th.)
HARTING—Maria Catharina, d. Michael & Anna Maria; b. Jan. 1, 1781; bap. Feb. 18, 1781; sp. Catharina Bohmer.
HASSLER—Sebastian, s. Peter & w. Margretha; b. July 19, 1783; bap. Aug. 10, 1783; sp. Sebastian Hassler, Sr. & w. Barbara.

HASSLER—Anna Maria, d. Sebastian; b. ———; bap. Mch. 10, 1764; sp. Anna Maria Keller.
HASSLER—Heinrich, s. Sebastian & w. Anna; b. Sept. 25, 1777; bap. Feb. 15, 1778; sp. Heinrich Hoschaar & w. Margretha.
HASSLER—Magdalena, d. Sebastian, Jr. & w. Anna; b. Mch. 5, 1778; bap. Mch. 6, 1779; sp. Widow Magdalena Schlechty. Johannes, s. of above; b. Aug. 26, 1781; bap. Dec. 9, 1781; sp. The Parents.
HASSLER—Johannes, d. Sebastian & w. Barbara; b. July 19, 1767; bap. Aug. 22, 1767; sp. The Parents.
HASSLER—Johannes, s. Stofel & w. Catharina; b. Dec. 20, 1783; bap. Apr. 11, 1784; sp. Johannes Dautrich & w. Catharina.
HASLER—Joh. Jacob, s. Stephany & w. Magretha; b. Dec. 27, 1779; bap. Mch. 23, 1780; sp. Jacob Hassler & Magdalena Ketzemeyer.
HASSLER—Elisabeth, d. Stephain & w. Margretha; b. Aug. 31, 1781; bap. Sept. 16, 1781; sp. Ludwig Katzemayer & Elisabeth, d. of Bastian Hassler, both single.
HAUFER—Elisabeth, d. Jacob & w. Barbara; b. Dec. 4, 1752; bap. Dec. 24, 1752; sp. Michael Stoltz & Elisabeth Kohl.
HAUSER—Barbara, d. Jacob & w. Barbara; b. Dec. 15, 1754; bap. Dec. 24, 1754; sp. Gorg Miller & w Barbara.
HAUSSER—Johann Jacob, s. Jacob & w. Susanna; b. Aug. 20, 1770; bap. Nov. 17, 1770; sp. Jacob Zinn & w. Catharina.
HEER (HARE)—Anna Catharina, d. Peter & w. Christina; b. June 15, 1753; bap. July 22, 1753; sp. Friedrich Steindorff & Anna Catharina Thielmann.
HEFFT—Sara, d. Phillipus & w. Sara; b. June 27, 1769; bap. Aug. 15, 1769; sp. Christofel Hauerr & w. Anna Maria.
HEIL—Catharina Barbara, d. Heinrich & w. Margretha; b. Aug. 17, 1783; bap. Sept. 14, 1783; sp. Philip Heil & w. Catharina, the grandparents.
HELL—Johannes, s. Gorg Michael; b. ———; bap. Mch. 27, 1759; sp. Johann Fischer & Elisabeth Schmal.
HELL—Maria Catharina, d. Heinrich & w. Anna Elisabeth; b. May 3, 1760; bap. June 15, 1760; sp. Johann Nicolaus Baass & w. Maria Elisabeth.
HELLMAN—Joh. Daniel, s. Gorg and w. Christina; b. Nov. 17, 1760; bap. Dec. 23, 1760; sp. Daniel Lang & w. Maria Catharina.
HEILBERGER—Christina, d. Conrad & w. Catharina; b. Feb. 4, 1757; bap. Mch. 6, 1757; sp. Gorg Michael Weiss & w.

REV. JOHN WALDSCHMIDT—1752-1786. 173

Christina. Johann Jacob, s. of above; b. Oct. 14, 1759; bap. Nov. 11, 1759; sp. Rudolph Bullinger & w. Margretha.

HEGY—Johann Gorg, s Jacob & w. Friedrica Magdalena; b. June 14, 1755; bap. Aug. 9, 1755; sp. Lorentz Weber & w. Anna Maria.

HOSHAAR—Heinrich's wife; bap. 1750.

HERBACH—Maria Elisabeth, d. Johannes & w. Maria Elisabeth; b. Nov. 23, 1760; bap. Jan. 1, 1761; sp. Jost Herbach & w. Maria Elisabeth.

HERBACH—Elisabeth, d. Peter & w. Sophia; b. Dec. 28, 1777; bap. Mch. 15, 1778; sp. Adam Traxel & w. Elisabeth.

HERBEN—Daniel, s. Peter & w. Maria Magdalena; b. Feb. 19, 1780; bap. Apr. 23, 1780; sp. Daniel Zacharias & w.

HERCKE—Wilhelm, s. John & w. Maria; b. Jan. 4, 1775; bap. Jan. 19, 1775; sp. ———.

HERING—Johannes, s Johannes & w. Anna Elisabeth; b. Aug. 18, 1763; bap. Oct. 12, 1763; sp. Johannes Froschauer & w. Eva.

HERR—Johann Peter, s. Johan Peter Herr "und N. N."; b. Oct. 7, 1755; bap. Nov. 16, 1755; sp. Friedrich Steindorff & w. Anna Magdalena.

HERRY—Jacob, s. Johannes & w. Elisabeth; b. Apr. 8, 1777; bap. Dec. 25, 1778; sp. Jacob Klingemann & Eva Hoffmann. (The Father died seven weeks before.)

HERTZ—Johannes, s. Conrad & w. Elisabeth; b. Dec. 26, 1781; bap. July 2, 1782; sp. Melchoir Seqner & w. Catharina, who were married on same day, July 2, 1782. Conrad, s. of above; b. June 16, 1783; bap. Aug. 3, 1783; sp. Gorg Adam Schuck & w. Anna Maria. Fillippius s. of above; b. Feb. 6, 1785; bap. May 22, 1785; sp. Melchoir Seqner & w. Catharina.

HERTZ—Elisabeth, d. David & w. Christina; b. Oct. 6, 1783; bap. Oct. 26, 1783; sp. Peter Hertz & Elisabeth, d. Jacob Miller, decd. Johannes, s. of above; b. Jan. 30, 1786; bap. Mch. 26, 1786; sp. Bernhart Behler & w. Elisabeth.

HERTZ—Anna Maria, d. Peter & w. Elisabeth; b. June 15, 1785; bap. July 17, 1785; sp. Gorg Jacob Muller & sister Anna Maria.

HERTZOG—Maria Catharina, d. Johann Michael; b. ———; bap. Jan. 11, 1767; sp. Michael Hertzog & w.

HERTZOG—Sophia, d. Nicolaus & Margretha; b. Apr. 27, 1777; bap. May 19, 1777; sp. Christofel Reinhold & w. Sophia. Christine, d. of above; b. Nov. 5, 1779; bap. Apr. 16, 1780; sp. Christofel Scherb & w. Christine.

HETZLER—Christina, s. Balser & w. Barbara; b. Feb. 26, 1778; bap. Nov. 24, 1778; sp. The Sponsorship was performed by Magdalena Schlechty, with and for her son Christian.

HEYBERGER—Conrad, s. Conrad & w. Catharina; b. Oct. 3, 1753; bap. Oct. 7, 1753; sp. Rudolf Bollinger & w. Margretha.

HEYDSCHUK—Margaretha, d. Jacob & w. Dorothea; b. Oct. 2, 1756; bap. Oct. 31, 1756; sp. Fillipp Schmidt & Margaretha Vornwald, both single, but were married Dec. 14, 1756, in Reading.

HICCENELL—Heinrich, s. David & Anna Maria; b. Oct. 22, 1783; bap. Aug. 1, 1784; sp. The Parents.

HICKENELL—Johannes, s. ———; b. ———; bap. Apr. 8, 1781; sp. Johannes Bechthol & w. Anna Maria. (Parents' name and date of birth omitted in the original.)

HILLEBRAND—Catharina, d. Christian & w. Maria Catharina; b. Mch. 9, 1778; bap. Mch. 10, 1778; sp. Catharina Zwally. (The Parents married at this time.)

HIMBERGER—Jacob, s. Balser & Eva; b. Oct. 17, 1784; bap. Nov. 14, 1784; sp. Jacob Blanckebichler & Regina Rufner, both single.

HINSSY—Johann Adam, s. Christofel & w. Anna Maria; b. Jan. 8, 1783; bap. Mch. 29, 1783; sp. Johann Adam Weitzel & w. Catharina.

HISTER—Johann Wilhelm, s. Jost & w. Anna Elisabeth; b. Nov. 11, 1770; bap. Dec. 26, 1770; sp. The Father.

HOFFER—Heinrich, s. Jacob & w. Anna; b. May 7, 1783; bap. Dec. 5, 1784; sp. Johannes Heberling & w. Magdalena.

HOFFER—Jacob, s. Johannes; b. Nov. 6, 1755; bap. Feb. 11, 1756; sp. Jacob Hassler & w. Anna Maria. Johan Heinrich, s. of above; b. ———; bap. May 13, 1759; sp. Heinrich Walter & w. Anna Margretha. Isaac, s. of above; b. ———; bap. Dec. 20, 1761; sp. Isaac Wittmeyer & w.

HOFFER—Susanna, d. Johannes & w. Elisabeth; b. Feb. 5, 1765; bap. Mch. 20, 1765; sp. Casper Kabel & w. Susanna.

HOFFER—Fronica, d. Matthias & w. Anna Maria; b. Feb. 15, 1754; bap. Mch. 17, 1754; sp. Rudolf Vollweiler & w. Catharina.

HOFMAN—Anna Elisabeth, d. Heinrich & w. Eva; b. May 11, 1785; bap. July 3, 1785; sp. Balser Hoffman & Anna Elisabeth, d. of Christian Eschelmann.

HOFFMAN—Johann Conrad, s. Wilhelm & w. Catharina; b. Sept. 3, 1783; bap. Nov. 9, 1783; sp. Conrad Ruhl & w. Christina.

REV. JOHN WALDSCHMIDT—1752-1786. 175

HOFFMANN—Maria, d. Heinrich & w. Eva; b. July 11, 1780; bap. Aug. 13, 1780; sp. The Grandparents, Jacob Hoffmann & w. Maria.

HOLL—Jacob, s. Gorg Michael & w. Susanna; b. Nov. 10, 1763; bap. Apr. 6, 1766; sp. Jacob Kriech & w. Catharina. Rosina, d. of above; b. Nov. 6, 1765; bap. Apr. 3, 1766; sp. Peter Grauel & w. Rosina.

HORNBERGER—Johann Adam, s. Friedrich & w. Anna; b. Dec. 31, 1777; bap. Apr. 20, 1778; sp. Conrad Hornberger & w. Anna Catharina.

HORNBERGER—Joh. Carl, s. Gorg Friedrich & w. Anna; b. June 18, 1785; bap. July 3, 1785; sp. Jacob Hoffer & w. Anna.

HOSCHAAR—Johann Peter, s. Friedrich & w. Christina; b. Dec. 21, 1780; bap. Mch. 11, 1781; sp. Andreas Gartner & w. Elisabeth.

HOSCHAAR—Catharina, d. Friedrich & w. Christina; b. Nov. 4, 1783; bap. Apr. 12, 1784; sp. Johannes Zerbe & w. Catharina.

HOSCHAAR—Anna, d. Heinrich & w. Margretha; b. Mch. 12, 1777; bap. Apr. 27, 1777; sp. The Parents.

HOSSCHAUER—Johan Heinrich, s. Heinrich & w. Anna; b. Apr. 30, 1768; bap. May 4, 1768; sp. Jost Heinrich Schneider & w. Catharina. (The Mother died May 6, 1768.) Heinrich, s. of above; b. Apr. 17, 1764; bap. May 27, 1764; sp. Heinrich Ache & w. Anna.

HUBER—Margretha, d. Johannes & Maria Elisabeth; b. Sept. 18, 1760; bap. Oct. 6. 1760; sp. Peter Ritscher & w. Anna Margretha.

HUBNER—Anna Margretha, d. Solomon & w. Christine; b. Jan. 21, 1780; bap. Jan. 30, 1780; sp. Anna Margretha, d. of David Kummers.

HUSTER—Johannes, s. Johannes & w. Catharina; b. July 15, 1783; bap. Sept. 7, 1783; sp. The Parents.

HYGENELL—Jacob, s. David & Anna Maria; b. July 8, 1778; bap. Aug. 23, 1778; sp. Philip Hess & w. Sara.

ISCHUNG—Christian, s. Peter & w. Magdalena; b. June 14, 1760; bap. July 6, 1760; sp. Matthias Hoffer & w. Anna Maria.

SCHWEITZER (?)—Fronica, d. Christian & Fronica; b. Mch. 21, 1764; bap. May 27, 1764; sp. The Parents. (The child was not Schweitzer's own, as Fronica was pregnant by another man, but Schweitzer married her.)

176 BAPTISMAL AND MARRIAGE RECORDS.

ILLEGITIMATE—Johann Michael, s. Michael Battdorf & Margretha, d. Adam Bohmer, decd.; b. Jan. 23, 1782; bap. Feb. 9, 1783; sp. Michael Bohmer & w. Maria Barbara.

ILLEGITIMATE—Elisabetha, d. Elias Raird-Deurs-(Davis?) & Anna Maria, d. Heinrich Hahn; b. Jan. 2, 1784; bap. May 11, 1784; sp. Heinrich Hahn & w. Anna Christina. (This Elias Dairds afterwards married a d. of Johannes Gernants.)

ILLEGITIMATE—Catharina; d. ------ & Dorothea Hefft, widow; b. Aug. 8, 1778; bap. June 18, 1779; sp. Magdalena Getz.

ILLEGITIMATE—Johannes, s. Jacob Joner & Augustina Duss; b. Apr. 29, 1753; bap. May 17, 1753; sp. Johannes Duss.

ILLEGITIMATE—Maria Catharina, s. Heinrich Muller & Magdalena Kessler; b. Dec. 22, 1783; bap. May 24, 1784; sp. Johannes Dautrich & w. Anna Maria.

ILLEGITIMATE—Johan Gorg, s. Johannes Rempsberger & Catharina Davis; b. Apr. 9, 1777; bap. Aug. 25, 1777; sp. Gorg Spat & w. Anna Maria.

ILLEGITIMATE—Johannes, s. James Ritsher & Fronica, d. Paul Ebrecht; b. Feb. 1, 1783; bap. Mch. 29, 1783; sp. The Mother.

ILLEGITIMATE—On the 23rd. of Nov. 1773, a son of the widow of Jost Filtzmeyer was baptized. The Father of the child was Filip Wehrheim, a married man. The child was born Nov. 9, 1773; sp. Henry Hetterich & w. Catharina.

JACK—Catharina, d. Thomas & w. Maria; b. Mch. 19, 1783; bap. June 1, 1783; sp. Jacob Anweg & w. Catharina.

JACOB—Abraham, s. Philip; b. Oct. 9, 1761; bap. Oct. 9, 1761; sp. Abraham Hassler & w.

JACOB—Heinrich, s. Philip & w. Elisabeth; b. Jan. 11, 1781; bap. Feb. 18, 1781; sp. Michael Schauer & w. Maria.

JACOBI—Johann Adam, s. Adam & w. Anna Margretha; b. Apr. 22, 1755; bap. May 13, 1755; sp. Matthias Jacobi & w. Elisabeth, after whose marriage the child was baptized. (The child died 1759.) Maria Catharina, d. of above; b. Nov. 9, 1756; bap. Dec. 5, ------; sp. Jacob Van Kiman & Maria Catharina Laber. Anna Elisabeth, d. of above; b. Mch. 27, 1760; bap. Apr. 20, 1760; sp. Jacob Enck & w. Anna Maria.

JACOBI—Johannes, s. Matthias & w. Elisabeth; b. Mch. 17, 1756; bap. Mch. 29, 1756; sp. Adam Jacobi & w. Anna Margretha.

JOST—Johannes, s. Nicolaus, Jr. & w. Regina; b. Apr. 18, 1779; bap. May 2, 1779; sp. Johannes Klingeman & w. Christina.

JUNG—Johannes, s. Johannes; b. ------; bap. Apr. 3, 1757; sp. Johannes Ache & w.

REV. JOHN WALDSCHMIDT—1752-1786. 177

JUNG—Johannes, s. Johannes & w. Maria Elisabetha; b. Aug. 27, 1753; bap. Sept. 16, 1753; sp. Johannes Eberhart & Catharina Schuts.

JUNG—Dorrothea, d. Michael & w. Susanna; b. Mch. 5, 1779; bap. June 13, 1779; sp. Dorrothea, widow of Gorg Hefft.

KABEL—Abraham, s. Casper; b. ———; bap. Apr. 1, 1753; sp. Abraham Hassler & his Mother. Isaac, s. of above; b. ———; bap. June 1, 1755; sp. Abraham Hassler & Catharina Weller. Jacob, s. of above; b. ———; bap. June 1, 1755; sp. Joh. Siegfried Billing & Juliana Weller. Maria Magdalena, d of above; b. ———; bap. Nov. 19, 1757; sp. Michael Schafer & w. Susanna Catharina, d. of above; b. ———; bap. Mch. 14, 1759; sp. Gorg Nagel & w. Anna Catharina.

KABEL—Elisabeth, d. Casper & w. Susanna; b. Mch. 20, 1761; bap. Apr. 15, 1761; sp. Wilhelm Fischer & w. Elisabeth. Daniel, s. of above; b. Nov. 25, 1763; bap. Dec. 25, 1763; sp. Daniel Kabel & w. Barbara.

KACHEL—Elisabetha, d. Lenhart & w. Catharina; b. Jan. 26, 1779; bap. May 23, 1779; sp. Gorg Schlabach & Elisabetha Eschelmann, both single.

KAFROTH—Maria Dorothea, d. Gerhart & w. Maria Barbara; b. Nov. 2, 1752; bap. Dec. 17, 1752; sp. Mathias Beckel & w. Dorothea. Johann Jacob, s. of above; b. Dec. 2, 1754; bap. Dec. 22, 1754; sp. Matthias Beckel & w. Dorrothea.

KAMLER—Elisabeth, d. Jacob & w. Elisabeth; b. Nov. 21, 1779; bap. Mch. 26, 1780; sp. The Parents.

KAUFFER—Maria Catharina, d. Johann Heinrich & w. Anna Margretha; b. Dec. 15, 1752; bap. Jan. 4, 1753; sp. Maria Catharina Richter.

KEILER—Thomas, s. Heinrich; b. ———; bap. Oct. 22, 1752; sp. Thomas Scherb & w. Maria Barbara, d. of above; b. ———; bap. July 29, 1758; sp. Ludwig Schweitzer & w.

KEGEREISS—Name omitted, s. Christian, omitted; b. (no date); bap. Aug. 1, 1779; sp. Gorg Michael Brunner & w.

KELLER—Johannes, s. Heinrich & w. Anna Catharina; b. Mch. 3, 1781; bap. Mch. 18, 1781; sp. The Parents.

KELLER—Anna Christina, d. Heinrich & w. Christine; b. July 23, 1786; bap. same day; sp. Catharina, d. (Rev.) John Waldschmidt. Catharina Margretha, d. of above; b: Nov. 1, 1782; bap. Nov. 16, 1782; sp. Catharina Margretha, d. Rev. John Waldschmidt.

KELLER—Elisabeth; d. Johannes & w. Dorrothea; b. July 2, 1773; bap. July 11, 1773; sp. The Parents. Anna Maria,

12—Vol. VI—6th Ser.

d. of above; b. July 26, 1775; bap. Sept. 17, 1775; sp. Anna Maria, Johannes Rub's d., for whom child was named.

KELLER—Johannes, s. Johannes & w. Dorrothea; b. Apr. 24, 1777; bap. Apr. 27, 1777; sp. The Father. Margretha, d. of above; b. Jan. 18, 1779; bap. Feb. 7, 1779; sp. Maria Catharina Schweicker. Jacob, s. of above; b. Dec. 19, 1780; bap. Dec. 26, 1780; sp. The Parents. Anna Catharina, d. of above; b. July 19, 1782; bap. Aug. 29, 1782; sp. Peter Zimmermann & Anna Catharina Schlichty. Johannes, s. of above; b. Feb. 16, 1784; bap. Mch. 28, 1784; sp. Johannes Schweicker & Barbara Schlecht, both single. Heinrich, s. of above; b. Feb. 10, 1786; bap. Mch. 19, 1786; sp. The Parents.

KELLER—Elisabeth, d. Lehnhard & w. Elisabeth; b. Jan. 30, 1780; bap. May 15, 1780; sp. The mother-in-law, Elisabeth, w. of Johannes Muhleisen.

KELLER—Margretha, d. Martin; b. ———; bap. Nov. 24, 1750; sp. Jacob Schatz & Anna Margretha Brunner. J. Heinrich, s. of above; b. ———; bap. June 22, 1755; sp. Heinrich Ache & Margretha Brunner. Cath. Elisabetha, d. of above; b. ———; bap. Oct. 4, 1759; sp. George Ache & w. Catharina. Anna Barbara, d. of above; b. ———; bap. Mch. 3, 1762; sp. Hanss Kumler & w. Anna Maria.

KELLER—Johannes, s. Michael & w. Maria; b. Mch. 30, 1782; bap. May 28, 1782; sp. The Parents.

KELLER—Peter, s. Michael & w. Maria; b. June 9, 1783; bap. July 20, 1783; sp. Peter Brunner & Adam Schlechty, both single. Johannes, s. of above; b. Sept. 24, 1784; bap. Dec. 19, 1784; sp. The Parents.

KEPPLINGER—Barbara, d. Peter & w. Christina; b. Dec. 29, 1785; bap. June 25, 1786; sp. Jacob Kepplinger & w. Eva.

KEPPLINGER—Magdalena, d. Peter & w. Magdalena; b. Mch. 17, 1785; bap. Apr. 10, 1785; sp. Matthias Frey & w. Peter's sister. (The Mother d. eight days after the child was born.)

KERN—Johann Jacob, s. Thomas & w. Sophia; b. Jan. 18, 1771; bap. Mch. 3, 1771; sp. Jacob Kumler.

KESSLER—Daniel, s. Heinrich & w. Susanna; b. Dec. 13, 1782; bap. Aug. 10, 1783; sp. Daniel Becht & w. Catharina.

KIEFFABER—Anna Maria, d. Peter & w. Catharina; b. Jan. 18, 1754; bap. Jan. 21, 1754; sp. Maria Margaretha, w. of Johann Nicolaus Ensmenger. (The child died Jan. 24, 1754.)

KIEFFER—Christian, s. Friedrich & w. Sabina; b. Sept. 11, 1762; bap. Oct. 12, 1762; sp. Stefy Bart & w. Catharina.

KISSINGER—Gorg Michael, s. Adam & w. Elisabeth; b. Feb. 18, 1780; bap. May 28, 1780; sp. Gorg Michael Hull & w. Susanna. Johannes, s. of above; b. Feb. 17, 1782; bap. Sept. 15, 1782; sp. Johannes Hell & Barbara, d. Gorg Ruhm.
KISSINGER—Alexander, s. Alexander & w. Elisabeth; b. Mch. 28, 1777; bap. May 8, 1777; sp. Gorg Filip Kissinger & m. Catharina.
KIEFFER—Johann Gorg, s. Daniel & w. Catharina; b. Apr. 7, 1779; bap. May 23, 1779; sp. Gorg Burckhaus & w. Anna Margretha.
KISSINGER—Johann Phillippus, s. Filip & w. Catharina; b. Jan. 4, 1781; bap. July 15, 1781; sp. Johan Philip Hefft & w. Sara.
KISSINGER—Anna Maragretha, d. Friedrich & w. Barbara; b. May 11, 1785; bap. Oct. 2, 1785; sp. Fillip Schweicker & Anna Margretha, d. Gorg Siegethaler.
KISSINGER—Elisabetha, d. Gorg Filip & w. Catharina; b. Mch. 15, 1777; bap. May 8, 1777; sp. Alexander Kissinger & w. Elisabeth. Heinrich, s. of above; b. June 26, 1779; bap. Sept. 13, 1779; sp. Jacob Amweg & w. Catharina.
KISSINGER—Johan Friedrich, s. Phillip; b. ———; bap. Feb. 25, 1762; sp. Abraham Kissinger.
KISSINGER—Johannes, s. Philip & w. Catharina; b. Nov. 8, 1783; bap. Feb. 29, 1784; sp. Friedrich Kissinger & Sophia, d. Gorg Brunner. Johan Gorg, s. of above; b. July 7, 1786; bap. Aug. 20, 1786; sp. Gorg Brunner & w. Anna Maria.
KLEIN—Johannes, s. Fredrich & w. Elisabeth; b. Jan. 9, 1782; bap. Apr. 28, 1782; sp. Johannes Schneider & w. Margretha.
KLEIN—Catharina Elisabeth, d. Fredrich & w. Elisabeth; b. Jan. 9, 1782; bap. Apr. 28, 1782; sp. Jacob Schmid & w. Catharina. Daniel, s. of above; b. Sept. 14, 1783; bap. Nov. 30, 1783; sp. Daniel Albrecht & Elisabeth, d. Ludwig Tobias.
KLEIN—Anna Maria, d. Marx; b. ———; bap. Apr. 22, 1753; sp. Friedrich Muller & w.
KNAUFF—Anna Elisabeth, d. Johannes & w., Anna Elisabeth; b. Aug. 15, 1763; bap. Oct. 12, 1763; sp. Anna Graber & w. Anna Elisabeth.
KOCH—Heinrich, s. Adam & w. Anna Maria; b. Oct. 28, 1783; bap. Nov. 23, 1783; sp. Heinrich Fidler & w. Eva.
KOCH—Christofel, s. Johannes & w. Magdalena; b. Dec. 17, 1785; bap. Mch. 7, 1786; sp. Christofel Hassler & w. Catharina.
KOHL—Johannes, s. Gorg & w. Margretha; b. Feb. 10, 1781; bap. Apr. 1, 1781; sp. Johannes Stiehl & Maria Elisabeth

180   BAPTISMAL AND MARRIAGE RECORDS.

Kohl, both single. Gorg, s. of above; b. Jan. 12, 1784; bap. Apr. 12, 1784; sp. Gorg Kohl, Sr. & w. Catharina, the grandparents.
KOHLMANN—Jacob, s. Johannes & w. Christina; b. Mch. 27, 1772; bap. Apr. 21, 1772; sp. Jacob Frey & w. Anna Maria. (The parents were m. Nov. 26, 1771, 5 months.)
KONIG—Johannes, s. Jacob & w. Maria; b. Oct. 12, 1782; bap. Dec. 29, 1782; sp. Filltpus Heil & w. Catharina.
KOPF—Anna Elisabeth, w. of Ludwig; b. ———; bap Jan. 17, 1784. (She was of Mcnnonist origin.)
KOPPENHEFER—Maria Catharina, d. Thomas & w. Catharina; b. July 8, 1760; bap. Aug. 19, 1760; sp. Peter Feder & Regina Mosser.
KRAUS—Eva, d. Johannes & w. Anna Maria; b. ———; bap. Nov. 24, 1754; sp. Eva Muller.
KRICK—Anna Maria, d. Peter & w. Catharina; b. Nov. 9, 1784; bap. Jan. 1, 1785; sp. Heinrich Schneider & w. Catharina.
KROM—Elisabeth Margretha, d. Simon & w. Maria Catharina; b. Dec. 11, 1760; bap. Jan. 1, 1761; sp. Johannes Schonberger & Margretha Hahn.
KROMMLAUFF—Gottlieb, s. Jacob & w. Christina; b. Jan. 9, 1784; bap. Apr. 12, 1784; sp. Adam Gramlin & w. Elisabeth.
KRUMBEIN—Anna Maria, d. Lenhart & w. Catharina; b. July 3, 1755; bap. July 29, 1755; sp. Gorg Backer & w. Anna Maria.
KRUMLAUFF—Jacob, s. Jacob & w. Christina; b. Mch. 19, 1779; bap. May 2, 1779; sp. Jacob Hoffer & Cathara Gramlin.
KUCHEL—Elisabetha, d. Jacob & w. Fronica; b. Nov. 4, 1758; bap. Nov. 11, 1758; sp. Michael Meyer & w. Elisabeth.
KULLINGER—Johann Peter, s. Andreas & w. Anna; b. Apr. 27, 1759; bap. Dec. 13, 1759; sp. Peter Rittscher & w. Anna Margretha.
KUMMERS—Anna, about 19 yrs. old, d. Daniel; bap. May 3, 1780; sp. ———.
KUNTZ—Maria Margreth, d. Johannes; b. ———; bap. Aug. 20, 1771; sp. Engel Becker & w.

LABER—Christina, d. Balsar & w. Elisabeth; b. Dec. 30, 1754; bap. Feb. 23, 1755; sp. Michael Laber & w. Regina.
LABER—Anna Maria, d. Michael & w. Regina; b. Dec. 11, 1753; bap. Dec. 23, 1753; sp. Balser Laber & Anna Maria, d. of the decd. Johann Wendel Laber.

LANG—Peter, s. Chilian & w. Magdalena; b. Mch. 10, 1760; bap. Oct. 6, 1760; sp. Jacob Dutz & w. Rebecca.

LANG—Margreth, d. Daniel & w. Maria Catharina; b. Nov. 9, 1760; bap. Dec. 28, 1760; sp. Johann Adam Fissler & w. Margretha.

LAUB—Johan Gorg, s. Conrad & w. Elisabeth; b. Oct. 1, 1778; bap. Apr. 10, 1779; sp. Nicolaus Jost, Jr. & w. Regina.

LAUDESCHLAGER—Johan Gorg, s. Heinrich & w. Anna Elisabeth; b. Oct. 20; 1764; bap. Sept. 17, 1765; sp. Were parents of the mother, Jacob (Muts) Mutes & w. Appollonia.

LAYER—Maria Elisabeth, d. Gorg & w. Barbara; b. Mch. 10, 1782; bap. Apr. 14, 1782; sp. Carl Schenckel & w. Maria Elisabeth.

LEHNHART—Anna Catharina, d. Jacob & w. Eva; b. June 21, 1752; bap. Aug. 29, 1752; sp. Adam Oberling & w. Catharina.

LEHNHERR—Filip Christian, s. Jacob & w. Eva; b. Oct. 7, 1762; bap. Nov. 21, 1762; sp. Filip Kreig & w. Catharina.

LEHRUH—Peter, s. Peter & w. Elisabeth; b. Oct. 22, 1752; bap. Dec. 3, 1752; sp. The Parents.

LERUE—Catharina, d. Peter & Anna Maria; b. Oct. 11, 1754; bap. Dec. 15, 1754; sp. Ignatius Leidner & w. Margaretha.

LERUH—Anna Barbara, d. Peter & w. Elisabeth; b. Jan. 2, 1757; bap. Mch. 29, 1757; sp. The Parents.

LEYSY—Johannes, s. Joseph & w. Sophia; b. June 2, 1785; bap. July 10, 1785; sp. His brother-in-law, Peter Schneider.

LIED—Catharina, d. Jacob & w. Catharina; b. Apr. 7, 1782; bap. May 26, 1782; sp. Peter Fischer & w. Catharina.

LINCK—Johannes s. Jchannes & w. Margretha; b. Dec. 16, 1769; bap. Mch. 25, 1770; sp. Filip Gebel & w. Margretha.

LITSH—Johann Daniel, s. Sebastian (Catholic Religion) & w. Magdalena; b. Mch. 23, 1754; bap. Apr. 14, 1754; sp. Thomas Geissler & Anna Eva, d. Filip Eckert.

LOSCHER—Anna Maria, d. Johannes & w. Elisabeth; b. Dec. 7, 1783; bap. Apr. 11, 1784; sp. Johann Nicolaus Loscher & Anna Maria, d. Heinrich Binckle.

LOSER—Christine, d. Andreas & w. Christine; b. Feb. 25, 1777; bap. Apr. 27, 1777; sp. Wilhelm Brendel & w. Anna Maria.

LOSSER—Johann Joseph, s. Nicolaus & w. Elisabeth; b. Mch. 1, 1784; bap. Mch. 20, 1785; sp. The brother-in-law, Johannes Fuhrmann.

LOTZ—Susanna Catharina, d. Johannes & w. Barbara; b. Nov. 23, 1776; bap. Feb. 2, 1777; sp. Johannes Schaub & Susanna, d. Christofel Kern.

LUCKHART—Anna Barbara, d. Conrath & w. Anna Maria; b. Sept. 22, 1782; bap. Nov. 24, 1782; sp. Gorg Muller & w. Anna Barbara.

LUCKHART—Conrath, s. Conrad & w. Anna Maria; b Oct. 6, 1783; bap. Nov. 30, 1783; sp. Wilhelm Vogel, a widower.

LUCKORT—Eva, d. Conrath & w. Anna Maria; b. Oct. 1, 1781; bap. Dec. 2, 1781; sp. Casper Wecht & w. Eva.

LUTZ—Johann Adam, s. Daniel & w. Margretha; b. Aug. 16, 1782; bap. Sept. 29, 1782; sp. Jost Schonauer & w. Catharina.

MACHAMER—Phillip, s. Nicolaus & w. Rosina; b. Sept. 29, 1781; bap. Oct. 21, 1781; sp. Phillip Machamar & Margretha Lauer.

MACHAMER—Christian, s. Henry & w. Elisabeth; b. Dec. 1, 1779; bap. Apr. 23, 1780; sp. Christian Lauer, his brother-in-law, yet single.

MACHAMER—Anna Maria, d. Nicolaus & w. Rosina; b. Sept. 21, 1779; bap. Oct. 31, 1779; sp. Bastian Berlet & w. Anna Maria.

MACHMER—Daniel, s. Fillip & w. Elisabeth; b. Oct. 23, 1782; bap. Nov. 24, 1782; sp. Johannes Diehl & w. Catharina.

MACHMER—Nicolaus, s. Heinrich & w. Elisabeth; b. Jan. 20, 1783; bap. May 18, 1783, p. Nicolaus Machmer & w. Rosina.

MACHMER—Catharina, d. Nicolaus & w. Rosina; b. Jan. 1, 1784; bap. Apr. 9, 1784; sp. Abraham Riesser & w. Catherina.

MANTEL—Catharina Elisabeth, d. Christofel & w. Catharina; b. Mch. 17, 1785; bap. ———; sp. Andreas Schmidt & Catharina, w. of Heinrich Muller.

MARCHALL—Sara, d. Dietrich & w. Juliana; b. Sept. 23, 1785; bap. Nov. 20, 1785; sp. Hector Pahn & w. Margretha.

MAST—Johann Heinrich, s. Conrath & w. Christina; b. Mch. 9, 1781; bap. June 17, 1781; sp. Heinrich Muller & w. Elisabeth.

MASTALLART—Anna Maria, d. Ludwig & w. Anna Elisabeth; b. ———; bap. Mch. 17, 1765; sp. David Wildermuth & w. Anna Maria.

MAYER—Barbara, d. Gorg & w. Barbara; b. June 16, 1760; bap. July 6, 1760; sp. Valentine Kremer & w. Barbara.

MAYER—Catharina, d. Heinrich & w. Catharina; b. June 30, 1778; bap. Nov. 8, 1778; sp. David Mayer & w. Anna Maria.

MAYER—Jacob, s. Jacob & w. Maria Sara; b. Feb. 2, 1782; bap. Apr. 28, 1782; sp. Jacob Spatz & w. Anna Maria.

MAYER—Maria Barbara, d. Michael & w. Elisabeth; b. Feb. 22, 1782; bap. ———; sp. Maria Barbara, widow of Gorg Mayer & Mother of Michael.

MELL—Elisabeth, d. Carl & w. Anna Maria; b. Dec. 8, 1774; bap. Dec. 26, 1774; sp. Melchoir Mell & w. Elisabeth. Johannes, s. of above; b. Apr. 15, 1776; bap. Apr. 30, 1776; sp. Johannes Mell & w. Susanna. Johann Heinrich, s. of above; b. Feb. 1, 1778; bap. Apr. 4, 1778; sp. Heinrich Fischer & w. Christina. Joh. Wilhelm, s. of above; b. Oct. 5, 1779; bap. Oct. 11, 1779; sp. Joh Wilhelm Michael & w. Elisabeth.

MELLEN—Valentine, s. Samuel & w. Susanna; b. Oct. 11, 1783; bap. Nov. 9, 1783; sp. Valentine Moser & w. Rosina.

MENGER—Johann Jacob, s. Jacob & w. Elisabeth; b. May 9, 1780; bap. June 11, 1780; sp. Johannes Strack & w. Catharina.

MESSNER—Filip Jacob, s. Filip Jacob & w. Catharina; b. Feb. 19, 1781; bap. Apr. 1, 1781; sp. The Grandparents, viz, Casper Messner & w. Barbara.

MESSNER—Anna Catharina, d. Johannes & w. Catharina; b. Oct. 6, 1783; bap. Oct. 26, 1783; sp. Anna Barbara Mosser. Elisabeth, d. of above; b. Mch. 1, 1786; bap. Apr. 16, 1786; sp. Johannes Mosser & w. Elisabeth.

MEYER—Joh. Gorg, s. Gorg & w. Barbara; b. Nov. 14, 1758; bap. Dec. 31, 1758; sp. Gorg Meyer & Catharina Meyer, both single.

MEYER—Maria Eva, d. Gorg & w. Anna Maria; b. Sept. 4, 1776; bap. Apr. 2, 1780; sp, Friedrich Bengel & w. Maria Eva. Gorg Friedrich, s. of above; b. June 4, 1779; bap. Apr. 2, 1780; sp. Friedrich Bengel & w. Maria Eva.

MEYER—Catharina, d Jacob & w. Margretha; b. Nov. 26, 1752; bap. Apr. 29, 1753; sp. Johannes Bender & Catharina Rudolf.

MEYER—Catharina, d. Jacob & w. Sara; b. June 19, 1777; bap. June 4, 1780; sp. Paul Derst & w. Catharina. Elisabeth, d. of above; b. Sept. 7, 1779; bap. June 4, 1780; sp. Michael Meyer & w. Elisabeth.

MEYGER—Johann Peter, s. Henry & w. Barbara; b. Dec. 29, 1753; bap. Mch. 13, 1754; sp. Johann Peter Ravensberger & w. Juliana.

MODEREISS—Heinrich, s. Heinrich & w. Margretha; b. Nov. 14, 1778; bap. Apr. 5, 1779; sp. Heinrich Reding & Eva Gicker.

MOHN—Margretha, d. Ludwig & w. Catharina; b. Aug. 30, 1763; bap. Sept. 11, 1763; sp. Johann Adam Krick & Margretha, d. Gorg Hain.

MOOR—Elisabeth, d. John & w. Elisabetha; b. Oct. 3, 1778; bap. June 6, 1779; sp. Magdalena Sieb.

MOSER—Joh. Casper, s. Casper & w.; b. ———; bap. Nov. 21, 1749; sp. Friedrich Wurtz & w.

MOSER—Anna Maria, d. Nicolaus & w. Anna Maria; b. Oct. 4, 1783; bap. Oct. 26, 1783; sp. Anna Barbara, widow John Moser.

MOSER—Anna Elisabeth, d. Nicolaus & w. Elisabeth; b. Dec. 25, 1780; bap. Jan. 28. 1781; sp. Johannes Moser & Anna Elisabeth, d. Christian Eschelmann.

MOSER—Johannes, s. Valentine & w. Rosina; b. Dec. 27, 1782; bap. Jan. 26, 1783; sp. Johannes Moser, brother of Valentine, single.

MOSER—Catharina, d. Weyerich & w. Margretha; b. May 24, 1779; bap. June 6, 1779; sp. The Parents.

MOSSER—Johannes, s. Johannes & w. Elisabeth; b. Feb 15, 1785; bap. Mch. 6, 1785; sp. The Parents. Anna Margretha, d. of above; b. Feb. 19, 1786; bap. Mch. 26, 1786; sp. Anna Margretha Schorp.

MOSSER—Maria Barbara, d. Nicolaus & w. Anna Maria; b. Feb. 27, 1779; bap. Apr. 11, 1779; sp. Gorg Schlapbach & Margretha, d. of the decd. Johannes Mosser. Johannes, s. of above; b. Aug. 20, 1785; bap. 9 Oct, 1785; sp. Johannes Messner & w. Anna Catharina.

MOTHER—Amali, d. Daniel & w. Amali; b. Jan. 16, 1783; bap. Mch. 29, 1783; sp. The Parents.

MULLER—Catharina, d. David & w. Elisabeth; b. June 28, 1785; bap. Aug. 14, 1785; sp. Gorg Trostel & w. Rosina. (Troxtel if the Father-in-law.)

MULLER—Johann Jacob, s. Filip Gorg & w. Barbara; b. Feb. 16, 1754; bap. Mch. 6, 1754; sp. Jacob Hausser & w. Barbara.

MULLER—Martin, s. Heinrich & w. Anna; b. Dec. 1, 1759; bap. June 10, 1760; sp. Odemann Schnebele & w. Barbara.

MULLER—Johann Philipp, s. Henry & w. Susanna Margaretha; b. Feb. 5, 1754; bap. Mch. 27, 1754; sp. Johannes Philipp Ensmenger & Elisabetha Merckll.

MULLER—Johann Theobald, s. Johannes; b. ———; bap. Oct. 8, 1761; sp. Theobald Kuntz.

MULLER—Catharina, d. Jeremias & w. Angnes; b. Dec. 11, 1779; bap. Aug. 20, 1780; sp. Conrath Schneider & Anna Eva Achebach, both single.

MULLER—Johannes, d. Jeremias & w. Elisabeth; b. Jan. 4, 1783; bap. Apr. 6, 1783; sp. The Father.

MULLER—Anna Maria, Christina, drs. Lehnhart & w. Catharina; b. Sept. 19, 1753; bap. Oct. 14, 1753; sp. Lehnhart Stein & w. Anna Maria; sp. Johann Jacob Wernss & Christina, d. Johannes Diefendorffer.

MULLER—Jacob, s. Nicolaus & w. Christina; b. Sept. 7, 1780; bap. Jan. 7, 1782; sp. Adam Hissner, the Father-in-law.

NAASS—Johannes, s. Matthias & w. Magdalena, b. Apr 6, 1781; bap. June 3, 1781; sp. Johannes Muhleisen & w. Eva.

NEIDIG—David, s. Solomon & ———; b. ———; bap. Oct. 25, 1783; sp. ——— Grunewald & w.

NEIDIG—Johan Abraham, s. Salomon & w. Elisabeth; b. Nov. 26, 1778; bap. Dec. 25, 1778; sp. Jacob Siegfried & Dorrothea Wolff.

NEIDIG—Johan Abraham, s. Solomon & w. Maria Elisabeth; b. Jan. 17, 1780; bap. Mch. 26, 1780; sp. Abraham Ruhm & w. Elisabeth.

NICKEL—Johann Ludwig, s. Johann Gorg & w. Anna Magdalena; b. Apr. 3, 1753; bap. Apr. 22, 1753; sp. Johann Ludwig Zimmerman & w. Maria Elisabetha, w. of Johannes Schneido.

NICODEMUS—Joh. Adam, s. Adam & w. Maria Christine; b. July 6, 1757; bap. Aug. 6, 1757; sp. Friedrich Steindorff & w. Magdalena.

NICODEMUS—Joh. Bernard, s. Conrad & w. Anna Maria; b. Jan. 21, 1761; bap. Feb. 1, 1761; sp. Bernhard Pfeiffer & w. Maria Margretha.

NICODEMUS—Anna Magdalena, d. Friedrich & w. Catharina; b. Apr. 12, 1758; bap. Apr. 23, 1758; sp. Friedrich Steindorff & w. Anna Margretha.

NICODEMUS—Johannes Conrath, s. Friederich & w. Elisabeth; b. Oct. 15, 1755; bap. Oct. 26, 1755. The God Parents were Peter Schaaff & w. Anna Elisabetha, Johann Conrath Nicodemus, Johann Heinrich Kuntz & Catharina Elisabetha Steindorff.

NEU—Anna Maria, d. Josef & w.; b. ———; bap. Nov. 21, 1749; sp. Balser Hissung & w.

NEUKOMMER—Peter, s. Frantz & w. Regina; b. May 24, 1760; bap. June 15, 1760; sp. The Doctor Peter Gudelius & w. Anna Maria.

PATTON—Johannes, s. Jacob; b. Feb. 25, 1782; bap. June 16, 1782; sp. Gorg Kohl & w. Margretha. (Wife's name not given in Record.)
PETER—Catharina, Anna Maria, ds. Casper & w.; b. not stated; bap. May 7, 1783; sp. The Parents.
PFEIFER—Catharina Elisabetha, d.'Jacob & w. Catharina Margaretha; b. Dec. 4, 1756; bap. Dec. 25, 1756; sp. Johann Peter Lebo & Catharina Elisabetha Riegel.
PFIEFFER—Johann Martin, s. Josef & Fronica; b. Mch. 18, 1758; bap. Apr. 23, 1758; sp. Johann Martin Hegy & Elisabetha, d. of Martin Wallayser.
PHEIFER—Johannes, s. Adam & w. Fronica; b. Oct. 22, 1758; bap. Dec. 3, 1758; sp. Johannes Schultz & Elisabetha, d. Adam Kuhner.
PICKENS—Samuel, s. Samuel & w. Elisabeth; b. Feb. 1, 1813; bap. Mch. 21, 1813; sp. Johannes Waldschmidt & w. Susanna.
PONTIUS—Anna Maria, d. David & w. Anna Elisabeth; b. Aug. 11, 1784; bap. Sept. 12, 1784; sp. Jacob Hoffer & w. Anna.
PRACHT—Joh. Peter, s. Daniel & w. Anna Margretha; b. May 10, 1758; bap. June 18, 1758; sp. Peter Klein & w. Barbara.
PRILLINGER—Peter, s. Peter & w. Elisabeth; b. Apr. 29, 1760; bap. June 15, 1760; sp. Peter Cudellus & w. Anna Maria.

RAGELE—Johannes, s. Adam & w. Margretha; b. Jan. 31, 1753; bap. Feb. 11, 1753; sp. Johannes Zimmerman & Anna Catharina Burmann.
RANCK—Maria Barbara, d. Filipp, Junr. & w. Magdalena; b. Nov. 15, 1754; bap. Nov. 24, 1754; sp. Durst Ammen & Barbara Ranck, both single.
RAPP—Wilhelm, d. Wilhelm & w. Catharina; b. Aug. 13, 1778; bap. Sept. 3, 1778; sp. Wilhelm Guting & Elisabeth Neukering. Anna, d. of above; b. Aug. 26, 1781; bap. Oct. 14, 1781; sp. Nicolaus Riehl & Anna Maria, d. Weyerick Moser.
RAVENSBERGER—Martinus, s. Peter & Juliana; b. Jan. 31, 1753; bap. Feb. 11, 1753; sp. Martin Braun & w. Catharina. Jacob, s. of above; b. June 4, 1755; bap. June 15, 1755; sp. Jacob Geiger & Eva, d. Jacob Huber. Maria Elisabeth, d. of above; b. Nov. 4, 1759; bap. Jan. 6, 1760; sp. Peter Meyer & w. Maria Elisabeth.
REDIG—Johann Filip, s. Joh. Gorg; b. ———; bap. May 13, 1753; sp. Filip Laubenschlager & w.

REICH—Maria Magdalena, d. Heinrich & w. Magdalena; b. Sept. 16, 1753; bap. Sept. 30, 1753; sp. Johannes Meddauer & Maria Magdalena, w. of Philip Roth.
REICH—(Christian name omitted), d. Heinrich Reich & his w.; b. Nov. 6, 1757; bap. Dec. 22, 1757; sp. Filip Roth & Johannes Wittauers's wife.
REINHART—Barbara, d. Joh. Gorg & w. Anna Margretha; b. Mch. 9, 1756; bap. Mch. 17, 1756; sp. Joh. Nicolaus Schmid & w. Martin, s. of above; b. Jan. 11, 1759; bap. Jan. 27, 1759; sp. Martin Tschudy & w. Anna.
REINHART—Anna Margaretha, d. Johann Gorg & w. Elisa Margaretha; b. Mch. 16, 1754; bap. Mch. 31, 1754; sp. Johann Adam Jacobi & w. Anna Margaretha.
REINHOLD—Johan Heinrich, s. Christof Heinrich; b. ———; bap. Mch. 26, 1758; sp. Henry Walter & w. Margaretha.
REINHOLD—Jacob Freidrich, s. Heinrich Stofel; b. ———; bap. May 12, 1762; sp. Jacob Amweg & w. Anna Elisabeth.
REISS—Johan, s. Adam; b. ———; bap. Sept. 23, 1759; sp. Johannes Keller & Anna Catharina Jacob.
REITEL—Elisabeth, d. Jost; b. ———; bap. July 24, 1762; sp. Gorg Geyer & w. Catharina.
REITEL—Juliana, d. Jost & w. Magdalena; b. Nov. 7, 1759; bap. Jan. 6, 1760; sp. Heinrich Cafroth & Juliana Ravensberger.
REITTENBACH—Catharina, d. Peter & w. Elisabeth; b. Dec. 25; 1778; bap. Feb. 5, 1779; sp. Johannes Meister & w. Catharina.
RESSLER—Jacob, s. Gorg; b. ———; bap. Dec. 25, 1767; sp. Jacob Kumler & Elisabeth Motz.
REUTER—Anna Margaretha, d. Philip Jacob & w. Anna Maria; b. Sept. 6, 1753; bap. Sept. 16, 1753; sp. Eberhard Thomas & Anna Margaretha, w. of Johann Heinrich Schramm.
REYGER—Eva Christina, d. Johann Heinrich & Maria Elisabeth; b. Aug. 24, 1753; bap. Sept. 16, 1753; sp. Jacob Neef & w. Eva Christina.
RIECH—Maria Catharina, d. Daniel & Anna Maria; b. Jan. 12, 1779; bap. Apr. 2, 1779; sp. Chiljan Kehl & w. Anna Maria.
RIECHER—Anna Maria, d. Jacob & w. Magdalena; b. Feb. 16, 1783; bap. June 15, 1783; sp. Elisabeth, d. Gorg Trostel.
REIG—Johannes, s. Daniel & w. Anna Maria; b. July 10, 1777; bap. Aug. 25, 1777; sp. Heinrich Voliker & w. Barbara.

188   BAPTISMAL AND MARRIAGE RECORDS.

RIEHL—Juliana, d. Johannes & w. Catharina; b. July 23, 1779; bap. Sept. 5, 1779; sp. Solomon Neidig & w. Maria Elisabetha. Maria Christina, d. of above; b. Nov. 29, 1780; bap. Nov. 26, 1780;—sie—sp. Gorg Bender & Christina Kleh.

RIEHM—Johannes, s. Abraham & w. Elisabeth; b. July 23, 1779; bap. Sept. 17, 1779; sp. Andreas Burckert & w. Anna Barbara. Esther, d. of above; b. Sept. 25, 1781; bap. Aug. 14, 1785; sp. The Parents. Abraham, s. of above; b. Aug. 1, 1784; bap. Aug. 14, 1785; sp. The Parents.

RIEHM—Johann Filip, s. Andreas & Susanna; b. Aug. 23, 1760; bap. Aug. 27, 1760; sp. Jacob Riehm & w. Christina.

RIEHM—Johannes, s. Friedrich & Magdalena; b. Sept. 26, 1783; bap. Oct. 14, 1784; sp. The Parents.

RIEHM—Magdalena, d. Gorg & w. Magdalena; b. Dec. 18, 1781; bap. Apr. 7, 1782; sp. Johannes Hahn & w. Magdalena.

RIEHM—Anna Maria, d. Johannes & w. Maria Eva; b. Sept. 30, 1752; bap. Dec. 13, 1752; sp. Marx Egly & w. Elisabetha.

RIESS—Johan Adam, s. Adam; b. ———; bap. Oct. 16, 1757; sp. Filip Jacob & Maria Elisabeth Binckle.

RIESSER—Susanna, d. Abraham & w. Catharina; b. Jan. 25, 1782; bap. Aug. 7, 1782; sp. Johann Christ Hiester & w. Susanna.

RIETH—Joh. Martin, s. Peter; b. ———; bap. Dec. 31, 1762; sp. Martin Driesbach & Catharina Schneider.

RIETH—Anna Maria, d. Peter & w. Elisabeth; b. Dec. 22, 1783; bap. Jan. 18, 1784; sp. Jacob Schneider & Anna Maria, d. Heinrich Binckle.

RIMMEL—Catharina, d. Gorg & w. Barbara; b. June 24, 1778; bap. June 13, 1779; sp. Gorg Keller & Catharina Gotz, both single.

RISS—Gorg Michael, s. Adam Riss; b. Mch. 27, 1756; bap. Apr. 24, 1756; sp. Gorg Brunner & w.

ROBERT—Maria Barbara, d. Johannes & w. Anna Maria; b. ———; bap. Apr. 27, 1765; sp. Thomas Robert & Maria Barbara Arbegert.

ROHLAND—Maria Elisabetha, d. Abraham & w. Maria Eva; b. Dec. 28, 1753; bap. Jan. 13, 1754; sp. Jacob Bullinger & w. Maria Elisabeth.

ROHRER—Johannes, s. Johannes & w. Barbara; b. Oct. 1, 1760; bap. Oct. 6, 1760; sp. Johannes Huber & w. Maria Elisabeth.

ROSENBERGER—Johann Daniel, s. Abraham & w. Juliana; b. Dec. 30, 1752; bap. June 20, 1753; sp. Daniel Besshaar & Catharina Becker.   Abraham, s. of above; b. Jan. 31, 1754;

bap. Feb. 17, 1754; sp. Johann Ludwig Chiljan Long & Anna Margaretha, d. Philip Eckert.

ROTH—Joh. Heinrich, s. Filip & w. Margretha; b. May 11, 1760; bap. June 8, 1760; sp. Heinrich Reich & Maria Catharina, w. of Johann Meddauer.

ROTH—Johannes, s. Johannes & w. Anna Maria; b. Apr. 4, 1786; sp. Ludwig Schweitzer & w. Anna Maria Rothacker.

RUB—Anna Maria, d. Jacob & w. Juliana; b. Aug. 26, 1761; bap. Sept. 23, 1761; sp. Anna Maria, w. Abraham Riehm. (The Father & Mother were married Aug. 10, 1761.)

RUCHER—Jacob, s. Jacob & w. Magdalena; b. Dec. 10, 1785; bap. Aug. 16, 1786; sp. The Father.

RUDOLF—Johann Conrad, s. Emmerick & w. Catharina; b. Mch. 20, 1753; bap. Apr. 29, 1753; sp. Felix Schutz & w. Fronica.

RUDY—Johannes, s. Emig & w. Catharina; b. Jan. 8, 1755; bap. Feb. 16, 1755; sp. Johannes Schutz & w. Margretha. Samuel, s. of above; b. Oct. 2, 1762; bap. Nov. 9, 1762; sp. Daniel Dieff & w. Juliana, who were married the day the child was baptized.

RUDY—Andreas, s. Johann Heinrich & w. Catharina; b. Dec. 6, 1756; bap. Dec. 19, 1756; sp. Johannes Kuntz.

RUHL—Elisabeth, d. Conrath & Christina; b. Feb. 2, 1782; bap. Apr. 7, 1782; sp. Gorg Reber & w. Elisabeth. Johannes, s. of above; b. Nov. 16, 1783; bap. Nov. 30, 1783; sp. Johannes Epler & w. Elisabeth.

RUHM—Anna Barbara, Johannes, Joh. Friedrich, Abraham; b. date omitted; bap. May 13, 1759; sp. Gorg Becker & w. Anna Maria, Johannes Ruhm & w. Maria Eva, Eberhart Ruhm, The Parents.

RUHM—Rosina, d. Abraham, Jr. & Rosira; b. Sept. 11, 1778; bap. Nov. 4, 1778; sp. The Parents.

RUP—Anna Maria, d. Nicolaus; b. ———; bap. Apr. 2, 1759; sp. Johannes Rup & w. Elisabeth, d. of above; b. ———; bap. Jan. 9, 1762; sp. Jost Walter & w. Elisabeth

RUP—Anna Barbara, d. Nicolaus; b. ———; bap. Sept. 16, 1763; sp. Hanss Billman & w. Heinrich, s. of above; b. ———; Dec. 25, 1767; sp. Christof Reinhold & w. Gorg, s. of above; b Sept. 12, 1769; bap. Sept. 12, 1770; sp. Gorg Roth & w. Christine. Catharina, d. of above; b. ———; bap. May 7, 1771; sp. Gorg Schneider & w.

RUP—Anna Maria, d. Nicolaus & w. Anna Maria; b. July 28, 1765; bap. Sept. 8, 1765; sp. Anna Maria Rup.

RUTH—Maria Barbara, d. Michael & w. Anna Maria; b. Aug. 19, 1763; bap. Sept. 11, 1763; sp. Maria Barbara, d. Peter Ruth.

SALATE—Johannes, s. Friedrich & w. Barbara; b. May 30, 1754; bap. Sept. 1, 1754; sp. Heinrich Bartholemay Schafer.

SALGEBE—Anna Barabra, d. Salomo & w. Anna Barbara; b. Jan. 14, 1776; bap. May 23, 1779; sp. Anna Margretha Scherb & Johannes Moser & Elisabeth Kleinkinnes. Elisabeth, d. of above; b. Nov. 1, 1778; bap. May 23, 1778; sp. Anna Margretha Scherb & Johannes Moser & Elisabeth Kleinkinnes.

SALGLY—Susanna, d. Samuel & w. Barbara; b. Sept. 14, 1779; bap. Oct. 17, 1779; sp. Johannes Moser & Elisabeth Kleinkonig.

SAUBER—Elisabetha, d. Heinrich & w. Eva; b. Dec. 10, 1778; bap. Apr. 11, 1779; sp. Bernhard Behler & w. Elisabeth.

SAUBERT—Elisabeth, d. Heinrich & w. Elisabeth; b. Apr. 20, 1783; bap. Aug. 3, 1783; sp. Jacob Saubert & w. Elisabeth.

SCHAB—Mathaus, s. Andreas; b. ———; bap. May 26, 1751; sp. Mathaus Beckle & w.

SCHAFFER—Peter, s. Gorg & w. Anna Maria; b. Sept. 29, 1759; bap. June 10, 1760; sp. Peter Wallmer & w. Margretha.

SCHAFFER—Elisabeth, d. Heinrich & w. Margretha; b. Dec. 20, 1782; bap. Dec. 22, 1782; sp. Michael Roth & w. Elisabeth, the parents of the child's mother.

SCHAFFNER—Catharina, d. Johann Jacob & w. Eva; b. Mch. 7, 1760; bap. July 7, 1760; sp. Jacob Schmeid & w. Catharina.

SCHAFNER—Catharina, d. Heinrich; b. ———; bap. Mch. 16, 1751; sp. Peter Fischer & Catharina Hoschaar. Elisabeth, d. of above; b. July 26, 1756; bap. Aug. 10, 1756; sp. Hans Billmann & w. Martin, s. of above; b. ———; bap. Sept. 23, 1759; sp. Martin Burckholder & w. Anna Barbara, d. ofo above; b. ———; bap. Nov. 27, 1762; sp. Bastian Hassler & w.

SCHAUB—Johann Christian, s. Andreas & w. Susanna Elisabetha; b. June 27, 1753; bap. Aug. 5, 1753; sp. Peter Ravensberger & w. Juliana.

SCHAUER—Elisabeth, d. Johann Nicolaus & w. Maria; b. May 5, 1780; bap. June 11, 1780; sp. Fillipus Schlebach & w. Elisabeth.

SCHAUER—Daniel, s. Nicolaus & w. Maria; b. Feb. 19, 1783; bap. Aug. 13, 1783; sp. the Parents.

SCHEIBLE—Anna Maria, d. Daniel & w. Barbara; b. Oct. 2, 1752; bap. Mch. 4, 7153; sp. Johann Peter Burgener & Juliana Kohl.

SCHEIBLE—Johan Jacob, s. Johannes; b. ———; bap. Apr. 6, 1751; sp. Jacob Creutz & Magdalena Domm,

REV. JOHN WALDSCHMIDT—1752-1786. 191

SCHENKEL—Catharina, d. Filipp & w. Juliana; b. Nov. 17, 1782; bap. Dec. 22, 1782; sp. Christian Waldschmidt & w. Catharina.

SCHENCKEL—Christian, s. Johann Filipp & w. Barbara; b. Apr. 18, 1785; bap. June 19, 1785; sp. Christian Schenckel & w. Magdalena.

SCHENCKEL—Johannes, s. Philip & w. Juliana; b. Dec. 7, 1780; bap. Dec. 24, 1780; sp. Stefany Bollander & w. Margretha.

SCHENCKEL—Johannes, s. Philip Jacob & w. Barbara; b. Feb. 23, 1783; bap. Mch. 16, 1783, sp. Michael Walter & w.

SCHENCKEL—Maria Barbara, d. Phillip Jacob & w. Maria Juliana; b. O—ct. 30, 1784; bap. Jan. 2, 1785; sp. Johan Filipp Schenckel & w. Maria Barbara.

SCHEURER—Anna Elisabeth, d. Johann Jacob & w. Catharina; b. Sept. 8, 1753; bap. Sept. 30, 1753; sp. Jacob Hollinger & w. Anna Elizabeth.

SCHIMPB—Johann Gorg, s. Casper & w. Elisabeth; b. Apr. 28, 1780; bap. July 23, 1780; sp. Gorg Geiger (Schimpb's Father-in-law) & w. Anna Margretha.

SCHLEBACH—Wilhelm Heinrich, s. Gorg & w. Rosina; b. Aug. 25, 1780; bap. Nov. 5, 1780; sp. the Parents (of Gorg), Heinrich Schlebach & w. Elisabeth. Maria Elisabeth, d. of above; b. Sept. 18, 1782! bap. Nov. 10, 1782; sp. Johannes Moser & Elisabeth, d. Christian E. Schelmann. Gorg, s. of above; b. Apr. 14, 1786; bap. June 25, 1786; sp. Gorg Heft & Barbara Schlabach.

SCHLEBACH—Anna Barbara, d. Philip & w. Elisabeth; b. June 1, 1783; bap. Aug. 3, 1783; sp. the Mother-in-law (Anna Barbara Gering) a widow.

SCHLEEHTY—Barbara, d. Christian & w. Magdalena; b. Nov. 12, 1763; bap. Nov. 24, 1778; sp. Not given. Anna, d. of above; b. Aug. 14, 1765; bap. Nov. 24, 1778; sp. Not given. Christian, s. of above; b. Nov. 11, 1768; bap. Nov. 24, 1778; sp. Not given.

SCHLOTTER—Johan Jacob, s. Sebastian & w. Barbara; b. Nov. 13, 1759; bap. Dec. 26, 1759; sp. Bernhart Franck & Elisabeth, d. Christofel Imben.

SCHLOTTERBECK—Anna, d. Johann Gorg & w. Christina; b. Nov. 17, 1759; bap. Dec. 26, 1759; sp. Friedrich Salentin & w. Anna.

SCHMID—Catharina, d. Jost Heinrich w. Anna Maria; b. June 27, 1767; bap. July 12, 1767; sp. Heinrich Ache & w. Catharina.

SCHMID—Wilhelm, s. Peter & w. Susanna; b. Feb. 3, 1783; bap. June 15, 1783; sp. Peter Blaasser & w. Elisabeth.

SCHMIDT—Susanna, d. Peter & w. Susanna; b. Nov. 23, 1780; bap. Feb. 18, 1781; sp. the Parents in law, viz: Peter Fischer & w. Catharina.

SCHMITT—Susanna, d. Johannes & w. Catharina; b. Apr. 17, 1798; bap. June 3, 1798; sp. Johannes Waldschmidt & w. Susanna.

SCHNEBEL—Johan Heinrich, s. Heinrich & w. Elisabeth, b. July 10, 1754; bap. July 21, 1754; sp. Johannes Schwab & w. Elysa Catharina.

SCHNEBLE—Anna Maria, d. Jacob & w. Elisabeth; b. June 30, 1781; bap. Nov. 17, 1782; sp. the Parents.

SCHNEIDER—Anna Maria, d. Adam & w. Maria Sara; b. Nov. 6, 1750; bap. Aug. 19, 1760, on the Schwadera; sp. Martin Kuffer & w. Elisabeth. Anna, d. of above; b. Sept. 3, 1754; bap. Aug. 19, 1760, on the Schwarara; sp. Heinrich Muller & w. Anna. Catharina Elisabeth, d. of above; b. Feb. 18, 1756; bap. Aug. 19, 1760, on the Schwadara; sp. Adam Wagner & w. Catharina Elisabeth. Anna Barbara, d. of above; b. Oct. 18, 1759; bap. Aug. 19, 1760, on the Schwadara; sp. Otto Schnebel & w. Barbara.

SCHNEIDER—Joh. Heinrich, s. Arnold; b. ———; bap. Mch. 7, 1756; sp. Heinrich Walter & w.

SCHNEIDER—Johanues, s. Conrath & w. Catharina; b. Feb. 6, 1785; bap. May 15, 1785; sp. Josef Gehr & w. Anna Maria.

SCHNEIDER—Johann David, s. Daniel & w. Maria Catharina; b. Dec. 13, 1759; bap. Jan. 1, 1760; sp. David Fortene & w. Catharina.

SCHNEIDER—Wilhelm, s. Gorg & w. Catharina; b. June 9, 1779; bap. July 25, 1779; sp. Phillipus Witmann & w. Catharina. Jacob, s. of above; b. Jan. 2, 1781; bap. Mch. 11, 1781; sp. Nicolaus Schub & w. Eva. Gorg, s. of above; b. Feb. 29, 1782; bap. Nov. 14, 1784; sp. Gorg Adam Schub & w. Anna Maria.

SCHNEIDER—Jacob, s. Jacob & w. Anna Maria; b. Nov. 22, 1758; bap. Dec. 6, 1758; sp. Christian Schneder & w. Anna Eva Ranck.

SCHNEIDER—Peter, s. Johannes & w. Susanna; b. Jan. 14, 1785; bap. Jan. 23, 1785; sp. Christian Waldschmidt & w. Chatarina.

SCHNEIDER—Johannes, s. Johannes & w. Susanna Elisabeth; b. Nov. 2, 1783; bap. Nov. 16, 1783; sp. Johannes Waldschmidt, Jr.

SCHNEIDER—Johannes, s. Wilhelm & w. Elisabeth; b. Aug. 13, 1780; bap. Sept. 10, 1780; sp. Christof & w. Catharina. Sophia, d. of above; b. Sept. 27, 1782; bap. Oct. 27, 1782; sp.

Peter Schneider & Sophia, d. Gorg Michael Brunner. Wilhelm, s. of above; b. Dec. 25, 1784; bap. Apr. 24, 1785; sp. Martin Kissinger & w. Margretha.

SCHNEIDO—Catharina, d. Johannes & w. Maria Elisabeth; b. Oct. 28, 1752; bap. Nov. 26, 1752; sp. Michael Mayer & w. Catharina.

SCHNELL—Joh. Heinrich, s. Filip & w. Dorothea; b. Mch. 20, 1758; bap. Apr. 16, 1758; sp. Heinrich Cafroth & Elisabeth Benss.

SCHNELL—Anna Dorrothea, d. Filip & w. Maria; b. Apr. 4, 1756; bap. ———; sp. ———.

SCHOP—Salomon, s. Gorg & w. Christina; b. Mch. 19, 1781; bap. June 17, 1781; sp. Johann Gorg Neumann & Elisabeth, d. Bastian Hassler.

SCHREINER—Johannes, s. Matthias & w. Elisabeth; b. Mch. 1, 1781; bap. Sept. 12, 1782; sp the Parents. Maria Elisabeth, d. ob above; b. May 7, 1782; bap. Sept. 12, 1782; sp. the Parents.

SCHRODER—Johannes, s. Heinrich & w. Maria; b. May 16, 1780; bap. May 28, 1780; sp. Ludwig Schweitzer, Jr. & Elisabeth Thiel. Christine, d. of above; b. Mch. 22, 1783; bap. May 11, 1783; sp. Johannes Loscher & w. Elisabeth.

SCHRODER—Maria Catharina, d. Heinrich & w. Elisabeth Maria; b. May. 30, 1773; bap. Aug. 22, 1773; sp. Fillip Jacob Schenckel & w. Maria Juilana.

SCHUB—Anna Maria, d. Gorg Adam & w. Anna Maria; b. Apr. 12, 1777; bap. May 11, 1777; sp. Thomas Moor & Anna Maria Mosser, both single.

SCHUCKER—Johannes, s. Henry & w. Margretha; b. Feb. 14, 1768; bap. Feb. 29, 1768; sp. Johannes Kennetsch & Maria Magdalena, d. Heinrich Fiedler.

SCHUERER—Dewalt, s. Johann Jacob & w. Catharina; b. July 23, 1760; bap. Aug. 17, 1760; sp. Dewalt Schank.

SCHUMACKER—Elisabeth, d. Peter & w. Elisabeth; b. Oct. 17, 1776; bap. Sept. 7, 1777; sp. the Parents. Johannes, s. of above; b. Aug. 25, 1778; bap. Sept. 4, 1779; sp. the Parents.

SCHUNG—Matthias, s. Peter & w. Magdalena; b. Sept. 2, 1757; bap. Oct. 23, 1757; sp. Matthias Hoffer & w. Anna Maria.

SCHWALMY—Maria Elisabeth, d. Antonius; b. ———; bap. Feb. 26, 1760; sp. Carl Scheneckel & w. Maria Elisabeth.

SCHWARTZ—Johannes, s. Daniel & w. Anna Maria; b. Jan. 11, 1769; bap. Jan. 17, 1769; sp. Johannes Schwartz & Elisabeth, d. Gorg Brunner. (The mother died Jan. 16, 1769, she was the only d. of Josef Neue.)

SCHWEIGER—Johannes, s. Ludwig & w. Anna; b. Jan. 12, 1785; bap. Mch. 28, 1785; sp. Johannes Schweiger & d. Catharina.

SCHWEITZER—Margretha, d. Christian; b. ———; bap. Dec. 27, 1760; sp. Martin Keller & w. Joseph, s. of above; b. ———; bap. Sept. 26, 1770; sp. Johannes Billman & w.

SCHWEITZER—Luisa Rahel, d. Frantz Stephanus & w. Maria Magdalena; b. Feb. 28; 1753; bap. Mch. 11, 1753; sp. Isaac Barre & w. Rahel.

SCHWEITZER—Maria Barbara, d. Ludwig; b. ———; bap. Feb. 11, 1756; sp. Peter Bollinger & w. Heinrich Ludwig, s. of above; b. ———; bap. Dec. 22, 1758; sp. Heinrich Bucher & w.

SCHWEITZER—Magdalena, d. Peter & w. Elisabeth; b. Nov. 2, 1781; bap. Mch. 30, 1782; sp. Wilhelm Geickle & w. Anna Maria.

SCHWITZGEBEL—Maria Elisabeth, d. Vincens & w. Catharina; b. Dec. 8, 1767; bap. Aug. 23, 1768; sp. Christian & Anna Maria Starck.

SEGETHALER—Anna Barbara, d. Gorg; b. ———; bap. Aug. 24, 1758; sp. Abraham Hassler & w.

SEGLER—Jacob, s. Melchoir & w. Catharina; b. Dec. 12, 1785; bap. June 25, 1786; sp. Filipp Funck & w. Catharina.

SEGNER—Elisabeth, d. Melchoir & w. Catharina; b. Feb. 16, 1784; bap. Apr. 11, 1784; sp. Johannes Nicolaus Schub, Jr. & Barbara Segner.

SEILER—Gorg Michael, s. Alexander & ————; b. Feb. 23, 1752; bap. Feb. 23, 1752; sp. Gorg Michael Brunner.

SEITNER—Johan Martin, s. Martin; b. ———; bap. Feb. 25, 1762; sp. Lorentz Maurer & w. Anna Barbara.

SELL—Catharina, d. Johann & Dorrothea; b. May 5, 1762; bap. Oct. 12, 1762; sp. Catharina Eckert.

SELTENREICH—Maria Margretha, d. Gorg & w. Maria Gegunta; b. Oct. 10, 1754; bap. Nov. 24, 1754; sp. Andreas Seltenreied & w. Fronica.

SIEGENDAHLER—Catharina, d. Gorg & w. Barbara; b. Nov. 4, 1773; bap. Jan. 27, 1775; sp. the Parents.

SIEGENTHALER—Anna Margretha, d. Gorg; b. ———; bap. Aug. 31, 1760; sp. Heinrich Walter & w. Margretha.

SIEGETHALER—Catharina, d. Gorg; b. ———; bap. Dec. 20, 1761; sp. Peter Franckhauser & w. Gorg, s. of above; b. Feb. 25, 1763; bap. Mch. 13, 1763; sp. Gorg Brunner & w. Elisabeth, d. of above; b. Aug. 3, 1769; bap. Oct. 15, 1769; sp. Johan Kuntz & w. Elisabeth. Peter, s. of above; b. ———; bap. Nov. 19, 1771; sp. Nicolaus Rup & w. Anna Maria.

SIEGETHALER—Margreth, d. Gorg & w. Anna Barbara; b. Nov. 8, 1764; bap. June 16, 1765; sp. Jacob Wuest & w. Catharina.

SIEGENTHALER—Johannes, s. Gorg & w. Barbara; b. Nov. 7, 1776; bap. Nov. 21, 1776; sp. the Parents.

SIMMER—Heinrich, s. Heinrich & w. Catharina; b. Mch. 4, 1780; bap. Apr. 9, 1780; sp. Heinrich Sohl & w. Catharina. Andreas, s. of above; b. Apr. 6, 1782; bap. May 12, 1782; sp. Andreas Burckert & w. Barbara.

SODER—Wilhelm Heinrich, s. Johannes & w. Catharina; b. Sept. 18, 1765; bap. Nov. 3, 1765; sp. Wilhelm Heinrich Biegel & Anna Maria, d. of Valentine Epler.

SOTER—Maria Catharina, d. Johannes w. Maria Margretha; b. May 27, 1779; bap. Aug. 29, 1779; sp. Susanna, d. of Peter Reitenbach.

SPAR—Johannes, Elisabeth, ch. Christian & w. Anna Maria; b. not given; bap. May 2, 1784; sp. Jacob Seifer & w. Elisabeth

SPINTLER—Michael, s. Matthias & w. Anna Maria; b. Aug. 4, 1782; bap. Aug. 14, 1782; sp. Michael Funffrock & w. Elisabeth.

SPRINGER—Johannes, s. Filip & w. —— name omitted; b. ———; bap. Mch. 17, 1765; sp. Johannes Soder & w. Catharina.

STAUFFER—Fronica, d. Vicens & w. Fronica; b. Mch. 17, 1764; bap. Mch. 29, 1764; sp. Johnnes Drachsel & w. Catharina.

STECHLER—Catharina, d. Jacob & w. Barbara; b. Aug. 22, 1783; bap. Oct, 5, 1783; sp. Heinrich Hart & Catharina Stichler.

STEFE—Anna Maria, d. Gorg & w. Catharina; b. Apr. 15, 1784; bap. May 30, 1784; sp. Michael Stephane & w. Anna Maria. Maria Catharina, d. of above; b. May 6, 1786; bap. June 25, 1786; sp. Peter Funck & w. Catharina.

STEFE—Catharina, d. Heinrich & w. Anna Maria; b. Mch. 11,1785; bap. Apr. 11, 1785; sp. Philip Kissinger & w. Catharina.

STEIN—Lehnhart, s. Lehnhart & w. Anna Maria; b. July 20, 1754; bap. Sept. 1, 1754; sp. Lehnhart Muller & w. Catharina. Eva Elisabeth, d. of above; b. Dec. 9, 1756; bap. Dec. 19, 1756; sp. Johannes Dieffendorffer & Eva Elisabeth Lang, both single.

STEINDORFF—Maria Susanna or Maria Johenette, d. Friedrich& Anna Magdalena; b. Apr. 3, 1753; bap. Apr. 30, 1753; sp. Johannes Waldschid, V. D. M. & Maria Elisabeth, d. Christian Grube.

STEINER—Johannes, s. Eberhartus & Maria Elisabeth; b. Jan. 12, 1755; bap. Jan. 18, 1755; sp. Eberhardus Thomas.

STEPHANI—Daniel, s. Gorg & w. Catharina; b. June 16, 1780; bap. Aug. 13, 1780; sp. Friedrich Steff & w. Elisabeth.
STEPHANI—Adam, s. Heinrich & w. Anna Maria; b. Mch. 5, 1786; bap. Apr. 16, 1786; sp. Peter Brunner & w. Eva.
STEPHE—Elisabeth, d. Goorg & w. Catharina; b. Dec. 5, 1781; bap. June 5, 1782; sp. Anna Elisabeth w. of Johannes Diess.
STICHLER—Gorg, s. Gorg; b. ———; bap. Sept. 12, 1780; sp. ———.
STOLTZ—Barbara, d. Michael & w. Anna Barbara; b. May 10, 1779; bap. Nov. 7, 1779; sp. the parents themeselves.
STRAABHAUER—J. Gorg, s. Johannes; b. ———; bap. Dec. 23, 1759; sp. Johann Gorg Reddig & w.
STRUBHAAR—Johannes, s. Johannes; b. ———; bap. May 16, 1757; sp. Johan Flicking (er?) & w.

THEIL—Joh. Heinrich, s. Heinrich; b. ———; bap. May 13, 1753; sp. Theobald Bruan & w.
THOMAS—Johann Heinrich, s. Eberhard & w. Elisabeth; b. Oct. 22, 1753; bap. Noov. 1, 1753; sp. Johann Heinrich Hoffman & Anna Maria, w. of Philip Jacob Reuter.
TOBIAS—Andreas, s. Ludwig & w. Sophia; b. Apr. 29, 1783; bap. June 14, 1778; sp. Andreas Bender.
TROSTEL—Abraham, s. Gorg & w. Rosina; b. Apr. 26, 1783; bap. June 15, 1783; sp. Johannes Laub & w. Elisabeth.
TROSTEL—Barbara, d. Heinrich & w. Catharina; b. Feb. 6, 1786; bap. May 7, 1786; sp. Johannes Trostel & Barbara Schweicker.
TSCHUDY—Johann Rudolf, s. Johannes & Fronica; b. July 11, 1753; bap. July 22, 1753; sp. Rudolf Brobeck & w. Margretha.
TSCHUDY—Eva Catharina, d. Martin & w. Anna; b. June 21, 1755; bap. Aug. 31, 1755; sp. Johann Michael Leydig & w. Appollonia. Joh. Friedrich, s. of above; b. July 30, 1758; bap. Sept. 10, 1758; sp. Johann Friedrich Martin & w. Maria Catharina.

ULHE—Christian Conrad, s. Daniel Gottfried; b. ———; bap. Mch. 4, 1753; sp. Conrad Bingener & w.
ULRICH—Christine, d. Peter & w. Christine; b. July 24, 1780; bap. Aug. 20, 1780; sp. the Parents.
UNGER—Anna Elisabeth, d. Johannes & w. Anna Catharina; b. Jan. 8, 1753; bap. Feb. 11, 1753; sp. Johannes Schutz & w. Anna Elisabeth.
UNGER—Joh. Nicolaus, s. Johannes & Eva; b. Aug. 20, 1759; bap. Oct. 29, 1759; sp. Johannes Nicolaus Hennicke & w. Anna Maria.

URY—Susanna, d. Gorg & w. Margaretha; b. Oct. 1, 1780; bap. Nov. 12, 1780; sp. Johannes Kohlmann & w. Christine.

VALENTINE—Elisabetha, d. Conrad & w. Catharina; b. Oct. 30, 1752; bap. Nov. 26, 1752; sp. Adam Jacobi & Elisabetha Herckelroth. Heinrich, s. of above; b. Sept. 1, 1759; bap. Sept. 16, 1759; sp. Heinrich Leinweuer & w. Juliana.

VAN ALLMAN—Conrad, s. Conrad & w. Anna; b. Mch.15, 1772; bap. Nov. 15, 1773; sp. the Father answered for both parents.

VETTERLING—Michael, s. Gorg & w. Susanna; b. Nov. 21, 1784; bap. Apr. 10, 1785; sp. Lehnhart Kepplinger.

WACHT—Jacob, s. Casper & w. Eva; b. Jan. 26, 1782; bap. Apr. 28, 1782; sp. Jacob Gipre & w. Elisabeth.

WAGNER—Tobias, s. Friedrich & w. Elisabetha; b. May 21, 1777; bap. Sept. 4, 1779; sp. the Parents themselves. (Owing to the War, the child was not baptized before.) Jacob, s. of above; b. Dec. 10, 1778; bap. Sept. 4, 1779; sp. the Parents themselves.

WAHL—Elisabeth, d. Martin & w. Christina; b. Jan. 14, 1779; bap. Nov. 7, 1779; sp. Elias Rittsher & w. Rosina.

WALDSCHMIDT—Catharina Elisabeth, d. Christian & w. Catharina; b. Sept. 16, 1781; bap. Oct. 7, 1781; sp. Susanna Elisabeth d. (Rev.) John Waldschmidt. Peter, s. of above; b. June 8, 1783; bap. June 29, 1783; sp. Peter Zimmermann & Catharina, d. (Rev.) John Waldschmidt. Anna Maria, d. of above; b. May 14, 1786; bap. June 5, 1786; sp. Elisabeth Bollender.

WALDSCHMID—Johannes Christianus, s. (Rev.) John & w. Maria Elisabetha; b. Mch. 23, 1755; at 10 P. M.; bap. Mch. 29, 1755; sp. Johann Christian Grube & w. Susanna Gerderaut. My wife, Maria Elisabeth was b. Mch. 17, 1733. Susanna Elisabetha, d. of above; b. Apr. 26, 1757; bap. May 8, 1757; sp. My sister (Rev. J. W.) appointed to stand in place of the mother. Anna Christine, d. of above; b. July 14, 1759; bap. Aug. 1, 1759; sp. Anna Magdalena, w. of Michael Andreas.

WALDSCHMIDT—Catharine Margretha, d. (Rev.) John & w. Maria Elisabetha; b. Jan. 10, 1762; bap. Jan. 21, 1762; sp. Catharatina Margretha, sister of Rev. J.W. Johannes, s. of above; b. Feb. 12, 1765; bap. Mch. 20, 1765; sp. the Father, Rev. J. W. Anna Maria, d. of above; b. Apr. 3, 1767; bap. May. 10, 1767; sp. the Father, Rev. J. W. Wilhelm, s. of above; b. June 30, 1769; bap. Aug. 25, 1769; sp. the Father, Rev. J. W.

WALDSCHMIDT—Chatarine, d. John & w. Susanna; b. Oct. 27, 1788; bap. Dec. 7, 1788; sp. Wilhelm Waldschmidt & w. Barbara. Susanna, d. of above; b. June 13, 1791; bap. June 26, 1791; sp. the Parents; by Pastor Amman. (She died June 26, 1791 at 6 P. M.) Christine, d. of above; b. Aug. 30, 1792; bap. Sept. 30, 1792; sp. Abraham Hassler & w. Chatarine, by Christian Wilms (?) Barbara, d. of above; b. July 15, 1795; bap. Aug. 9, 1795; sp. Heinrich Kumler & Barbara Hahn by Christian Wilms in his church. Elisabeth, d. of above; b. Oct. 12, 1797; bap. Oct. 25, 1797; sp. Elisabeth Geleinger; by Christian Wilms in house. Johannes, s. of above; b. Nov. 1799; bap. Jan. 11, 1800; sp. the Parents; by Christian Wilms. Susana, d. of above; b. June 17, 1805; bap. July 1, 1805; sp. the Parents; by Carl Helbenstein.

WALDSCHMIDT—Wilhelm, d. John & w. Susana; b. Dec. 28, 1809; bap. Feb. 4, 1810; sp. the Parents; by Rev. Faber.

WALDSCHMIDT—Johannes, s. Wilhelm & Barbara; b. Jan. 13, 1785; bap. Mch. 20, 1785; sp. Johannes Waldschmidt & w. Susana; by Rev. Boos. Anna Barbara, d. of above; b. Mch. 25, 1790; bap. Apr. 22, 1790; sp. Johannes Waldschmidt & w. Susana; by Mr. Amman. Elisabeth, d. of above; b. May 16, 1791; bap. May 24, 1791; sp. Casper Hassler & w. Elisabeth; by Rev. Conrad Amman. Anna Maria, d. of above; b. May 3, 1794; June 15, 1794; sp. Gorg Weinhold & w. Elisabeth; by Rev. Christian Willem in the Schwara Ch.

WALLFSEN—Catharina, d. Michael & w. Catharina; b. Apr. 8, 1780; bap. Apr. 23, 1780; sp. Elisabeth Haas.

WALTER—Susanna, d. Gergard & w. Anna Maria; b. ——, 1781; bap. Apr. 8, 1781; sp. Johannes Gehr w. Susanna.

WALTER—Juliana Maria, d. Heinrich; b, ——; bap. June 1, 1755; sp. Jacob Hasler & w. Barbara, d. of above; b. July 17, 1768; bap. July 17, 1768; sp. Jacob Wust & w. Barbara. Heinrich's daughter; bap. May 5, 1782; (Neither name of child nor date of birth stated in the original).

WALTER—Elisabeth, d. Heinrich & w. Eva; b. Aug. 19, 1777; bp Aug. 20, 1780; sp. Elisabeth Amweg. Johannes, s. of above; b .Aug. 22, 1779; bap. Aug. 20, 1780; sp. the Father. Johann Heinrich, s. of above; b. Sept. 14, 1782; bap. Dec. 25, 1783; sp. Ahraham Hassler & Neuman, his step daughter.

WALTER—Juliana, d. Jacob & w. Juliana; b. Mch. 8, 1760; bap. June 8, 1760; sp. Peter Ravensberger & w. Juliana.

WALTER—Anna Eva, d. Jost Walter; b. ——; bap. Mch. 10, 1759; sp. Martin Driespach & w. Eva.

WALTER—Johannes, Sophia, ch. Michael & w. Catharina; b. Aug. 19, 1783; bap. Sept. 21, 1783; sp. Carl Schenkel & w. & Filip Jacob Schenkel & w. Juliana.
WALTER—Johan Jacob, s. Nicolaus & his wife; b. ———; bap. July 20, 1749; sp. Jacob Brunner & w. (Copied by (J. W.) from a Baptism Book at Michael Amwegs.)
WALTER—Simon, s. Wilhelm; b. June 15, 1770; bap. July 1, 1770; sp. Christofer Schindler & Elisabeth Walter. Johan Heinrich, s. of above; b. ———; bap. Aug. 16, 1772; sp. Johannes Gerhard & w. Susanna.
WALTER—Johannes, s. Wilhelm & w. Catharina; b. July 22, 1779; bap. Aug. 22, 1779; sp. Gorg Roth & w. Christine.
WEBER—Catharina, d. Bastian & w. Anna Maria; b. Feb. 17, 1783; bap. June 8, 1783; sp. Jacob Wirthenberger & w. Catharina.
WEBER—Maria Margaretha, d. Gorg & w. Maria Elisabetha; b. Feb. 8, 1755; bap. Feb. 18, 1755; sp. Phillipus Grunewald & w. Maria Margaretha.
WEBER—Johann Adam, s. Heinrich & w. Margretha; b. Sept. 24, 1759; bap. Oct. 24, 1759; sp. Stophel Henicke & w.
WEBER—Heinrich, s. Johannes & w. Susana; b. Apr. 13, 1786; bap. May. 14, 1786; sp. Heinrich Eberling.
WEBER—Christina, d. Johan Gorg & w. Maria Elisabetha; b. July 30, 1752; bap. Sept. 3, 1752; sp. Gorg Michael Weiss & w. Christina.
WEETLE—Johannes, s. Michael & w. Dorrothea; b. Sept. 17, 1779; bap. Nov. 7, 1779; sp. Salomon Westle & w. Regina.
WEINHOLD—Anna Maria, d. Michael & w. Susanna Margretha; b. Oct. 29, 1780; bap. Dec. 10, 1780; sp. Conrath Althauser & Anna Maria, d. of Nicolaus Weinhold, both single.
WEISS—Felix, s. Gorg Michael & w. Christina; b. Oct. 22, 1752; bap. Oct. 29, 1752; sp. Felix Schutz & w. Fronica. Margretha Catharina, d. of above; b. Mch. 29, 1761; bap. Apr. 15, 1761; sp. Joh. Jacob Bullinger & w. Anna Maria.
WEISS—Anna Barbara, d. Michael & w. Anna Barbara; b. Jan. 25, 1755; bap. Mch. 30, 1755; sp. Gorg Fackler & Anna Barbara Lang.
WERNER—Anna Maria, d. Casper & w. Anny; b. ? Jan. 18, 1760; bap. Apr. 27, 1760; sp. Peter Kodelein & w. Anna Maria.
WERNS—Johann Martin, s. Gorg & w. Barbara; b. Dec. 26, 1753; bap. Jan. 13, 1754; sp. Johann Martin Urich & Elisabeth Rohland.
WIELAND—Catharina Elisabetha, d. Peter & w. Margretha; b. Aug. 6 ,1757; bap. Nov. 6, 1757; sp. Margretha, d. of Gerhart Huybschman.

WISSENANT—Anna Barbara, d. Adam & ———; b. ———; bap. Sept. 22, 1751; sp. Gorg Brunner & w.
WITTMANN—Sara, d. Ahraham & w. Elisabeth; b. Mch. 6, 1779; bap. May 2, 1779; sp. Lehnhart Kessler & w. Anna Maria.
WITTMANN—Magdalena, d. Wilhelm & w. Catharina; b. Dec. 16, 1780; bap. Feb. 18, 1781; sp. Lehnhard Kepler & w. Anna Maria.
WOHLFART—Elisabetha, d. Conrath & w. Margretha; b. Mch. 12, 1755; bap. Mch. 23, 1755; sp. Ulrich Mischler & w. Elisabetha.
WOHLLEBEN—Johann Heinrich, s. Frantz & w. Catharina; b. Oct. 6, 1778; bap. Oct. 29, 1778; sp. Heinrich Muller & w. Catharina.
WOHLWEIN—Johannes, s. Philipus & w. Elisabeth; b. Apr. 24, 1767; bap. May 31, 1767; sp. Johannes Meyer & Catharina Schafer, both single.
WOLFF—Maria, d. Jacob & w. Magdalena; b. Jan 2, 1781; bap. Apr. 22, 1781; sp. Salomon Westler & w. Regina.
WOLFSKIEHL—Marie Magdalena, d. Fillipp & w. Wandelina; b. Oct. 8, 1754; bap. Oct. 13, 1754; sp. Maria Magdalena Wengert.
WOLLWEIN—Barbara, d. Filip & w. Elisabeth; b. Feb. 7, 1769; bap. Mch. 5, 1769; sp. Marx Binckle & Barbara Bulmann.
WOMMER—Johann Michael, s. Michael & w. Barbara; b. Oct. 12, 1765; bap. Nov. 3, 1765; sp. Michael Wommer & w. Anna Maria.
WORST—Johann Jacob, s. Jacob Worst; b. ———; bap. ———, 1749; sp. Marx Klein, Jr. & w. (Copied by Rev. J. W. from a Baptism Book at Michael Amwegs.) Maria Juliana, d. of above; b. ———; bap. Apr. 6, 1751; sp. Michael Binckle & w. Heinrich, s. of above; b. ———; bap. June 22, 1755; sp. Heinrich Binckle & Catharina Killian.
WURST—Johan Peter, s. Jacob; b. ———;bap. June 8, 1753; sp. Peter Klein & Margretha Brunner.
WURTZ—Gorg Michael, s. Friedrich; b. ———; bap. Aug. 12, 1753; sp. Gorg. Brunner & w.
WURTZ—Elizabeth, d. Heinrich; b. ———; bap. Jan. 2, 1769; sp. Jacob Bauer & Elisabeth Walter. Anna Christine, s. of above; b. ———; bap. Nov. 24, 1750; sp. Theobald Seltenreich & w.

ZACHERIAS—Peter, s. Daniel & w. Anna Elisabeth; b. Jan. 13, 1765; bap. Mch. 17, 1765; sp. Peter Herben & Elisabeth, d. of Michael Grauel.

ZEBACH—Juliana Rosine, d. Bartholomay; b———; bap. July 22, 1760; sp. Juliana Rosina Urig.

ZELL—Christian, s. Thomas & w. Catharina; b. Apr. 4, 1784; bap. June 20, 1784; sp. Bernhard Zell.

ZELLER—Heinrich, s. Filip Jacob & w. Dorrothea; b. Aug. 10, 1781; bap. Oct. 14, 1781; sp. Heinrich Weid & w. Catharina.

ZELLER—Daniel Adam, s. Jacob & w. Dorrothea; b. May 1, 1784; bap. July 11, 1784; sp. Adam Bohmer & Barbara Schlebach.

ZELLER—Peter, s. Peter & w. Elisabeth; b. Jan. 16, 1784; bap. May 10, 1784; sp. Michael Pitz & w. Elisabeth.

ZIBACH—J. Paul, s. Bartholamay; b. ———; bap. May 8, 1761; sp. Johannes Pauly Gimperlin & w.

ZIEGLER—Anna Maria, d. Christian & w. Anna Maria; b Dec. 18, 1783; bap. Apr. 11, 1784; sp. Samuel Kachel & w. Barbara.

ZIEGLER—Samuel, s. Gorg & w. Anna Margretha; b. Apr. 11, 1786; bap. June 25, 1786; sp. Abraham Ziegler & Anna Barbara Keppler.

ZIEGLER—Abraham, s. Gorg & w. Margretha; b. Nov. 4, 1784; bap. Feb. 13, 1785; sp. Abraham Ziegler & Anna Barbara, d. of Lehnhart Kepplinger, both single.

ZIGLER—Elisabeth, d. Gorg & w. Maria Margreth; b. Sept. 13, 1778; bap. Nov. 22, 1778; sp. Elias Riche & w. Rosina.

ZIMMERMANN—Juliana, d. Adolf; b. ———; bap. Mch. 16, 1760; sp. Michael Binckle & w.

ZIMMERMANN—Maria Margaretha, d. Christian & w. Maria Margretha; .b Oct. 2, 1780; bap. Nov. 12, 1780; sp. the Parents.

ZIMMERMANN—Johan Gorg, s. Heinrich & w. Barbara; b. June 2, 1785; bap. Aug. 21, 1785; sp. Johann Gorg Wagner & w. Anna Maria.

ZIMMERMANN—Maria Catharina; d. Michael & w. Anna Maria; b. Dec. 13, 1782; bap. Feb. 9, 1783; sp. Gorg Klees & Catharina, d. Heinrich Hetzel.

ZIMMERMANN—Heinrich, s. Peter & w. Anna; b. Oct. 30, 1784; bap. Nov. 28, 1784; sp. Marx Garner & Barbara Schluhli, both single.

ZIMMERMANN—Barbara, d. Peter & w. Elisabeth; d. Dec. 31, 1781; bap. Apr. 21, 1782; sp. Adam Wurdeburger & Barbara Wild.

ZIN—Johan Jacob, s. Jacob & Catharina; b. Oct. 21, 1756; bap. Apr. 5, 1757; sp. Jacob Grieck & Rosina Fischer.

ZOLLER—Johan Peter, s. Philip Jacob & w. Dorrothea; b. Jan. 13, 1779; bap. Apr. 11, 1779; sp. Gorg Stefy & w. Catharina.

ZUBER—Abraham, s. Abraham & w. Maria; b. Sept. 14, 1780; bap. Jan. 7, 1782; sp. the Parents.

ZULAUFF—Jacob, s. Johannes & w. Anna Margreth; b.
Nov. 24, 1783; bap. Mch. 21, 1784; sp. Jacob Wicklein & w.
Catharina.

ZWALLY—Thomas, s. Johannes & Anna Catharina; b.
July 30, 1767; bap. Mch. 3, 1771; sp. Catharina Zwally, child
named for Thomas Kern. Catharina, d. of above; b. Aug. 22,
1769; bap. Mch. 3, 1771; sp. Catharina Zwally. Johannes, s. of
above; b. Oct. 17, 1770; bap. Mch. 3,1771; sp. Gorg Ury & w.
Eva Margretha.

MARRIAGES.

MARRIAGES.

AACHE—Goorg, and Elisabeth, d. of Gorg Scheider; Dec. 2, 1772.

AACHE—Gorg, s. Johannes Aache, and Catharine Elisabetha, d. of Georg (Illegible); Dec. 17, 1754.

AACHE—Jacob, s. of decd. Lehnhard Aache, and Elizabeth, d. of Conrad Breneisen; Apr. 20, 1782.

AACHE—Johannes, widower, and Maria Christine, d. of Adolph Zimmerman; July 21, 1767. (In Heinrich Aache' house.)

ACHEBACH—Anna Maria, d. of Matthias Achebach, and Gorg Brunner, s. of Gorg Michael Feb. 12, 1779.

ACHEBACH—Maria Margaretta, d. of Matthias Achebach, and Peter Naumann, s. of Peter Naumann; Feb. 2, 1779.

ACKERMANN—Balser, s. of the decd. Wendel Ackermann, and Elisabeth, widow of Gorg Albrecht; June 18, 1771.

ADAM—Johannes, s. of Bernhard Adam and Elisabeth d. of the decd. Heinrich Seidenbander; June 13, 1779.

ADAM—Nicolaus, s. of Bernhard Adam, and Anna Maria, d. of Gorg Kohl; Nov. 22. 1782.

ALBRECHT—Anna Maria, widow of David Albrecht, and Bernhardus Neizer; June 25, 1754.

ALLBRECHT—Catharina, d. of Johann Christ Allbrecht, and Johannes Huster, s .of Jost Huster; Sept. 5, 1780. (In Pastor's house.)

ALBRECHT—Elisabeth, widow of Gorg Albrecht, and Balser Ackerman, s. of Wendel Ackerman, decd.; June 18, 1771.

ALBRECHT—Gorg, s. of the decd. Joh. Gorg Albrecht, and Agada, d. of the decd. Christofel Gister; Feb. 14, 1758.

ALBRECHT—Johan Gorg, widower, and Anna Maria, d. of Peter Lehr; Apr. 6, 1777.

ALBRECHT—Johan Gorg, and Elisabetha, d. of Martin Walless; Mch. 27, 1759.

ALBRECHT—Stophel, and Catharina Zuber; Sept. 22, 1761.

ALLSTADT—Catharina, d. of Martin Allstadt, and Johannes Soder, s. of Nicolaus Soder, decd.; Nov. 8, 1764. In the Church at Reading.

ALTHAUS—Conrad, s. of Jacob Althaus, and Barbara, d. of Nicolaus Weinhold; May 29, 1781.

AMME—Phillippus, s. of the decd. Johannes Amme, and Magdalena, d. of Jacob Bosser; Jan. 21, 1755.

BAPTISMAL AND MARRIAGE RECORDS.

AMWEG—Elisabeth, d. of Jacob Amweg, and Jeremias Muller, widower, Oct. 14, 1782.

ANDREAS—Anna Maria, d. of Abraham Andreas, decd., and Peter Dunckel, s. of Peter Dunckel, decd.; May 16, 1785.

AUGENSTEIN—Catharina, d. of Johannes Augenstein, and Gorg Philip Kissinger, s. of Filip Kissinger; June 2, 1772.

ANGWITCH—Jacob, s. of the decd. James Angwitch, and Susanna, d. of the decd. Heinrich Mohler; Dec. 2, 1783.

AUMULLER—Anna Elisabetha, d. of Conrad Aumuller, and Matthias Buchmann, s. of Gorg Buchmann; Dec. 26, 1757.

AUMULLER—Elisabeth, d. of Johannes Aumuller, and Johannes Dock, s. of Henry Dock; Apr. 29, 1782.

APPEL—Johannes, s. of the decd. Heinrich Appel, and Maria Elisabeth, d. of Gorg Weber; Aug. 8, 1780; in Weber's house and in the presence of Mary Weber.

ARNOLD—Jacob, widower, and Catharina, widow of Martin Schreck; Aug. 23, 1785.

BAACKEN—Johannes, s. of the decd. Jacob Baacken, and Salome, widow of Valentine Schneider; Sept. 24, 1782.

BAHMER—Elisabeth, d. of Adam Bahmer, decd., and Valentine Fehl, s. of Gorg Fehl; June 30, 1776.

BALSER—Anna Maria, d. of Peter Balser, decd., and Wilhelm Broadstock, s. of Bernhard Broadstock; Oct. 23, 1783.

BANDER—Gorg, s. of the decd. Gorg Bander, and Margaretha, d. of Johannes Gerner; June 20, 1786.

BARET—Joseph, and Anna Maria, d. of Jacob Magly; Apr. 24, 1757.

BART—Michael, s. of Gorg Bart, and Magdalena, d. of the decd. Heinrich Beer (Bear); Nov. 22, 1785.

BAUENBACH—Frantz, s. of the decd. Melchoir Bauenbach, and Elisabeth, d. of the decd. Paul Gehr; Aug. 5, 1777.

BAUER—Adam, s. of Henry Bauer, and Sabina, widow of Samuel Zerfass; Mch. 1, 1774; in Hein Muller's house among many witnesses.

BAUER—Catharina, d. of Heinrich Bauer, and David Meintzer, s. of Gorg Meintzer; Feb. 18, 1771.

BAUER—Jacob, s. of Heinrich Bauer, and Anna Maria, d. of Heinrich Lieder; Jan. 25; 1774.

BAUERR—Abraham, s. of Heinrich Bauer, and Elisabeth, d. of Johannes Beyer; May 10, 1774.

BAUMANN—Catharina, d. of Heinrich Baumann, and Gorg Meyer, s. of Christophel Meyer, decd.; Apr. 15, 1760 .

BAUMANN—Christine, d. of Heinrich Baumann, and Jacob Hegy, s. of Jacob Hegy, decd.; Aug. 23, 1763.

BAUMANN—Elisabeth, d. of Martin Baumann, and Hermann Schneider, s. of Mattheus Schneider; Jan. 1, 1781.
BAUMANN—Elizabeth, d. of Samuel Baumann, and Balsar Laber, s. of George Wendel Laber; Mar. 13, 1754.
BAUMANN—Magdalena, d. of Jacob Baumann, decd., and Gorg Manner, s. of Paul Manner, decd.; Apr. 24, 1755.
BAUMANN—Margretta, d. of Heinrich Baumann, and Martin Hegy, s. of Jacob Hegy, decd.; Apr. 15, 1760.
BAYER—Johannes, s. of Adam Beyer, and Maria, d. of Nicolaus Rupp; Aug. 16, 1785.
BAYER—Joohannes, and Anna Maria Sauerbrey; Nov. 29, 1768.
BAYER—Valentin, s. of Valentin Bayer, and Elisabeth, d. of Jacob Kuhn; Aug. 20, 1785.
BECHTOL—Maria Elisabeth, d. of Nicolaus Bechtol, decd., and Peter Rieth, s. of Peter Rieth, decd.; Feb. 15, 1780.
BECK—Elisabeth, d. of Jacob Beck, decd., and Johannes Reight, s. of Thomas Reight; June 16, 1784.
BECK—Jacob, s. of the decd. Jacob Beck, and Catharine, d. of Christian Luther; May 22, 1781.
BECK—Johan Jacob, s. of the decd. Peter Beck, and Anna Maria, widow of Peter Kafroth; Mch. 18, 1753.
BECKER—Anna Margaretta, d.* of Adam Becker, and Jacob Graff; Apr. 12 1768. (In Wilhelm Hedrick's house.)
BECKER—Anna d. of Christofel Becker decd. and Filip Miss, s. of Balsar Miss, decd.; Apr. 1, 1783.
BECKER—Barbara, d. of Johan Gorg Becker, and Friedrich Kissinger, s. of Philip Kissinger, decd.; Feb. 22, 1785.
BECKER—Catharine, d. of Peter Becker, and Lenhart Eckert, s. of Philip Eckert; Apr. 1, 1755.
BECKER—Jacob, s. of Peter Becker, and Sara, d. of Stofel Reiger; Sept. 24, 1782.
BECKER—Johannes, s. of the decd. Christofel Becker, and Salome, d. of Jacob Keller; Sept. 5, 1784.
BECKER—Johannes, s. of Michael Becker, and Magdalena, widow of Ludwig Zwernss; Nov. 5 ,1771.
BECKER—Sophia, d. of Christofel Becker, decd. and Ignatius Ernst, s. of Johannes Ernst; Nov. 21, 1780.
BECKLY—Margaretta Dorrothea, d. of Ulrich Beckly, and Johannes Bonnet, s. of Johannes Bonnet, decd.; Apr. 22, 1755.
BEER—Abraham, s. of the decd. Michael Beer, and Juliana, d. of the decd. Heinrich Walter; Jan. 25, 1774.
BEER—Barbara, d. of Adam Beer (Bear), and Gorg Stober, s. of Gorg Stober; Feb. 17, 1784.

---

*(else Henry Hedrick's wife's daughter which she bore in dishonor.)

BEER—Martin, s. of Ulrich Beer, and Catharina, d. of Jacob Schnurler; May 6, 1781.

BEER—(Bear) Catharine, widow of Adam Beer (Bear), and Christofel Scherbm, widower; Aug. 16, 1785.

BEER—(Bear) Catharine, d. of Jacob Beer (Bear), and Christofel Scherb; Apr. 3, 1783.

BEER—(Bear) Catharine, d. of Johannes Beer (Bear), and Andreas Rudy, s. of Emmig Rudy; July 3, 1785.

BEER—(Bear) Magdalena, d. of Heinrich Beer (Bear), decd., and Michhael Bart, s. of Gorg Bart; Nov. 22, 1785.

BEER—(Bear) Margaretta, d. of Michael Beer (Bear), and Joseph Mischler, s. of Jacob Mischler; Feb. 25, 1783.

BEHL—Ludwig, s. of Ludwig Behl, and Catharina, d. of Peter Pfeil; Jan. 1, 1760.

BEHRINGER—David, s. of the decd. Adam Behringer, and Elisabeth, d. of the decd. Christian Muller; June 9, 1783.

BELTZ—Andreas, s. of Peter Beltz, and Juliana, d. of the decd. Johannes Herchelroth; on Easter Monday, Apr. 4, 1763. (On the Middle Creek).

BEMER—Friedrich, s. of Michael Baymer, and Julianna, d. of Johannes Jung; July 5, 1756.

BENDER—Christine, d. of Samuel Bender, decd., and Abraham Riehm, s. of Matthias Riehm; Dec. 9, 1783.

BENDER—David, s. of the decd. Johannes Bender, and Barbara, d. of Gorg Wernss, June 26, 1770.

BENDER—Maria, d. of Johannes Bender, and Casper Jordan, s. of Elias Bender; Aug. 8, 1786.

BENSS—Anna Maria, d. of Weyrich Benss. and Gorg Ruth, s. of Peter Ruth; Jan. 21, 1766.

BENSS—Catharina, d. of Weirig Benss, and Jacob Keller, s. of Johann Lehnhart Keller, decd.; Apr. 15, 1755.

BENSS—Elisabeth, d. of Peter Benss, and Jacob Schweickert, s. of Gorg Schweickert; Dec. 7, 1784.

BENSS—Gorg, s. of Weyrich Benss, and Maria Elis Holsinger; Dec. 8, 1761.

BERCKER—Salome, d. of Christofel Bercker, decd., and Gorg Feuerstein, s. of Johannes Feuerstein; Feb. 5, 1782.

BERGHAUSER—Michael, s. of the decd. Johannes Berghauser, and Catharine, d. of Christy Harting, Apr. 4, 1775.

BERNHARD—Samuel, s. of the decd. Adam Bernhard, and Margaretta, d. of Frantz Schallt; July 4, 1785.

BERNHART—Peter, s. of the decd. Christian Bernhart, and Barbara, d. of the decd. Jacob Merckel; Apr. 17, 1775, on Easter Monday in Pastor's house.

BERNHART—Matthias, s. of the decd. Matthias Bernhart, and Anna Margaretha, d. of the decd. Wilhelm Heinrich Bugel; Apr. 27, 1765; in Eppler's church.

BERTHEL—Anna Maria, d. of Peter Berthel, and Gorg Michael Voltz, widower; Apr. 20, 1773.

BETZ—Friedrich, and Anna Maria, d. of Casper Werner; Dec. 27, 1763.

BETZ—Wilhelm, s. of the decd. Johannes Betz, and Margaretha, d. of the decd. Martin Illi; Aug. 2, 1785.

BELTZER—Anthonius, s. of Christofel Beltzer, and Anna Maria, d. of Heinrich Otto; May 23, 1781.

BEYER—Elisabeth, d. of Johannes Beyer, and Abraham Bauer, s. of Heinrich Bauer; May 10, 1774.

BEYER—Peter, s. of the decd. Adam Beyer, and Anna Maria, d. of the decd. Martin Schultz, Apr. 20, 1762.

BIEGEL—Maria Sybilla, d. of Wilhelm Heinrich Biegel, decd., and Ludwig Gautzler, s. of Johann Gorg Gautzler; Dec. 8, 1765.

BIEGEL—Wilhelm, Heinrich, s. of the decd. Wilhelm Heinrich Biegel, and Magdalena, d. of Philip Hoff; July 24, 1768.

BILLING—Johann Siegfried, and Juliana, d. of Heinrich Weller; Oct. 27, 1755.

BINCKLEY—Elisabeth, d. of Heinrich Binckley, and Johannes Loscher, s. of Nicolaus Loscher; Feb. 4, 1783.

BINCKLY—Marx, s. of Michael Binckly, and Magdalena, d. of the decd. Johannes Diessler; Nov. 27, 1770.

BINGEMANN—Carl, s. of the decd. Peter Bingemann, and Anna Margaretha, d. of the decd. Peter Schmidt; Sept. 18, 1766.

BIRCKENHAUSER—Maria, d. of Johannes Birckenhauser, decd., and Nicolaus Harding, s. of Christian Harding; Apr. 5, 1774.

'BITZER—Catharina, d. of Johannes Bitzer, and Johan Martin Wenss, s.of Gorg Wenss, decd.; June 3, 1783.

BIXLER—Christian, widower, and Margaretha, widow of Jacob Schlauch; Sept. 6 1785.

BLAKE—Joseph, and Anna Mitchell; Mch. 28, 1759.

BLECHER—Catharina, widow of Jost Blecher, and Philippus Dunnes, widower; Dec. 20, 1760.

BLUMER—Gorg, widower, and Deyanna, widow of Edwart Gultin; Aug. 5, 1784.

BOHM—Eva, d. of Jacob Bohm, and Jacob Marshall, s. of Dietrich Marshall; Dec. 10 1780.

14—Vol. VI—6th Ser.

BOHMER—Anna Maria, d. of Adam Bohmer, and Johan Michael Harting, s. of Christian Harting; July 28, 1778.

BOHN—Maria Rosina, d. Johann Adam Bohn, and Johann Adam Vollmer, s. of Michael Vollmer; Feb. 25, 1782.

BOHMER—Johann Adam, s. of the decd. Adam Bohmer, and Elisabeth, d. of Abraham R.ehm; Apr. 18, 1786.

BOHMER—Johann Adam, s. of the decd. Adam Bohmer, and Elisabeth, d. of Rudolf Heberling; Mch. 29, 1785.

BOLLENDER—Catharina, d. of Peter Bollender, decd., and Christian Waldschmidt, s. of Rev. John Waldschmidt; Aug. 15, 1780; by Rev. Boos in Reading Town.

BOLLINGER—Rudolph, s. of Christian Bollinger, Margaretha, d of Abraham Dorr; Oct. 17, 1752.

BONNET—Johannes, s. of the decd. Johannes Bonnet, and Margaretha Dorrothea, d. of Ulrich Beckly; Apr. 22, 1755.

BORDER—Johannes, s. of the decd. Johannes Border, and Susanna, widow of Jacob Mullinger; May 16, 1780.

BOSSER—Magdalena, d. of Jacob Bosser, and Phillipus Amme, s. of Johanne Amme, decd.; Jan. 21, 1755.

BOSSER—Margaretta, d. of Heinrich Bosser, decd., and Johanes Schrack, s. of Aadam Schrack; Feb. 11, 1777.

BOSSHAAR—Daniel, s. of the decd. Johann Bosshaar, and Catharina, d. of the decd. Rudolf Rudy; Mch. 30, 1756.

BOSSHART—Margaretta, d. of Johannes Bosshart, and Gorg Zoller, s. of Nicolaus Zoller; Aug. 2, 1781.

BOSSHAAR—Michael, s. of Goorg Bosshaar, and Margaretha, d. of the decd. Gorg Rettig; Mch. 27, 1785.

BRAUN—Anna Maria, d. of Joh. Engel Brann, and Abraham Weidman, s. of Rudolf Weidman; June 5, 1764.

BRAUM—Gerteraub, d. of Joohann Engel Braum, and Heinrich Buckle, s. of Adam Buckle; Dec. 19, 1768.

BRAUN—James, s. of the decd. Martin Braun, and Anna Maria, d. of the decd. Etwert Crosby; Jan. 15, 1784.

BRAUN—Peter, and Catharina, widow of William Cerl; Apr. 1, 1766. "Als nur der östn frau copuliret wurden."

BRAUN—Wilhelm, s. of the decd. Peter Braun, and Catharina, d. of Frantz Grick; Aug. 3, 1777.

BRANNAN—John, and Hanna, widow of Ritchser Dixen; June 25, 1770.

BRAUNINGER—Anna Eva, d. of Martin Brauninger, and Jacob Dussinger, s. of Adam Duddinger, decd.; Apr. 24, 1770.

BRECHT—Sara, d. of Michael Brecht, and Lehnhard Ruppert, s. of Philip Ruppert; Mar. 24, 1786.

BREITENSTEIN—Anna Eva, d. of Lenhard Breitenstein, decd., and Jacob Dornbach, s. of Jacob Dornbach, decd.; May 18, 1765.

BREITENSTEIN—Maria Margaretta, d. of Lehnhard Breitenstein, decd., and Michael Rank, s. of Philip Ranck. Date of marriage not mentioned. The Record stands between one dated May 20, 1755, the other Oct. 21, 1755.

BREITENSTEIN—Philip, and Margaret Brunner; Nov. 4, 1755.

BREININGER—Rosina, d. of Martin Breininger, and Johannes Gilsinger, s. of Gorg Gilsinger; June 9, 1767.

BRENEISEN—Julianna, widow of Jacob Breneisen, and Justus Hauch, s. of Daniel Hauch; Apr. 18, 1785.

BRENDEL—Elisabeth, d. of Philip Brendel, and Heinrich Klapp, s. of Johannes Klapp, decd.; Nov. 27, 1781.

BRENDEL—Barbara, d. of Philipp Brendel, and Samuel Meder, s. of Dewalt Meder; Aug. 9, 1785.

BRENDEL—Susanna, d. of Philip Brendel, and Gorg Seidenbauder, s. of Heinrich Seidenbauder, decd.; Feb. 18, 1784.

BRENEISEN—Elisabeth, d. of Conrad Breneisen, and Jacob Aache, s. of Lehnhard Aache, decd.; Apr. 20, 1782.

BRENNERMANN—Maria Catharina, d. of Christian Brennermann, decd., and Friedrich Diehbold, s. of Johann Gotofried Diehbold, decd.; Feb. 6, 1783.

BRITSCH—Jacob, s. of the decd. Jacob Britsch, and Anna, d. of Johannes Feuerstein; Jan. 16, 1781.

BROADSTOCK—Wilhelm, s. of Bernhard Broadstock, and Anna Maria, d. of the decd. Peter Balser; Oct. 3, 1783.

BRUBACHER—Abraham; widower, and Christina Gut, widow of Daniel Gut; Dec. 22, 1778.

BRUCKER—Barbara, d. of Jacob Brucker, and Nicolaus Weinhold, widower; Apr. 3, 1770.

BRUCKER—Christine, d. of Jacob Brucker, and Johannes Kohlman, s. of Bastian Kohlman, decd.; Nov. 26, 1771; in Gorg Ury house.

BRUCKER—David, s. of the decd. Peter Brucker, and Magdalena, d. of Jacob Erb; Nov. 8, 1780.

BRUCKER—Jacob, s. of the decd. Peter Brucker, and Margaretha, widow of Heinrich Walter; Mch. 14, 1769.

BRUHA—Adam, s. of the decd. Adam Bruha, and Margaretha, d. of Heinrich Feder; Feb. 25, 1783.

BRUMBACH—Margaretta, d. of Melchoir Brumbach, and Christian Conrad, s. of Lehnhard Conrad; Marty 6, 1770; in Riehms Town in Andreas Riehm's house.

BRUNNER—Gorg, s. of Gorg Michael Brunner, and Anna Maria, d. of Matthias Achebach; Feb. 12, 1782.
BRUNNER—Margaret, and Philip Breibenstein; Nov. 4, 1755.
BRUNNER—Peter, s. of Gorg Michael Brunner, and Eva, d. of Matthias Achebach; Sept. 2, 1783.
BUCH—Philip, s. of Gorg Nicolaus Buch, and Susanna, d. of Martin Eicholtz; Mch. 12, 1782.
BUCHER—Benedict, s. of Benedict Bucher, and Susanna, d. of the decd. Heinrich Mohler; Mch. 30, 1784.
BUCHER—Benedictus, or Benedict, or Benss-Bucher, second marriage, and Maria, widow of Johannes Frey; Sept. 8, 1778.
BUCHER—Heinrich, s. of the decd. Engelhard Bucher, and Catharina, d. of Christofel Kern; Apr. 21, 1783.
BUCHER—Johannes, widower, and Elisabeth, d. of the decd. Martin Keller; May 14, 1776.
BUCHER—Sabina, d. of Peter Bucher, decd., and Philip Weiss, widower 2n. m.; Mar. 9, 1785.
BUCHLER—Catharine, d. of David Buchler, and Martin Zuber; Nov. 10, 1760; in Johannes Huber's house in Ronnels Town.
BUCHMANN—Matthias, s. of Gorg Buchmann, and Anna Elisabetha, d. of Conrad Aumuller; Dec. 26, 1757.
BUCHSSLER—Anna, d. of Jacob Buchssler, and Christian Flickinger, s. of Joseph Flickinger; Apr. 21, 1783.
BUCKLE—Heinrich, s. of Adam Buckle, and Gerteraub, d. of Johann Engel Braun; Dec. 19, 1768.
BUGEL—Anna Margaretta, d. of Wilhelm Heinrich Bugel, decd., and Matthias Bernhart, s. of Matthias Bernhart, decd.; Apr. 27, 1765; in Eppters Church.
BULLINGER—Magdalena, d. of Christian Bullinger, decd., and Abraham Dorr, s. of Abraham Dorr, decd.; Feb. 28, 1758.
BUNSH—Magdalena, d. of Thomas Bunsh, and Gorg Kohl, s. of Gorg Kohl; Aug. 24, 1780.
BURCKHALTER—Heinrich, s. of Martin Burckhalter, and Rosina, d. of Friedrich Gerhart; Mch. 10, 1778.
BURCKHOLDER—Anna Eva, d. of Martin Burckholder, and Johannes Harnisch, s. of Samuel Harnisch; Apr. 7, 1781.
BURRER—Margretta, and Peter Lingenfelder; Feb. 20, 1759.
BUSS—Catharine, d. of Peter Buss, decd., and Jacob Weinhold, s. of Nicolai Weinhold, decd.; June 10, 1771.
BUSS—Peter s. of Thomas Buss, and Elizabetha, d. of Johannes Dentler; Nov. 11, 1755

BUTTS—Thomas, s. of the decd. Thomas Bubbs, and Catharina, d. of Tobias Metzger; Aug. 23, 1784.

CAFROTH—Elisabetha, d. of Gerhard Cafroth, and Peter Meyer, s. of Elias Meyer; Nov. 13, 1759.

CALLEN—Thomas, s. of the decd. Andreas Callen, and Catharina, d. of Gorg Conrad; May 7, 1781.

CARL—Conrad, and Magdalena Krammert, Aug. 3 1761.

CARL—Dorothea, d. of Jacob Carl, and Christian Hartmann; Aug. 3, 1761. Note states that on the 15th. Aug. the wife left her husband, & on the 19th sickened and died.

CAROLUS—Anna Maria, d. of Johannes Carolus, and Gottfried Scharb, s. of Johannes Scharb, decd.; Apr. 21, 1783.

CERL—Catharine, w. of Wilhelm Cerl, and Peter Braun; Apr. 1, 1766. Als. nur der 5ten frau Copuliret wurden.

CHILJAN—Michael, s. of the decd. Matthias Chiljan (Killian?), and Elisabeth, d. of the decd. Conrad Ziegler; May 26, 1778.

CHRIST—Ernst Wilhelm, and Anna Maria Schmist; Mch. 16, 1767.

CLEMSON—Elisabeth, d. of Thomas Clemson, and James Lewyton, s. of Wilhelm Lewyton, decd.; Dec. 6, 1782.

COLLHEN—(or Collken, Colleon) Rebecca, d. of Heinrich Collhen, and Jonas Leigen, s. of Peter Leigen; Oct. 24, 1754.

CONNER—Samuel, s. of the decd. Thomas Conner, and Elisabeth, d. of the decd. Salomon Mecreny (McCreary); Feb. 24, 1784.

CONRAD—Catharina, d. of Gorg Conrad, and Thomas Callen, s. of Andreas Callen, decd.; May 7, 1781.

CONRAD—Christian, s. of Lehnhard Conrad, and Margaretha, d. of Melchor Brambach; Marty 6, 1770.

CONRAD—Johann Gorg, s. of Johann Gorg Conrad, and Catharina Elisabetha, d. of Ludwig Kohl; Nov. 30, 1756.

CONRAD—Johannes, s. of the decd. Lehnnard Conrad, and Catharina, d. of Peter Schneider; Oct. 6, 1782.

CONRATH—Jacob, s. of the decd. Lehnhardt Conrath, and Barbara, d. of the decd. Martin Keller; Aug. 5, 1777.

CORNER—Johan, s. of the decd. Justus Borner, and Elisabeth, d. of the decd. Daniel Merckert; Dec. 8, 1783.

COSCHET—Bernhard, s. of Isaac Coschet, and Salome, d. of the decd. Daniel Gut; Mch. 31, 1785.

CROSBY—Anna Maria, d. of Edwart Crosby, decd., and James Braun, s. of Martin Braun, decd. Jan. 15, 1784.

DANNER—Jacob, his "daughter m. Oct. 4, 1763" (Nothing but the above on the Record—L. R. K.)

DANNER—Jacob, his "Daughter m. Oct. 4, 1763" (Nothing but the above on the Record—L. R. K.)

DAUBRICK—Barbara, d. of Jacob Daubrick, and Daniel Kabel, s. of Nicolaus Kabel, decd.; Mar. 15, 1760.

DAUDERICK—Elisabeth, d. of Jacob Dauderick, and Frantz Hahn, s. of Peter Hahn; May 31, 1753. Moden Creek Church.

DAUTH—Heinrich, s. of Peter Dauth, and Elisabetha, d. of the decd. Johannes Frantz; Nov. 1, 1758.

DAUTRICH—Barbara, d. of Johann Dautrich, and Jacob Hassler, s. of Sebastian Hassler; May 10, 1782.

DAVIS—Anna, d. of Wilhelm Davis, and Friedrich Gloss, s. of Adam Gloss; Apr. 12, 1785.

DAVIS—Margretta, d. of Gabriel Davis, and Zacharius Pursol, s. of Johannes Pursol, decd.; Aug. 17, 1779.

DAVIS—Rachel, and Wilhelm Hew; Nov. 30, 1778.

DAVIS—Rahel, d. of James Davis, and Johann Christophel Schneider; July 11, 1786.

DEAN—Caleb, s. of Nehimiah Dean, and Maria, d. of the decd. John Marlin; Feb. 16, 1785.

DECKER—Heinrich, s. of Valentine Decker, and Anna Maria, d. of Frantz Hermann; Aug. 21, 1764.

DESSTER—Jacob, widower, and Anna Maria, widow of Gorg Gottschall; m. in Desster's house; Apr. 20, 1767.

DEUTLER—Elizabetha, d. of Johannes Deutler, and Peter Buss, s. of Johannes Buss; Nov. 11, 1755.

DEYER—Johannes, s. of Gorg Deier, and Anna Christina, d. of Johannes Diefendorfer; Apr. 20, 1756.

DIEFENDORFER—Anna Christina, d. of Johannes Diefendorfer, and Johannes Deyer, s. of Gorg Deier; Apr. 20, 1756.

DIEFENDORFER—Johann Jacob, s. of Johannes Diefendorfer, and Eva, d. of the decd. Adam Muller; May 20, 1755.

DIEFENDORFER—Johannes, s. of Alexander Diefendorfer, and Magdalena Weick, d. of Joseph Weick; Dec. 2, 1755.

DIEHBOLD—Friedrich, s. of the decd. Johann Gottfried Diehbold, and Maria Catharina, d. of the decd. Christian Brennermann; Feb. 6, 1783.

DIEM—Wilhelm, s. of Peter Diehm, and Catharina, d. of Johannes Gloss; June 17, 1786.

DIEMER—Jacob, widower, and Anna Maria Linck, widow of Adam Linck; Feb. 5, 1780.

DIEMETH—Bastian, s. of Engelhart Diemeth, and Anna Maria, d. of the decd. Nicolaus Franck; Nov. 10, 1783.

DIESSLER—Magdalena, d. of Johannes Diessler, decd., and Mart. Binckly, s. of Michael Binckly; Nov. 27, 1770.

DIEST—Daniel, s. of the decd. Johannes Diest, and Juliana, d. of Peter Ravensberger; Nov. 9, 1762.

DIETRICH—Nicolaus, s. of the decd. Johann Jacob Dietrich, m. 31st Oct., 1752, Anna Margaretha, d. of Johann Gerhart Shafer. Rev. J. Waldschmidt.

DIETZ—Ernst, s. of the decd. Adam Dietz, and Catharina, d. of Johann Runckel; June 17, 1771.

DILL—Maria, d. of Casper Dill, and Wilhelm Waldschmidt, widower; Feb. 23, 1808. Added by some other than Rev. J. W., who d. 1786.

DIXEN—Hanna, w. of Ritchser Dixen, and John Brannan; June 25, 1770.

DOCK—Johannes, s. of the decd Henry Dock, and Elisabeth, d. of Johannes Aumuller; Apr. 29, 1782.

DOCK—Maragretta, d. of Fillipp Dock, and Adam Ulrich, s. of Gorg Ulrich, decd.; Jan. 11, 1784.

DOMMAIN—Magdelene, and Christian Schlechly; July 4, 1764.

DONOB—Carl August Maxiliamus, d. of Johann Matthias Donob, and Catharina, d. of Johannes Laub; Jan. 5, 1786.

DORNBACH—Anna Maria, d. of Anthon Dornbach, and Johan Christian Weber, s. of Christian Weber; Oct. 29, 1754.

DORNBACH—Dorrothea, d. of Anthony Dornbach, and Joseph Millinger, s. of Christofel Millinger, decd.; Apr. 6, 1762.

DORNBACH—Jacob, s. of Anthon Dornbach, and Anna Eva, d. of the decd. Lehnhard Breitenstein; May. 18, 1765.

DORR—Abraham, s. of the decd. Abraham Dorr, and Magdalena d. of the decd. Christian Bullinger; Feb. 28, 1758.

DORR—Catharina, d. of Abraham Dorr, and Conrad Heyberger, s. of Conrad Heyberger, decd.; by Rev. John Waldschmidt; Oct. 17, 1752.

DORR—Margaretha, d. of Abraham Dorr, and Rudolph Bollinger, s. of Christian Bollinger, m. 17th Oct., 1752; Rev. J. Waldschmidt.

DRACHSEL—Fronica, d. of Johannes Drachsel, and Vicens (Vincent) Stauffer; June 15, 1762.

DRITSCH—Jacob, widower, and Catharina, widow of Nicolaus Ruhm; Nov. 22, 1778.

DRUCKEBROD—Matthias, s. of Matthias Druckebrod, and Fronica, d. of the decd. Conrad Meinzer; Nov. 25, 1783.

DUMMY—Jacob, s. of Durst Dummy, and Maria Ursula, d. of Jacob Graff; May 19, 1760.

DUNCKEL—Peter, s. of the decd. Melchoir Dunckel, and Anna Maria, d.of the decd. Ahraham Andreas; May 16, 1785.

DUNNES—Philippus, widower, and Catharina, widow of Jost Blecher; Dec. 20, 1760.

DUPPEL—Lorenz, widower, and Barbara, widow of Valentin Schweigart; June 5, 1731.

DURST—Christina, d. of Casper Durst, decd., and Henry Fischer, s. of Wilhelm.Fischer; Sept. 28, 1761.

DUSSINGER—Jacob, s. of the decd. Adam Dussinger, and Anna Eva, d. of Martin Brauninger; Apr. 24, 1770.

DUSSINGER—Johannes, and Magdalena Elisabetha, d. of Philip Gebler; Apr. 27, 1779.

DUY—Simon, s. of Conrad Duy, and Catharina, d. of the decd. Thileman Schutz; Apr. 23, 1754.

EBERHARD—Catharina, d. of Christian Eberhard, and Jacob Lehnhard, s. of Jacob Lehnhard, decd.; Nov. 19, 1775; at 4 o'clock in the afternoon.

EBERHART—Christian, s. of Johan George Eberhart, and Sarah, d. of Christian Martin Wagmann; July 3, 1753.

EBERHERT—Agatha, d. of Christian Eberhert, and Heinrich Winckler; Sept. 21, 1783.

EBERLE—Christian, s. of Peter Ebler (sie), and Christina, d. of Joseph Flickinger; Mch. 27, 1785.

EBLER—Peter, s. of Peter Ebler, decd., and Anna, d. of Josef Flickinger; Feb. 3, 1780.

ECKART—Anna Eva, d. of Philip Eckert, and Jacob Epple, s. of Jacob Epple, decd.; May 21, 1754.

ECKART—Magdalena, d. of Lehnhart Eckart, decd., and Christophel Meyer, s. of Heinrich Meyer; May 16, 1781.

ECKERT—Anna Margaretta, d. of Philip Eckert, and Johann Casper Grube, s. of Christian Grube; May 15, 1754.

ECKERT—Anna Maria, d. of Casper Eckert, and Johann Michael Herold, widower; Mar. 9, 1773.

ECKERT—Lenhart, s. of Philip Eckert, and Catharina, d. of Peter Becker; Apr. 1, 1755.

EDWARDS—Elisabeth, d. of Ewen Edwards, decd., and Jacob Hinckel, s. of Gorg Hinckel; Feb. 13, 1775; in Christopher Friedrich's house.

EGLY—Susanna, d. of Marx Egly, and Phillippus Kohl, s. of Peter Kohl; Nov. 7, 1754.

EHBRECHT—Anna Maria, d. of Paul Ehbrecht, and Christofel Pinnsser, s. of Christofel Pinnsser, decd.; July 28, 1782.

EHRHART—Barbara, d. of Nicolaus Ehrhart, and Michael Mayer, s. of Michael Mayer; Aug. 31, 1761.

REV. JOHN WALDSCHMIDT—1752-1786.   217

EICHELBRENNER—Gottfried, s. of Daniel Eichelbrenner, and Juliana, d. of Casper Raush. (Not dated, but between July 28, 1760 & Oct. 28, 1760—L. R. K.)

EICHHOLTZ—Barbara, d. of Martin Eichholtz, and Heinrich Lausch, s. of Gabriel Lausch; Feb. 11, 1783.

EICHOLTZ—Susanna, d. of Martin Eicholtz, and Philip Buch, s. of Gorg Nicolaus Buch; Mch. 12, 1782.

EIGEREICHER—Judith, d. of Conrad Eigerreicher, and Daniel Ermold; Oct. 29, 1766. (At the same time a son was baptized.)

ENCK—Catharine, d. of Jacob Enck, and Martin Laber, s. of Joh. Wendel Laber, decd.; Oct. 13, 1761. Married by Rev. Stoy, when Rev. Waldschmidt. ("Uter der Suskehanna war.")

ENCK— Jacob, s. of Jacob Enck, and Anna Catharina, d. of the decd. Wendel Laber; Dec. 30, 1755.

ENCK—Johannes, s. of Jacob Enck, and Barbara, d. of the decd. Joh. Wendel Laber; Oct. 13, 1761.

ENDERS—Anna, d. of Wilhelm Enders, decd. and Jacob Gorges, s. of Joseph Gorges; May 10, 1786.

ENGALLEND—Johann Gotlieb, s. of Johann Gottlieb Engelland, and Anna Catharina, d. of the decd. Johann George Quickel; Aug. 21, 1753.

ENGEL—Magdalena, d. of Conrath Engel, decd., and Jacob Unger, s. of Johannes Unger; Feb. 19, 1785.

EPPLE—Jacob, s. of the decd. Jacob Epple, and Anna Eva, d. of Philip Eckert, Lancaster, Pa.; May 21, 1754.

EPPLER—Anna Maria, d. of Valentine Eppler, and Christofel Hacke, s. of Johannes Hacke, decd.; Oct. 11, 1768.

EPPRECHT—Rebecca, d. of Philip Epprecht, and Abraham Muller, s. of Anderas Muller, decd.; Jan. 29, 1765.

ERB—Magdalena, d. of Jacob Erb, and David Brucker, s. of Peter Brucker, decd.; Nov. 28, 1780.

ERNST—Ignatius, s. of Johannes Ernst, and Sophia, d. of the decd. Christofel Becker; Nov. 21, 1780.

ERMOLD—Daniel, and Judith Eyrricker, d. of Conrad Eigereicher; Oct. 29, 1766. At the same time a son was baptized.

ERWEN—Thomas, s. of the decd. John Erwen, and Sara, d. of Joseph Russel; Mch. 18, 1783.

ESCHBACH—Margaretta, d. of Friedrich Eschbach, decd., and Christian Walter, s. of Jacob Walter; Mch. 1, 1785.

ESCHELMANN—Anna Maria, d. of Christian Eschelmann, and John Nicolaus Mosser, s. of Johannes Mosser; July 2, 1776.

ESCHELMAN—Catharina, d. of Christian Eschelman, and Gorg Kappe, s. of Gorg Kappe; Oct. 2, 1781.

ESCHELMAN—Abraham, s. of Christian Eschelman, and Susanna, d. of the decd. Friedrich Horn; Feb. 20, 1781.

EULER—John Michael, s. of the decd. Adam Euler, and Sybilla, d. of the decd. Jost Fuchs; Jan. 3, 1769.

EURICH—Johann Gorg, and Anna Maria, d. of Dietrich Sehl; Dec. 20, 1769.

EYERICH—Conrad, s. of Conrad Eyerich, and Juliana Lauer, d. of Michael Lauer; Feb. 18, 1771.

FANCKHAUSS—Catharine, d. of ------ Franckhaus, and Peter Funck, s. of Gorg Funck, decd.; Nov. 9, 1771.

FARNY—Barbara, d. of Peter Farny, and Jacob Feder, s. of Bernhart Feder, decd.; Dec. 1, 1777.

FAUST—Elisabeth, d. of Anthon Faust, and Johan Jost Stamm, s. of Adam Stamm; Nov. 2, 1768.

FAUST—Elisabeth, d. of Peter Faust, and Daniel Maurer, s. of Christofel Maurer; June 12, 1769; in Pastor's (J. W.) house.

FAUST—Heinrich, s. of Peter Faust, and Magdalena, d. of Nicolaus Weimer; June 12, 1769.

FAUST—Magdalena, d. of Peter Faust, and Christen Theel; Mch. 24, 1767.

FEDER—Isaac, s. of the decd. Bernhard Feder, and Elizabeth, s. of Gorg Schumacher; May 29, 1780.

FEDER—Jacob, s. of the decd. Bernhart Feder, and Barbara, d. of Peter Farny; Dec. 1, 1777.

FEDER—Margaretha, d. of Heinrich Feder, and Adam Bruha, s. of Adam Bruha, decd.; Feb. 25, 1783.

FEDER—Peter, s. of Peter Feder, and Anna Maria, d. of Christian Oblinger; June 7, 1781.

FEHL—Salome, s. of Johannes Fehl, decd., and Nicolaus Kammer, s. of Peter Kammer; Sept. 28, 1784.

FEHL—Valentin, s. of Gorg Fehl, and Elisabeth, d. of the decd. Adam Bahmer; June 30, 1776.

FERRY—Elisabeth, d. of Wilhelm Ferry, and Wilhelm Shaw, s. of Samuel Shaw, decd.; June 12, 1780.

FEUERSTEIN—Anna, d. of Johannes Feuerstein, and Jacob Britsch, s. of Jacob Britsch, decd.; Jan. 16, 1781.

FEUERSTEIN—Daniel, s. of Johannes Feuerstein, and Anna, d. of Gorg Lang; Aug. 5, 1783.

FEUERSTEIN—Gorg, s. of Johannes Feuerstein, and Salome, d. of the decd. Christofel Bercker; Feb. 5, 1782.

FEUERSTEIN—Magdalena, d. of Johannes Feuerstein, and Johannes Lufft, s. of Peter Lufft, decd.; Sept. 12, 1773

FIEDLER—Anna Juliana, d. of Gottfried Fiedler, and Abraham Leynbach, s. of Johannes Leinbach; Apr. 12, 1768.

FIESS—Christine, d. of Johannes Fiess, and Michael Muller, s. of Hanss Ulrich Muller; Dec. 3, 1759.

FIESSER—Susanna, d. of Nicolaus Fiesser, and Andreas Ruhm, s. of Eberhard Riehm; July 12, 1759.

FILTSMEYER—Johann Jost, s. of Philip Filtsmeyer, and d. of Gabriel Rietscher; Apr. 5, 1757. (Christian name of d. omitted.)

FISCHER—Elisabeth, d. of Joseph Fischer, and Conrad Winckler, s. of Conrad Winckler; June 9, 1764.

FISCHER—Henry, s. of Wilhelm Fischer, and Christina, d. of the decd. Casper Durst; Sept. 28, 1761.

FISCHER—Peter, s. of Heinrich Fischer, and Magdalena, d. of Christian Weber; Oct. 8, 1783.

FISCHER—Peter, s. of Wilhelm Fischer, and Appolonia, d. of Michael Heckert. (Date omitted, but between two Records, one Apr. 17, 1758, the other May 16, 1758—L. R. K.)

FISCHER—Rosina, d. of Wilhelm Fischer, and Peter Grauel, s. of Michale Grauel, by me (Rev. J. Waldschmidt) in the presence of many witnesses; April 10, 1764.

FIX—Margaretta, w. of Samuel Fix, and Friedrich Wirtz, widower; May 27, 1784.

FLAUER—Dorrothea, and Jacob Lambert; Oct. 19, 1772. Both of the Catholic religion.

FLICKINGER—Anna, d. of Josef Flickinger, and Peter Ebler, s. of Peter Ebler, decd.; Feb. 8, 1780.

FLICKINGER—Christian, s. of Joseph Flickinger, and Anna, d. of Jacob Buchssler; Apr. 21, 1783.

FLICKINGER—Christina, d. of Joseph Flickinger, and Christian Eberle, s. of Peter Eberle; Mch. 27, 1785.

FLICKINGER—Johannes, s. of Joseph Flickinger, and Anna, d. of Heinrich Handschy; Mch. 30, 1784.

FORDINE—Wendel, s. David Fordine, and Anna Sophia Treutel; Nov. 6, 1759.

FORLOH—Johannes, s. of the decd. Ruppert Forloch, and Barbara, d. of Gorg Siegethaler; Jan. 25, 1785.

FORN (?)—Elisabeth, d. of Adam Forn (?), decd., and Peter Hettrig, s. of Peter Hetrig, decd.; Apr. 13, 1786.

FRANCK—Anna Maria, d. of Nicolaus Franck, decd., and Bastian Diemett, s. of Engelhart Diemett; Nov. 10, 1783.

FRANCK—Margaretta, d. of Nicolaus Franck, and Heinrich Muller, s. of Matthias Muller; Feb. 8, 1784.

FRANTZ—Abraham, s. of Michael Frantz, and Maria, d. of the decd. Casper Koch; Mch. 29, 1784.

BAPTISMAL AND MARRIAGE RECORDS.

FRANTZ—Adam, s. of the decd. Gorg Adam Frantz, and Sarah, d. of the decd. Ulrick Schorck; June 19, 1780.

FRANTZ—Barbara, d. of Gorg Adam Frantz, and Johannes Stiess, s. of Jacob Stiess; Feb. 20, 1781.

FRANTZ—Barbara, w. of Daniel Frantz, and Johannes Neumann, widower & m. for 3rd time; Feb. 4, 1777.

FRANTZ—Elisabeth, d. of Johannes Frantz, decd. and Heinrich Dauth, s. of Peter Dauth; Nov. 1, 1758.

FRANTZ—Gorg, s. of the decd. Daniel Frantz, and Maria, d. of the decd. Ulrich Schorck; Jan. 20, 1780.

FRANTZ—Jacob, s. of the decd. Daniel Frantz, and Anna, widow of Paul Gehr; Dec. 16, 1777.

FRANTZ—Magdalena, forsaken wife of Stophel Frantz, and Christian Urich, s. of Frantz Ury (sic), decd.; Sept. 11, 1764.

FREY—Catharina, d. of Johannes Frey, decd., and Johannes Hag, s. of Conrad Hag, lecd.; Aug. 7, 1781.

FREY—Elisabeth, d. of Jacob Frey, and David Mumma; s. of Lehnhard Mumma; Dec. 26, 1785. Pastor's house.

FREY—Fronica, d. of Rudolf Frey, and Peter Ressler, s. of Gorg Ressler, decd. Apr. 10, 1784.

FREY—Juliana, d. of Jacob Frey, and Conrad Hart, s. of Conrad Hart; Apr. 21, 1772. On Easter Tuesday.

FREY—Julianna, d. of Jcaob Frey, and Jacob Mumma, s. of Lehnhard Mumma; Feb. 28, 1786.

FREY—Ludwig, s. of Jacob Frey, and Susanna, d. of the decd. Johannes Kohl; Mch. 10, 1778.

FREY—Maria, w. of Johannes Frey, and Benedictus, Benedict, or Benss Bucher second Marriage; Sept. 8, 1778.

FREY—Maria Catharina, d. of Jacob Frey, and Andreas Surrerus, s. of Andreas Surrerus; Feb. 14, 1782.

FREY—Margaretta, d. of Jacob Frey, and Jacob Weith, s. of Heinrich Weith; Feb. 14, 1786.

FREY—Margaretta, d. of Jacob Frey, and Gorg Jacob Weinhold, s. of Nicolaus Weinhold, decd.; July 27, 1773. In the Pastor's house and in the presence of 3 witnesses: Jacob Frey, Nicolaus Weinhold & Conrad Hart.

FREY—Martin, s. of Rudolf Frey, and Elisabeth, d. of Lenhart Kepplinger; July 29, 1783. In his house, namely Lehnhart Kepplinger at the Allegenc.

FREY—Peter, s. of Jacob Frey, and Anna Maria, d. of Christian Weber; May 6, 1784.

FUCHS—Johann Adam, s. of the decd. Jost Fuchs, and Anna Maria, d. of Gorg Hain; Mch. 20, 1764.

FUCHS—Sybilla, d. of Jost Fuchs, decd., and Johan Michael Euler, s. of Adam Euler, decd.; Jan. 3, 1769.
FUHRMANN—Maria, d. of Paul Fuhrmann, and Nicolaus Losser, s. of Nicolaus Losser; Apr. 11, 1780.
FUHRMANN—Peter, s. of Paul Fuhrmann, and Juliana, b. of Jost Reitel; Apr. 19, 1783.
FUISSER—Maria Margaretta, d. of Nicolaus Fuisser, and Phillipus Grunewalt, widower; Apr. 16, 1754.
FUNCK—Catharina, d. of Gorg Funck, and Melchoir Seguet, s. of Thomas Segner, decd.; July 2, 1782.
FUNCK—Peter, s. of the decd. Gorg Funck, and Catharina, d. of Fankhauss———; Nov. 9 1771.
FUSSER—Susanna, d. of Peter Fusser, and Peter Schmid, s. of Ludwig Schmid, decd.; Mch. 21, 1780.

GABEL—Johannes, s. of Wilhelm Gabel, and Barbara, d. of Gorg Meyer, decd · Nov. 6, 1759.
GANTZLER—Ludwig, s. of Johann Gorg Gantzler, and Maria Sybilla, d. of the decd. Wilhelm Heinrich Biegel; Dec. 8, 1765.
GARTNER—Maria Elisabeth, and Elias Mayer, m. for 3d. time; Feb. 2, 1762.
GARTNER—Maria Margaretta, d. of Bernharth Gartner, and Johannes Hildebrand, s. of Christian Hildebrand, decd.; Oct. 12, 1780.
GEBLER—Magdalena Elisabetha, d. of Philip Gebler, and Johannes Dussinger; Apr. 27, 1779.
GEERISS—Elisabeth, d. of Adam Geeriss, and Phillipus Schlebach, s. of Heinrich Schlebach; Feb. 29, 1780.
GEHR—Andreas, s. of the decd. Paul Gehr, and Elisabeth, d. of the decd. Michael Ruth; Jan. 16, 1781.
GEHR—Anna, w. of Paul Gehr, and Jacob Frantz, s. of Daniel Frantz, decd.; Dec. 16, 1777.
GEHR—Daniel, s. of the decd. Andreas Gehr, and Catharina, d. of Gorg Rein; Jan. 13, 1784.
GEHR—Elisabeth, d. of Paul Gehr, decd., and Frantz Bauenbach, s. of Melchoir Bauenbach, decd.; Aug. 5, 1777.
GEHR—Gorg s. of the decd. Paul Gehr, and Elisabeth, d. of the decd. Jost Schnekler; Nov. 15, 1785.
GEHR—Johanna Christine, d. of Andreas Gehr, and was called Salome until her baptism, Apr. 15, 1767, and Rev. Johann Gorg Wittner; June 2, 1767
GEHR—Johannes, s. of the decd. Paul Gehr, and Elisabeth, d. of Samuel Hundicker; Apr. 3, 1780.

GEISSLER—Adam, s. of Adam Geissler, and Anna Barbara, d. of Johannes Lang; Dec. 2, 1755.
GERER—Catharina, d. of Johannes Gerer, and Casper Guiter; Oct. 28, 1760.
GERHART—Elisabeth, d. or Adam Gerhart, and Johannes Weiss, s. of Stophel Weiss; June 11, 1776.
GERHART—Rosina, d. of Friedrich Gerhart, and Heinrich Burckhalter, s. of Martin Burckhalter; Mar. 10, 1778.
GERNER—Friedrich, s of Marx Gerner, and Catharina, d. of the decd. Sebastian Kohl; Marty 13, 1770.
GERNER—Margaretta, d. of Johannes Gerner, and Gorg Bauder, s. of Gorg Bauder, decd.; June 20, 1786.
GERMAN—Johannes, and Maria Magdalena, d. of Jacob Springer; Apr. 27, 1760.
GERMANN—Barbara, d. of Lehnhard Germann, and Johannes Groll, s. of Adam Groll; Dec. 9, 1783.
GESSLER—Elisabeth, d. of Michael Gessler, decd., and Johannes Toll, s. of Johannes Toll; Nov. 24, 1763.
GEYER—Barbara, d. of Jacob Geyer, and Valentine Rauck, s. of Michael Rauck, decd.; Apr. 9, 1780.
GICKER—Eva, d. of Heinrich Gicker, and Conrath Koch, s. of Alexander Koch; Sept. 24, 1783.
GILSINGER—Johannes, s. of Gorg Glisinger, and Rosina, d. of Martin Breininger; June 9, 1767.
GINTER—Casper, and Catharina, d. of Johannes Gerer; Oct. 28, 1760.
GISTER—Agada, d. of Christofel Gister, decd., and Gorg Albrecht, s. of Joh. Gorg Albrecht, decd.; Feb. 14, 1759.
GLOSS—Catharina, d. of Johannes Gloss, and Wilhelm Diem, s. of Peter Diehm; June 17, 1786.
GLOSS—Friedrich, s. of Adam Gloss, and Anna David-Davis, Wilhelm Davis'-David's daughter; Apr. 12, 1785.
GOETT—Salome, w. of Carl Goett, and Abraham Hirschberger, widower (m. 2d. times); Nov. 28, 1780.
GOTTSCHALL—Anna Maria, w. of Gorg Gottschall, and Jacob Desster, widower, m. in Desster's House; Apr. 20, 1767.
GOTTSCHALL—Nicolaus, s. of Christofel Gottschall, and Elisabeth, d. of the decd. Jacob Nuss; Sept. 12, 1758.
GORG—Christian, s. of the decd. Heinrich Gorg, and Regina d. of the decd. Johan Jacob Juncker; July 24, 1781.
GORG—Rebecca, d. of Saul Gorg, and Johannes Zeller, s. of Nicolaus Zeller; June 15, 1786.
GORGES—Jacob, s. of the decd. Josef Gorges, and Anna, d. of the decd. Wilhelm Enders; May 10, 1786.

GOTZ—Gorg, s. of the decd. Andreas Gotz and Maria Sybilla, d. of Melchoir Stiehl; June 11, 1782.

GRAF—Samuel, s. of Joseph Graf, and Susanna, d. of Abraham Graf; Jan. 1, 1782.

GRAF—Susanna, d. of Abraham Graf, and Samuel Graf, s. of Joseph Graf; Jan. 1, 1782.

GRAF—Wilhelm, and Esther Leibrock; June 6, 1757.

GRAFF—Ester, d. of Wilhelm Graff, and Gorg Machmer, s. of Philip Machmer; decd.; May 3, 1786.

GARFF—Maria Ursulam, d. of Jacob Graff, and Jacob Dummy, s. of Durst Dummy; May 19, 1760.

GRAFF—Jacob, and Anna Margaretha, d. of ..Adam Becker; Apr. 12, 1768. ..else Henry Hedricks' wife's daughter, which she bore in dishonor.

GRAFF—Johannes, widower, and Maria Fronica, widow of Jacob Otttt; Nov. 27, 1770.

GRAFF—Peter, s. of Joseph Graff, and Magdalena, d. of the decd. Heinrich Huber; Aug. 20, 1786.

GRAMLING—Adam, s of Gorg Gramling, and Elisabeth, d. of Johannes Servi (Zerbe); Mch. 28, 1780.

GRAUEL—Peter, s. of Michael Grauel, and Rosina, d. of Wilhelm Fischer; by me (Rev. J. W.) in the presence of many witnesses; Apr. 10, 1764.

GRICK—Catharina, d. of Frantz Grick, and Wilhelm Braum, s. of Peter Braum, decd.; Aug. 3, 1777.

GRIGER—J. Jacob, s. of Gorg Grier, and Margaretha, d. of Ludwig Mohn; Jan. 1, 1771.

GRIGER—Jacob, s. of Jacob Griger, and Catharina, d. of Daniel Schuy; Oct. 11, 1757.

GROLL—Johannes, s. cf Adam Groll, and Barbara, d. on Lehnhard Germann; Dec. 9, 1783.

GRUB—Ludwig Peter, s. of Christian Grube, and Maria Barbara, d. of Lorenz Weber, in Christian Grube's house; May 6, 1755.

GRUBE—Johann Casper, s. of Christian Grube, and Anna Margaretha. d. of Philip Eckert; May 15, 1754.

GRUBE—Maria Elisabetha, d. of Christian Grube, and Rev. Johannes Waldschmidt; May 14, 1754.

GRUNEWALD—Phillipus, a widower, and Maria Margaretha, d. of Nicolaus Fusser; Apr. 16, 1754.

GUCKER—Daniel, s. of Henry Gucker, and Catharina, d. cf the decd. Matthias Weber; Apr. 2, 1782.

GULBIN—Deyanna, w. of Edwart Gulbin, and Gorg Blvmer, widower; Aug. 5, 1784.

GULT—Anna, d. of Edwart Gult, and Matthias Kohlronn, s. of Johannes Kohlronn, decd,; Mar. 6, 1781.

GULTIN—Johannes, s of the decd. Edwart Gultin, and Elisabeth, d. of Gorg Weber; Apr. 15, 1783.

GUNDEL—Maria Magdalena, d. of David Gundel, decd., and Wilhelm Schack, s. of Michael Schack.

GUSCHWAY—Anna Margretta, d. of Isaias Guschway, and Johannes Hahn, s. of Adam Hahn; May 15, 1769.

GUSCHWAY—Ester, d. of Isaias Guschway, and Johannes Hahn, s. of Peter Hahn, decd.; Oct. 25, 1768.

GUT—Christina, w. of Daniel Gut, and Abraham Brubacher, widower; Dec. 22, 1778.

GUT—Salome, d. of Danl. Gut, decd., and Bernhard Coschet, s. of Isaac Coschet; Mch. 31, 1785.

GUT—Heinrich, s. of Christian Gut, and Maria, d. of Christian Weber; Oct. 24, 1783.

GUT—Peter, s. of Peter Gut, and Anna, d. of Benedictus or Benss Horniss; Mch. 10, 1782.

HAAG—Magdalena, d. of Gorg Haag, decd., and Henry Riethe, s. of Johannes Rieth; Dec. 31, 1778.

HAASS—Catharina, d. of Conrath Haass, decd., and Heinrich Nuen, s. of Johan Heinrich Nuen, decd.; Aug. 2, 1785.

HAASS—Catharina, d. of Peter Haass, and Michael Walleisen, s. of Michael Walleisen, decd.; June 6, 1779.

HAB—Maria Christina, d. of Peter Hab, and Johann Gorg Schreiber (widower); July 23, 1774.

HABECKER—Jacob, s. of Jacob Habecker, and Barbara, d. of the decd. Michael Lehmann; June 13, 1784.

HACK—Barbara, d. of Johannes Hack, decd., and Johannes Schreib, s. of Englebert Scheib; Nov. 30, 1756.

HACKE—Christofel, s. of the decd. Johannes Hacke, and Anna Maria, d. of Valentin Eppler; Oct. 11, 1768.

HACKMAN—Heinrich, s. of Heinrich Hackmann and Susanna, d. of Johannes Seiler; Aug. 8, 1785.

HAFFNER—Anna Maria, d. of Friedrich Haffner, and Johann Jacob Weiss, s. of Jacob Weiss; July 8, 1770. At 6 o'clock at Jacob Weiss' house.

HAG—Johannes, s. of the decd. Conrad Hag, and Catharina, d. of the decd. Johannes Frey; Aug. 7, 1781.

HAGE—Heinrich, s. of the decd. Christian Hage, and Anna Maria Kehl; Sept. 19, 1784.

HAHN—Anna Margaretta, d. of Peter Hahn, decd., and Peter Ruth, s. of Peter Ruth; Apr. 5, 1768.

HAHN—Anna Maria, d. of Adam Hahn, and Phillipus Hecker; Jan. 27, 1767.

HAHN—Daniel, s. of Frantz Hahn, and Barbara, d. of the decd. Johannes Schweickert; Mch. 4, 1781.

HAHN—Frantz, s. of Peter Hahn, and Elisabeth, d. of Jacob Dauderick; May 31, 1753.

HAHN—Johannes, s. of Adam Hahn, and Anna Margaretha, d. of Isaac Guschway; May 15, 1769.

HAHN—Johannes, s. of the decd. Peter Hahn, and Ester, d. of Isaiac Guschwaq; Oct. 25, 1768.

HAHN—Margaretta, d. of Gorg Hahn, and Philip Krick, s. of Frantz Krick; Jan. 3, 1769.

HAHN—Margaretta, d. of Gorg Hahn, and Philip Wehrheim, s. of Conrad Wehrheim; Dec. 26, 1769.

HAIN—Anna Maria, l. of Gorg Hain, and Johanns Adam Fuchs, s. of Jost. Fuchs, decd.; Mar. 20, 1764.

HAM—Wolfgang, aus den landen Bern, m. Dorrothea, d. of George Hefft; Dec. 31, 1752—Moden Krick Church.

HAMSON—Wilhelm, s. of Hugh Justus Jost Hamson, and Catharina Lehnerr, forsaken wife of Jacob Lehnerr, who out of lovelessness, went into the War without compulsion, and who she now believes to be dead; June 24, 1779.

HANDSCHY—Anna, d. of Heinrich Handschy, and Johannes Flickinger, s. of Joseph Frickinger; Mar. 30, 1784.

HARDUNG—Nicolaus, s. of Christian Hardung, and Maria, d. of the decd. Johannes Birchenhauser; Apr. 5, 1774.

HARNISCH—Johannes, s. of Samuel Harnisch, and Anna Eva, d. of Martin Burckholder; Apr. 7, 1781.

HART—Conrad, s. of Conrad Hart, and Juliana, d. of Jacob Frey; Apr. 21 1772. On Easter Tuesday.

HART—Catharina, w. of Heinrich Hart and Andreas Schmitt, widower; Sept. 12, 1786.

HART—Juliane, d. of Conrad Hart and Dietrick Marshall, d. of Dietrick Marshall; Oct. 10, 1765.

HART—Margaretta, d. of Conrath Hart and Hector Pehn, s. of Wilhelm Pehn; June 5, 1785.

HARTING—Catharina, d. of Christing Harting, and Michael Berghauser, s. of Johannes Berghauser; Apr. 4, 1775.

HARTING—Johan Michael, s. of Christian Harting, and Anna Maria, d. of the decd. Adam Bohmer; July 28, 1778.

HARTMANN—Anna Catharina, w. of Heinrich Hartmann, and Nicolaus Riehm, widower; Aug. 15, 1769.

226   BAPTISMAL AND MARRIAGE RECORDS.

HARTMAN—Anna Maria, d. of Henry Hartmann, decd., and Joseph Leinbach, s. of Johannes Leinbach, decd.; July 12, 1773.

HARTMANN—Christian, and Dorrothea, d. of Jacob Carl; Aug. 3, 1761. Note states that on the 15th. Aug. the wife left her husband, on the 19th. sickened & died.

HARTMANN—Philip, s. of the decd. Gorg Hartmann, and Christina, d. of Peter Schaarmann; June 10, 1777.

HASSLER—Abraham, s. of the decd. Abraham Hassler, and Catharina Margaretha, d. of the decd. (Rev.) John Waldschmidt; Nov. 21, 1786.

HASSLER—Barbara, d. of Abraham Hassuer, decd., and Wilhelm Waldschmidt, s. of Rev. John Waldschmidt, decd.; Mar. 6, 1787. Recorder by J. W., son of Rev. J. W.

HASSLER—Jacob, s. of Sebastian Hassler, and Barbara, d. of Johann Dautrich; May 10, 1782.

HASSLER—Johan Friedrich, s. of Bastian Hassler, and Catharina Elisabeth, d. of Johannes Palm; May 26, 1772.

HASSLER—Magdalena, d. of Sebastian Hassler, and Philip Hoffmann, s. of Heinrich Hoffmann, decd.; Apr. 19, 1785.

HASSLER—Sebastian, s. of Sebastian Hassler, and Anna, d. of Daniel Kummer; May 10, 1774.

HASSLER—Stephanus s. of Sebastian Hassler, and Maria Margaretha, d. of Peter Katzemayer; Apr. 13, 1779.

HASSLER—Susanna, d. of Abraham Hassler, decd., and Johannes Waldschmidt, s. of Rev. John Waldschmidt decd.; Dec. 19, 1786. Rec. (?) by J. W., son of Rev. J. W.

HAUCH—Justus, s. of Daniel Hauch, and Julianna, widow of Jacob Breneisen; Apr. 18, 1785.

HAUR—Christina d. of Michael Haur, and Jacob Roth, s. of Philip Roth; May 18, 1776. In the new congregation in Bern.

HAUSSWIRTH—Maria Eva, d. of ——— Hausswirth, decd., and Samuel Oberholss, s. of Jacob Oberholss decd. Sept. 8, 1765.

HAUSSWIRTH—Margaretta, and Jacob Strouck; Mar. 7, 1765. In Jacob Ruth's House.

HAUTZ—Elisabeth, d. of Filip Hautz, and Johannes Weber; May 15, 1759.

HAUTZ—Magdalena, d. of Philip Hautz, and Johann Jacob Werns, s. of Conrad Werns; Mch. 22, 1757.

HEBERLING—Elisabeth, d. of Rudolf Heberling, and Valentine Bohmer, s. of Adam Bohmer, decd.; Mch. 29, 1785.

HEBERLING—Johannes, son of Gorg Heberling, and Magdalena, d. of Jacob Schmidt; Feb. 1, 1757.

HEBERLING—Rudolf, widower, and Anna Maria, d. of Friedrich Ráum; Jan. 19, 1768. In the decd. Casper Hahn's House.

HECKART—Elisabeth, d. of Johannes Heckart, and Jost Seiler, s. of Bastian Seiler; Mar. 10, 1777.

HECKER—Phillipus, and Anna Maria, d. of Adam Hahn; Jan. 27, 1767.

HEER—Nicolaus, s. of Heinrich Heer, and Barbara Merckel; Aug. 11, 1779.

HECKERT—Appolonia, d. of Michael Heckert, and Peter Fischer, s. of Wilhelm Fischer. (Date omitted, but between two Records, one Apr. 17, 1758, the other May 16, 1758—L. R. K.)

HEFFT—Dorothea, d of George Hefft, and Wolfgang Ham, aus dem lauden Bern; Dec. 31, 1752. Moden Krick Church.

HEGY—Jacob, s. of the decd. Jacob Hegy, and Christina d. of Heinrich Baumann; Aug. 23, 1763.

HEGY—Martin, s. of Jacob Hegy, decd., and Margretha, d. Heinrich Baumann; Apr. 15, 1760.

HEHN—Elisabeth, d. of Heinrich Hehn, and David Hermann, s. of Johannes Hermann, decd.; June 1. 1773.

HEID—Jacob, and Barbara Kempf; Oct. 25, 1757.

HEIL—Jacob, s. of Gorg Heil, and Anna Maria, d. of Jacob Schweickert; Apr. 21, 1782.

HEMLING—Casper, s. of the decd. Samuel Heml'ng, and Elisabeth, widow of Tobias Metzger; Aug. 9, 1785.

HEMMIG—Eva Catharina, d. of Johannes Hemmig, and Heinrich Seibert, s. of Conrad Seibert; July 9, 1769. In the Allegany Church.

HERCHELROTH—Elisabetha, d. of Johann Herchelroth, decd., and Matthias Jacobi, s. of Jacob Jacobi, decd.; May 13, 1755.

HERCHELROTH—Heinrich, s. of the decd. Johannes Herchelroth, and Anna Christina, d. of the decd. Christian Mumma; Apr. 17, 1770.

HERCHELROTH—Juliana, d of Johanna Herchelroth, decd., and Andreas Beltz, s. of Peter Beltz; Apr 4, 1763. Easter Monday, on the Middle Creek.

HERCHELROTH—Lohrens, s. of the decd. Johannes Herchelroth, and Anna Catharina, d. of the decd. Philip Quickel; Aug. 2, 1763.

HERMANN—Anna Maria, d. of Frantz Hermann, and Heinrich Dicker, s. of Valentine Decker; Aug. 21, 1764.

HERMANN—David, s. of the decd. Johannes Hermann, and Elisabeth, d. of Heinrich Hehn; June 1, 1773.

HEROLD—Johann Michael, widower, and Anna Maria, d. of Casper Eckert; Mch. 9, 1773.

HERTSELL—Catharina, w. of Johann Dietrich Hertsell, and Gorg Balsser Lehner, widower (m. 2nd. time); Nov. 16, 1799.

HERTZ—Anna, d. of Philip Hertz, and Christian Willand, sl, of Peter Willand; Sept. 6, 1775.

HERTZ—Conrad, s. of Philip Hertz, and Elisabeth, d. of Thomas Sagner; Sept. 18, 1781.

HERTZOG—Catharina, d. of Nicolaus Hertzog, and Gorg Wackerman, s. of Gorg Wackerman, decd.; Apr. 25, 1786.

HETERS—Catharina Elisabeth, d. of Christian Heters, decd., and Johann Adam Wagner, widower & school master in Quidobehil; Apr. 28, 1760

HETTRIG—Peter, s. of the decd. Peter Hettrig, and Elisabeth, d. of the decd. Adam Forn (?); Apr. 13, 1786.

HETZEL—Catharin, d. of Heinrich Hetzel, and Gorg Kloss, s. of Friedrich Kloss; Feb 13, 1785.

HETZEL—Elisabeth, d. of Mr. Henry Hetzel, and Johannes Schneder, s. of Jacob Schneder; Aug. 6, 1782.

HEW—Wilhelm, and Rachel Davis; Nov. 30, 1778.

HEYBERGER—Conrad, s. of the decd. Conrad Heyberger, m. 17th. Oct. 1752; Catharina, d. of Abraham Dorr, Rev. John Waldschmidt.

HEYER—Anna Maria, d. of Gorg Heyer, and Conrad Hix, s. of Heinrich Hix; May 15, 1768.

HILLLEBRAND—Christian, d. of the decd. Christian Hillebrand, and Maria Catharina, d. of Balser Wennerick; Mch. 10, 1778.

HILDEBRAND—Johannes, s. of the decd. Christian Hildebrand, and Maria Margaretha, d. of Bernharth Gartner; Oct. 12, 1780.

HILDEBRAND—Maria, d. of Peter Hildebrand, and Johannes Schneider, s. of Johannes Schneider; Oct. 31, 1782.

HINCKEL—Jacob, s. of Gorg Hinckle, and Elisabeth, d. of the decd. Ewen (sic) Edwards; Feb. 13, 1775. In Christofel Friedrich's House.

HINGKELL—Anna Maria, d. of Gorg Hingkell, and Johannes Wolff, s. of Bernhard Wolff; Dec. 28, 1783.

HIRSCHBERGER—Abraham, widower (m. 2d. time), and Salome, widow of Carl Goett; Nov. 28, 1780.

HIRSCHBERGER—Catharina, d. of Christian Hirschberger, and Johann Adolph Pann, s. of Casper Peter David Pann, decd.; Oct. 25, 1785.

HIRSCHBERGER—Heinrich, s. of the decd. Johannes Hirchberger, and Magdalena, d. of the decd. Michael Schenck; May 15, 1781.

HIRSCHBERGER—Susanna, d. of Isaac Hirschberger, and Jacob Zent, s. of Jacob Zent; May 3, 1785.

HISBAND—Elisabeth, d. of Heinrich Hisband, and Peter Weber, s. of Gorg Weber; Aug. 26, 1782.

HISSNER—Adam, s. of Adam Hissner, anr Magdalena, d. of Joseph Mellinger; Sept 29, 1782.

HISSNER—Margaretta, d. of Adam Hissner, and Jacob Muller, widower, second mairiage; Jan. 7, 1782.

HIX—Conrad, s. of Heinrich Hix, and Anna Maria, d. of Gorg Heyer; May 15, 1768.

HOCH—Susanna, d. of Martin Hoch, decd., and Johannes Zuck, s. of Rudy Zuck, decd.; Nov. 20, 1780.

HOCHWATER—Philip, and Elisabeth Shiffler; Dec. 6, 1768. In Reading.

HOFF—Magdalena, d. of Philip Hoff, and Wilhelm Henrich Biegel, s. of Wilhelm Heinrich Biegel, decd.; July 24, 1768.

HOFFELBAUER—Anna Maria, d. of Filip Hoffelbauer, and Johann Gorg Ley, widower; Feb. 19, 1760.

HOFFER—Jacob, s. of Johannes Hoffer, and Anna, d. of the decd. Jost Schonauer; Dec. 8, 1782.

HOFFMAN—Angnes, d. of Heinrich Hoffman, and Jeremiah Muller, decd.; July 20, 1779.

HOFFMANN—Anna Barbara, d. of Michael Hoffman, decd., and John Jacob Wagner, s. of Gorg Wagner, decd.; Oct. 21, 1755.

HOFFMANN—Anna Eva, d. of Heinrich Hoffmann, and Heinrich Walter, s. of Johan Jost Walter, s. of Heinrich Walter, decd.; Oct. 22, 1776.

HOFFMANN—Philip, s. of the decd. Heinrich Hoffmann, and Magdalena, d. of Sebastian Hassler; Apr. 19, 1785.

HOHL—Judith, d. of Iohannes Hohl, decd., and Johannes Lippert, s. of Johannes Lippert; Apr. 16, 1784.

HOLDERY—Matthias, s. of the decd. Johann Gorg Holdery, and Catharina, d. of Gabriel Lauss; Dec. 10, 1770.

HOLDRY—Peter, s. of the decd. Gorg Holdry, and Barbara, d. of Johannes Laub; Jan. 26, 1777.

HOLSINGER—Maria Elisabeth, and Gorg Benss, s. of Weyrich Benss; Dec. 8, 1761.

HOLTZEDER—Catharina, d. of Peter Holtzeder, and Balsar Ottenheim, s. of Gorg Ottenheim; Dec. 22, 1782.

HOLTZINGER—Johann Gorg, widower, and Magdalena, widow of Abraham Kessler; Oct. 21, 1783. Five years ago Miss Kessler was m. by Rev. Boos to Friedrich Luckart, but the latter went away about three years ago without any cause.

HORN—Anna Maria, d. of Christofel Horn, decd., and Gorg Otto, s. of Heinrich Otto: Dec. 21, 1784.

HORN—Susanna, d. of Frederich Horn, decd., and Abraham Eschelman, d. of Christian Eschelman; Feb. 20, 1781.

HORNISS—Anna, d. of Benedictus or Benss Horniss, and Peter Gut, s. of Peter Gut; Mch. 10, 1782.

HORST—Tobias, s. of the decd. Tobias Horst, and Margaretha, d. of Jacob Spring; Aug. 13, 1765. In the Pastor's House.

HOSCHAAR—Friedrick, s. of Dewald Hoschaar, and Christina, d. of Andreas Kreinert; Nov. 19, 1775. In Michael Stoltz's House.

HOSCHAAR—Heinrich, widower, and Margaretha, d. of Martin Keller; June 7, 1768.

HOSCHAAR—Johannes, s. of Heinrich Hoschaar, and Eva, d. of the decd. Johann Jost Walter; Apr. 17, 1781.

HUBLER—Frantz, s. of Jacob Hubler, and Carlina, d. of the decd. Johannes Kirner; May 1, 1757.

HUBER—Anna Maria, d. of Michael Huber, and Gerhard Walter, s. of Johann Jost Walter; Aug. 28, 1780.

HUBER—Barbara, d. of Michael Huber, and Jacob Keller, s. of Jacob Keller; Feb. 4, 1783.

HUBER—Magdalena, d. of Heinrich Huber, and Peter Graff, s of Joseph Graff; Aug. 20, 1786.

HUBSCH—Anna, d. of Daniel Hubsch, decd., and Jonas Muller, s. of Michael Muller; Nov. 2, 1777.

HUHN—Nicolaus, s. of Valentin Huhn, and Elisabeth, d. of Daniel Rudy; Nov. 19, 1782.

HUN—Gorg, s. of Valentin Hun, and Anna Maria, d. of the decd. Christian Lang; Jan. 7, 1781.

HUNDICKER—Elisabeth, d. of Samuel Hundicker, and Johannus Gehr, s. of Paul Gehr, decd.; Apr. 3, 1780.

HUSTER—Johannes, s of the decd. Jost Huster, and Catharina, d. of Johann Christ. Allbrecht; Sept. 5, 1780. In Pastor's House.

HUTH—Maria Margaretta, d. of Johannes Huth, decd., and Daniel Lutz, s. of Adam Lutz; Feb. 22, 1780.

ILLESS (ELLIS)—Elisabeth, d. of Martin Illess (Ellis), and Johannes Westheber, s. of Gorg Westheber; Dec. 23, 1782.
ILLI—Margaretta, d. of Martin Illi, decd., and Wilhelm Betz, s. of Johannes Betz, decd.; Aug. 2, 1785.
JACOBI—Jacob Adam, s. of the decd. Jacob Jacobi, and Anna Margaretha, d. of the decd. Johannes Wendel Lauber; 20th. Nov., 1753.
JACOBI—Matthias, s. of the decd. Jacob Jacobi, and Elisabetha, d. of the decd. Johann Herchelroth; May 13, 1755.
JONES—Mr. John, and Susanna, d. of Heinrich Muller; Apr. 9, 1776.
JORDAN—Casper, s. of Elias Jordan, and Maria, d. of Johannes Bender; Aug. 8 1786.
JOST—Elisabeth, d. of Nicolaus Jost, and Conrad Laub, s. of Michael Laub; June 15, 1773.
JOST—Johann Nicolaus, s. of Nicolaus Jost, and Regina, d. of Johann Philip Klingemann; July 13, 1773.
JUNCKER—Regina, d. of Johan Jacob Juncker, decd., and Christian Gorg, s. of Heinrich Gorg, decd.; July 24, 1781.
JUND—Johannes, widower, 2nd. m., and Rahel, d. of Jacob Schanschack; Aug. 16,1785.
JUNG—Anna, d. of Jacob Jung, decd., and Ludwig Schweiger, s. of Heinrich Schweiger; Apr. 4, 1784. He is a Brannechweiger.
JUNG—Dorrothea, w. of Jacob Jung, and Andreas Schaub, widower; Jan. 4, 1769.
JUNG—Elisabeth, d. of Johannes Jung, and Jacob Kumler, s of Jacob Kumler; Apr. 24, 1770. Pastor's House (J. W.)
JUNG—Julianna, d. of Johannes Jung, and Friedrich Bemer, s. of Michael Baymer; July 5, 1756.
JUNG—Lorentz, s. of Peter Jung, and Margaretha, d. of the decd. Johann Heinrich Lentz; June 23, 1771.

KABEL—Casper, widower, and Anna Maria, d. of the decd. Jacob Riehl; Oct. 31, 1768.
KABEL—Daniel, s. of Nicolaus Kabel, decd., and Barbara, d. of Jacob Dautrich, decd.; Mch. 15, 1760.
KAFROTH—Anna Maria, w. of Peter Kafroth, and Johan Jacob Beck, s. of Peter Beck, decd.; Mch. 18, 1753.
KAMMER—Nicolaus, s. of Peter Kammer, and Salome, d. of the decd. Johannes Feul; Sept. 28, 1784.
KAMPF—Barbara, and Jacob Heid; Oct. 25, 1757.
KAPPE—Gorg, s. of Gorg Kappe, decd., and Catharina, d. of Christian Eschelman; Oct. 2, 1781.

KARGESS—Anna Elisabeth, d. of Peter Kargess, decd., and Johann Wendel Martin, s. of Wiehand Martin, decd.; July 5, 1781.

KATZEMAYER—Maria Margaretta, d. of Peter Katzemayer, and Stephanus Hassler, s. of Sebastian Hassler; Apr. 13, 1779.

KATZEMEYER—Ludwig, s. of Peter Katzemeyer, and Anna Elisabeth, d. of Peter Romer; Jan. 22, 1782.

KATZEMEYER—Michael, s. of Peter Katzemeyer, and Christina, d. of the decd. Jacob Muller; Oct. 5, 1779.

KAUFMANN—Anna, d. of Jacob Kaufmann, and Abraham Stubschen, s. of Christian Stubschen; Dec. 14, 1783. In Pastor's House.

KEGEREIS—Maria, and Johannes Waldschmidt; Mar. 8, 1735. Added by someone, other than Rev. J. W., who d. 1786.

KEHL—Anna Maria, and Heinrich Hage, s. of Christian Hage, decd.; Sept. 19, 1784.

KEHLI—Chilyan, widower, and Elisabeth, widow of Peter Muller; June 16, 1734.

KELLER—Barbara, d. of Martin Keller, decd., and Jacob Conrath, s. of Lehnart Conrath, decd.; Aug. 5, 1777.

KELLER—Christina, w. of Lorentz Keller, and Gorg Reichmann, widower; Sept. 9, 1776.

KELLER—Elisabeth, d. of Martin Keller, decd., and Johannes Bucher; May 14, 1776.

KELLER—Heinrich, s. of the decd. Martin Keller, and Christina, d. of the Pastor Rev. John Waldschmidt; Aug. 15, 1780; by Rev. Boos in Reading Town.

KELLER—Jacob, s. of Jacob Keller, and Barbara, d. of Michael Huber; Feb. 4, 1783.

KELLER—Jacob, s. of Jacob Keller, and Barbara, d. of Michael Huber; Feb. 4, 1783

KELLER—Jacob, s. of the decd. Johann Lehnhart Keller, and Catharine, d. of Weirig Benss; Apr. 15, 1755.

KELLER—Johannes, s. of the decd. Martin Keller, and Dorrothea, d. of Johannes Rub; Oct. 4, 1772.

KELLER—Julianna, d. of Johannes Keller, and Tobias Reihm, s. of Johann Eberhard Riehm; May 16, 1758.

KELLER—Lenhart, widower, m. 2nd. time, and Elisabeth, d. of Johannes Muhleisen; Nov. 9, 1779.

KELLER—Margaretta, d. of Martin Keller, and Heinrich Hoschauer, widower; June 7, 1768.

KELLER—Michael, s. of the decd. Martin Keller, and Anna Maria, d. of the decd. Daniel Kummer; July 11, 1781.

KELLER—Salome, d. of Jacob Keller, and Johannes Becker, s. of Christofel Becker, decd.; Sept. 5, 1784.

KEMRING—Magdalena, d. of Peter Kemring, decd., and Peter Keplinger, s. of Lehnhard Keplinger; Sept. 24, 1781.

KEPLINGER—Peter, s. of Lehnhard Keplinger, and Magdalena, d. of the decd. Peter Kemring; Sept. 24, 1781.

KEPPLINGER—Elisabeth, d. of Lehnhart Kepplinger, and Martin Frey, s. of Rudolf Frey; July 29, 1783. In his house, namely Lehnhart Kepplinger, in the Allegem.

KEPPLINGER—Peter, widower, and Christina, w. of Jacob Krumlauff; Oct. 9, 1785.

KERN—Catharina, d. of Christofel Kern, and Heinrich Bucher, s. of Engelhard Bucher, decd.; Apr. 21, 1783.

KESSLER—Magdalena, d. of Abraham Kessler, decd., and Johannes Koch, s. of Christian Koch, decd.; Aug. 23, 1784.

KESSLER—Magdalena, w. of Abraham Kessler, and Johann Gorg Holtzinger, widower; Oct. 21, 1783. Five years ago this Kessler was m. by Rev. Bocs to Friedrich Luckart, but the latter went away about three years ago without any cause.

KEYSER—Valentin, s. of Michael Keyser, and Maria Catharina, d. of Melchoir Stiehl; June 11, 1782.

KIEFER—Ann Maria, d. of Daniel Kiefer, and Gorg Adam Schub; Jan. 17, 1773. In Allegheny Congragation.

KILLWELL—Christina, d. of Wilhelm Willwell, and Wilhelm Kinglywy, s. of Peter Kinglywy; Mar. 29, 1783. New rames to me, they are written in English & are verbatim. Uncertain what they are—L. R. K.

KINGLYWY—Wilhelm, s. of Peter Kilglywy, and Christina, d. of Wilhelm Killwell; Mch. 29, 1783. New names to me, they are written in English, and are verbatim. Uncertain what they are.—L. R. K.

KINTER—Gorg, widower, and Magdalena, widow of Stephany Lasch; Jan. 24, 1774.

KINZER—Elisabeth, d. of Jacob Kinzer, and Johannes Friedrich Mohr, s. of Gorg Mohr, decd.; July 2, 1765. In Millbach.

KIRCHSBATTER—Magdalena, w. of Martin Kirchsbatter, and Johannes Muller, m. for 3rd. time. May 19, 1760.

KIRNER—Carlina, d. of Johannes Kirner, decd., and Frantz Hubler, s. of Jacob Hubler; May 1, 1757.

KISSING—Martin, s. of the decd. Philip Kissing, and Margaretha, d. of the decd. Jost Heinrich Schneider; June 30, 1782.

KISSINGER—Friedrich, s. of the decd. Philip Kissinger, and Barbara, d. of Johan Gorg Becker; Feb. 22, 1785.

KISSINGER—Gorg Philip, s. of Filip Kissinger, and Catharina, d. of Johannes Augenstein; June 2, 1772.

KITZLY—Conrad, and Maria Rentz; Jan. 30, 1759.

KLAPP—Heinrich, s. of the decd. Johannes Klapp, anu Elisabeth, d. of Philip Brendel; Nov. 27, 1781.

KLEIN—Salome, d. of Gorg Klein, decd., and Johannes Martinus, s. of Jacob Marumu (sic); June 24, 1776 In my house in the presence of witnesses.

KLEIN—Wilhelm, and Margaretha, d. of Thilmann Schutz; Oct. 30, 1759.

KLEING—Elisabeth, 1. of Johannes Kleing, decd., and Johannes Mosser, s. of Johannes Mosser, decd.; Apr. 12, 1784.

KLINGEMANN—Regina, d. of Johann Philip Klingemann, and Johann Nicolaus Jost, s. of Nicolaus Jost; July 13, 1773.

KLOSS—Gorg, s. of Friedrich Kloss, and Catharina, d. of Heinrich Hetzel; Feb. 13, 1785.

KNOPFF—Jacob, s. of the decd. Johannes Knopff, and Maria, d. of Christian Knopff; May 1, 1785.

KNOPFF—Maria, d. of Christian Knopff, and Jacob Knopff, s. of Johannes Knopff, decd.; May 1, 1785.

KOCH—Conrath, s. of Alexander Koch, and Eva, d. of Heinrich Gicker; Sept. 24, 1783.

KOCH—Johannes, s. of the decd. Christian Koch, and Magdalena, d. of the decd. Abraham Kessler; Aug. 23, 1784.

KOCH—Johannes, s. of the decd. Johannes Koch, and Anna Barbara, d. of the decd. Jacob Maurer; Feb. 25, 1755.

KOCH—Maria, d. of Casper Koch, decd., and Abraham Frantz, s. of Michael Frantz; Mar. 29, 1784.

KOFER—Buby, —— Joseph, s. of the decd. Franz Buby Kofer, and Anna Maria, d. of the decd. Hans Jacob Ulrich; Aug. 1, 1756.

KOHE—Catharina, d. of Sebastian Kohe, decd., and Friedrich Gerner, s. of Marx Gerner; Marty 13, 1770.

KOHL—Gorg, s. of Gorg Kohl, and Magdalena, d. of Thomas Bunsh; Aug. 24, 1780.

KOHL—Anna Maria, d. of Geo. Kohl, and Nicolaus Adam, s. of Bernard Adam; Nov. 22, 1782.

KOHL—Catharina Elisabeth, d. of Ludwig Kohl, and Johann Gorg Conrad, s. of Johann Gorg Conrad; Nov. 30, 1756.

KOHL—Julianne, d. of Ludwig Kohl, and Heinrich Leinweber; Jan. 16, 1759.

KOHL—Phillipus, s. of Peter Kohl, and Susanna, d. of Marx Egly; Nov. 7, 1754.

KOHL—Susanna, d. of Johannes Kohl, decd., and Ludwig Frey; Mar. 10, 1778.

KOHLMAN—Johannes, s. of the decd. Bastian Kohlman, and Christina Brucker, d. of Jacob Brucker; Nov. 26, 1771.

KOHLRONN—Matthias, s. of the decd. Johannes Kohlronn, and Anna, d. of the decd. Etwart Gult; Mch. 6, 1781.

KOLB—Peter, s. of the decd. Krafft Kolb, and Barbara, d. of Casper Schweitzer; Aug. 11, 1781.

KOLLY—Johannes, s. of Heinrich Kolly, and Barbara, d. of Christian Scherrer; May 13, 1754.

KONIG—Christine, d. of Carl Konig, decd., and Jacob Krumlauff, s. of Gorg Krumlauff; Aug. 20, 1776

KONIG—Philip Jacob, s. of Nicolaus Konig, and Maria Barbara, d. of Jacob Wilhelm; Apr. 1, 1763; in Jacob Wilhelm's house.

KONNER—David, s. of the decd. Reinhart Conner, and Christina, d. of the decd. Friedrich Michael; Dec. 21, 1778.

KRAFFERT—Maria, d. of Philip Kraffert, and Johannes Meister, s. of Johannes Meister; July 25, 1785.

KRAMER—David, s. of the decd. Carl Kramer, and Isabella, d. of John Wherner; Apr. 23, 1782.

KRAMMERT—Magdalena, and Conrad Carl; Aug. 3, 1761.

KRAUSS—Johannes, s. of Johann Heinrich Krauss, and Anna Maria, d. of the decd. Johann Adam Miller; Dec. 11, 1752.

KREINER—Adam, s. of the decd. Martin Kreiner, and Maria Catharina, d. of the decd. Hans Wendel Laber; June 21, 1757.

KREINERT—Christina, d. of Andreas Kreinert, and Friedrich Hoschaar, s. of Dewald Hoschaar; Nov. 19, 1775; in Michael Holtz's house.

KRICK—Anna Catharine, d. of Adam Krick, and Heinrich Schneider, s. of Heinrich Schneider, decd.; Jan. 21, 1783.

KRICK—Frantz, s. of Frantz Krick, and Anna Maria, d. of Adam Spahn; Apr. 4, 1758.

KRICK—Philip, s. of Frantz Krick, and Margaretha, d. of Gorg Hahn; Jan. 3, 1769.

KRIEG—Catharine, d. of Johann Krieg, decd., and Friedrich Weiss, s. of Carl Weiss, decd.; Aug. 22, 1786.

KRING—David, s. of Gottfried Kring, and Anna Mary, d. of the decd. Rev. John Waldschmidt; Dec. 7, 1790.

KRUMLAUFF—Christine, w. of Jacob Krumlauff, and Peter Kepplinger, widower; Oct. 9, 1785.

KRUMLAUFF—Jacob, s. of Gorg Krumlauff, and Christine, d. of the decd. Carl Konig; Aug. 20, 1776.

KUHN—Elisabeth, d. of Jacob Kuhn, and Valentine Bayer, s. of Valentine Bayer; Aug. 20, 1785.

236   BAPTISMAL AND MARRIAGE RECORDS.

KUMLER—Jacob, s. of the decd. Jacob Kumler, and Elisabeth, d. of Johannes Jung; Apr. 24, 1770; Jastor's house (J. W.).

KUMMER—Anna, d. of Daniel Kummer, and Sebastian Hassler, s. of Sebastian Hassler; May 10, 1774.

KUMMER—Anna Maria, d. of Daniel Kummer, decd., and Michael Keller, s. of Martin Keller, decd.; July 11, 1781.

KUNER—Catherina Elizabeth, d. of Adam Kuner, and Johannes Schutz, s. of Thilmann Schutz; Nov. 27, 1759.

KUNTZ—Catherina,. d. of Johannes Kuntz, and Peter Schneider, s. of Jost Heinrich Schneider, decd.; Apr. 5, 1785.

KUNTZ—Gorg, s. of the decd. Johannes Kuntz, and Elisabeth, d. of the decd. Johannes Masser; Dec. 29, 1785.

KUNZ—Anna Elisabeth, d. of Heinrich Kunz, and Johannes Strickhauser, s. of Wilhelm Strickhauser; Oct. 19, 1762.

LABER—Anna Catharina, d. of Wendel Laber, decd., and Jacob Enck, s. of Jacob Enck; Dec. 30, 1755.

LABER—Barbara, d. of Joh. Wendel Laber, decd., and Johannes Enck, s. of Jacob Enck; Oct. 13, 1761.

LABER—Balsar, s. of George Wendel Laber, and Elizabeth, d. of Samuel Barmann, Mch. 13, 1754.

LABER—Maria Catharina, d. of Hans Wendel Laber, decd., and Adam Kreiner, s. of Martin Kreiner, decd.; June 21, 1757.

LABER—Martin, s. of the decd. Joh. Wendel Laber, and Catharina, d. of Jacob Enck; Oct. 13, 1761. Married by Rev. Stoy, when Rev. W. "uber der Suskihanue war."

LAMBERT—Jacob, and Dorrothea Flauer; Oct. 19, 1772; both of the Catholic religion.

LAMBERT—Margaretta, d. of Frantz Lambert, and Christian Schneider, s. of Bernhard Schneider; Nov. 7, 1775.

LANG—Anna, d. of Gorg Lang, and Daniel Feuerstein, s. of Johannes Feuerstein; Aug. 5, 1783.

LANG—Anna Barbara, d. of Johannes Lang, and Adam Geissler, s. of Adam Geissler; Dec. 19, 1755.

LANG—Anna Maria, d. of Christian Lang, and Gorg Hun, s. of Valentine Hun; Jan. 7, 1781.

LANG—Barbara, d. of Christian Lang, decd., and Daniel Rudy, s. of Daniel Rudy; Nov. 19, 1782.

LASCH—Magdalena, w. of Stephany Lasch, and Gorg Kinter, widower; Jan. 24, 1774.

LAUB—Barbara, d. of Johannes Laub and Peter Holdry, s. of Gorg Holdry; Jan. 26, 1777.

LAUB—Catharine, d. of Johannes Laub, and Carl August Maxilianus Donob, s. of Johann Matthaus Donob; Jan. 5, 1786.

REV. JOHN WALDSCHMIDT—1752-1786. 237

LAUB—Conrad, s. of Michael Laub, and Elizabeth, d. of Nicolaus Jost; June 15, 1773.

LAUBER—Anna Maigaretta, d. of Johannes Wendel Lauber, decd., and Jacob Adam Jacobi; Nov. 20, 1753.

LAUER—Elisabeth, d. of Michael Lauer, and Heinrich Macheuer, s. of Johannes Macheuer, decd.; Jan. 29, 1771.

LAUER—Juliana, d. of Michael Lauer, and Conrad Eyerich, s of Conrad Eyerich; Feb. 18, 1771.

LAUSCH—Heinrich, s. of Gabriel Lausch, and Barbara, d. of Martin Eichholtz; Feb. 11, 1783.

LAUSS—Catharina, d. of Gabriel Lauss, and Matthias Holdery, s. of Johann Gorg Holdery; Dec. 10, 1770; in Pastor's house.

LAW—Abraham, s. of the decd. John Law, and Margaretha, d. of Joseph Mucklery (McCleary?); Nov. 22, 1785.

LAW—Barbara, d. of John Law, decd., and John Tweed, s. of James Twed, decd.; Aug. 1, 1786; in John Zuber's house.

LEHMANN—Barbara, d. of Michael Lehmann, decd., and Jacob Habecker; June 13, 1784.

LEHNER—Catharine, forsaken wife of Jacob Lehner, who out of lovelessness, went into the war without compulsion & whom she now believes to be dead, and Wilhelm Hamson, s. cf Hugh Justus Jost Hamson; June 24, 1779.

LEHNER—Gorg Balsser, widower, m. 2d time, and Catharina, widow of Johann Dietrich Hertsell; Nov. 16, 1799.

LEHNHARD—Jacob, s. of the decd. Jacob Lehnhard, and Catharina, d. of Christian Eberhard; Nov. 19, 1775; at 4 o'clock in the afternoon.

LEHR—Anna Maria, d. of Peter Lehr, and Johan Gorg Albrecht, widower; Apr. 6, 1777.

LEHR—Peter, s. of Philip Lehr, and Sabina Witz; Oct. 9, 1763; by Rev. Otterbein.

LEIBROCK—Esther, and Wilhelm Graf; June 6, 1757.

LEICHT—Ludwig, s. of the decd. Johann Martin Leicht, and Catharina, d. of Johann Adam Neidig; Oct. 15, 1771; at the Allegence Church.

LEIDE—Heinrich, widower, and Catharine, widow of Jost Heinrich Scheider; Oct. 11, 1785.

LEIGEN—Jonas, s. of Peter Leigen, and Rebecca, d. of Heinrich Collhen or Collken or Collson; Oct. 24, 1757.

LEIN—Jacob, s. of the decd. Jacob Lein, and Barbara, d. of Wilhelm Schaack; Feb. 26, 1782.

LEINBACH—Joseph, s. of the decd. Johannes Leinbach, and Anna Maria, d. of the decd. Henry Hartmann; July 12, 1773.

BAPTISMAL AND MARRIAGE RECORDS.

LEINWEBER—Heinrich, and Juliana, d. of Ludwig Kohl; Jan. 16, 1759.

LEISS—Peter, widower, and Susanna, widow of Heinrich Muller; Apr. 21, 1781.

LENTZ—Margaretta, d. of Johann Heinrich Lentz, decd., and Lorentz Jung, s. of Peter Jung; June 23, 1771.

LE VAN—Zacharias, widower, confessiones ratione judacus vocatus, and Magdalena, widow of John Lusst; Mch. 21, 1780.

LEWYTON—James, s. of the decd. Wilhelm Lewyton, and Elisabeth, d. of Thomas Clemson; Dec. 6, 1782.

LEY—Johann Gorg, widower, and Anna Maria Barbara, widow of Filip Hoffelbauer; Feb. 19, 1760.

LEYNBACH—Ahraham, s. of Johannes Leinbach, and Anna Juliana, d. of Gottfried Fiedler; Apr. 12, 1768.

LIED—Adam, s. of Heinrich Lied, and Barbara, d. of Nicolaus Rupp, May 16, 1784.

LIED—Anna Maria, d. of Heinrich Lied, and Peter Schneider, s. of Peter Schneider; Aug. 2, 1785.

LIEDER—Anna Maria, d. of Heinrich Lieder, and Jacob Bauer, s. of Heinrich Bauer; Jan. 25, 1774.

LIEDER—Friedrich, s. of Heinrich Lieder, and Susanna, d. of Casper Schreid; Mch. 18, 1783.

LEISIG—Joseph, s. of the decd. Gorg Leisig, and Sophia, d. of Gorg Schneider; Sept. 19, 1784.

LIMBERT—Catharine, d. of Herman Limbert, decd., and Sebastian Stohler; Nov. 11, 1758.

LINCK—Anna Maria, w. of Adam Linck, and Jacob Diemer, widower; Feb. 5, 1780.

LINGENFELDER—Peter, and Margretha Burrer; Feb. 20, 1759.

LIPPEL—Johann Heinrich, s. of the decd. Andreas Lippel, and Anna, d. of the decd. Jacob Roth; July 25, 1785. "Eris ein Braunshweiger Soldat gewahren."

LIPPERT—Johannes, s. of the decd. Johannes Lippert, and Judith, d. of the decd. Johannes Hohl; Apr. 6, 1784.

LITZINGER—Johannes, s. of Conrad Litzinger, and Catharine, d. of Johann Adam Sontag; Aug. 9, 1766; in Wilhelm Hedrich's house, Berne Township.

LOSCHER—Johanes, s. of Nicolaus Loscher, and Elisabeth, d. of Heinrich Binckly; Feb. 4, 1783.

LOSSER—Nicolaus, s. of Nicolaus Losser, and Maria, d. of Paul Fuhrmann; Apr. 11, 1780.

LUFFT—Johannes, s. of the decd. Peter Lufft, and Magdalena, d. of Johannes Feuerstein; Sept. 12, 1773; in Ruhm's Stadtlein.

REV. JOHN WALDSCHMIDT—1752-1786. 239

LUSST—Magdalena, w. of John Lusst, and Zacharias Le Van, widower, "confessiones ratione judacus vocatus;" Mch. 21, 1780.

LUTHER—Catharina, d. of Christian Luther, and Jacob Beck, s. of Jacob Beck, decd.; May 22, 1781.

LUTZ—Daniel, s. of Adam Lutz, and Maria Margaretha, d. of the decd. Johannes Huth; Feb. 22, 1780.

MACHEMER—Heinrich, s. of the decd. Johannes Mechemer, and Elisabeth, d. of Michael Lauer; Jan. 29, 1771.

MACHMER—Gorg, s. of the decd. Philipp Machmer, and Ester, d. of Wilhem Graff; May, 3, 1786.

McDANIEL?—Daniel, and Angnes, widow of Moses Mecallner; Aug. 23, 1780.

MACK—Gottlieb, s. of Gottlieb Mack, and Anna, d. of the decd. Conrad Ziegler; Nov. 22, 1778; in Rhums Town.

McCRERY or McCREARY—Elisabeth, d. of Salomon McCrery or McCreary, decd, and Samuel Conner, s. of Thomas Conner, decd.; Feb. 24, 1784.

MAGLY—Anna Maria, d. of Jacob Magly, and Joseph Baret; Apr. 24, 1757.

MANN—Johann Christian, now twice married, and Anna, widow of Johann Adam Schrock; June 2, 1765; in Host Congregation.

MANNER—Gorg, s. of the decd. Paul Manner, and Magdalena, d. of the decd. Jacob Baumann; Apr. 24, 1755.

MARHOBER—Nicolaus, and Anna Christina, d. of Frantz Urich; Aug. 26, 1753.

MARLIN—Maria, d. of John Marlin, decd., and Caleb Dean, s. of Nehemiah Dean; Feb. 16, 1785.

MARSHALL—Dietrich, s. of Dietrich Marshall, and Juliana, d. of Conrad Hart; Oct. 10, 1765.

MARSHALL—Jacob, s. of Dietrich Marshall, and Eva, widow of Jacob Bohm; Dec. 10, 1780.

MARSHALL—Sara, d. of Dietrich Marshall, and Marx Worstel, s. of Jacob Worstel, decd.; Nov. 24, 1771; in Pastor's house.

MARTIN—Johann Wendel, s. of the decd. Wiehand Martin, and Anna Elisabeth, d. of the decd. Peter Kargess; July 5, 1781.

MARTINUS—Johannes, s. of Jacob Martine (sic) and Salome, d. of the decd. Gorg Klein; June 24, 1776; in my house, in the presence of witnesses.

MATTHAY—Maria, w. of Christofel Matthay, and Conrath Nun; July 8, 1783.

BAPTISMAL AND MARRIAGE RECORDS.

MAUNTZ—Johannes, s. of the decd. Johann Jacob Mauntz, and Maria Elisabeth, d. of Valentin Reintrel; Aug. 26, 1765; in Host Church.

MAURER—Anna Barbara, d. of Jacob Maurer, decd., and Johannes Kock, s. of Johannes Kock, decd.; Feb. 25, 1755.

MAURER—Daniel, s. of Christofel Maurer, and Elisabeth, d. of Peter Faust; June 12, 1769; in Pastor's (J. W.) house.

MAURER—Michael, s. of the decd. Michael Maurer, and Elisabeth, d. of the decd. Etwart Siel; July 24, 1785.

MAYER—Dorrothea, w. of Peter Mayer, and Christhof Wilbert, widower; Oct. 28, 1782; in Ruhm's Town in Lehnhard Keller's house.

MAYER—Elias, m. for the third time, and Maria Elisabeth Gartner; Feb. 2, 1762.

MAYER—Johannes, s. of the decd. Johannes Mayer, and Catharine, d. of the decd. Adam Oberly; Jan. 23, 1781.

MAYER—Magdalena, d. of Johannes Mayer, and Jacob Offenbach, widower; Mch. 7, 1786.

MAYER—Michael, s. of Michael Mayer, and Barbara, d. of Nicolaus Ehrhart; Aug. 31, 1761.

MECALLNER—Angnes, (Agnes) w. of Moses Mecallner, and Daniel McDaniel; Aug. 23, 1780.

MEDER—Phillipus Jacobus, M. D., of the Court Town of Manheim, s. of Nicolaus Meder, decd., m. 19th Dec., 1752; Maria, d. of Johannes Merckel; by. Rev. J. W.

MEDER—Samuel, s. of Dewalt Meder, and Barbara, d. of Philipp Brendel; Aug. 9, 1785.

MEICHSEL—Juliana, d. of Martin Meichsel, and Johannes Zuber, s. of Daniel Zuber, decd.; Aug. 7, 1785.

MEINTZER—Eva, d. of Gorg Meintzer, and Gorg Menner; July 3, 1764.

MEINTZER—David, s. of Gorg Meintzer, and Catharina, d. of Heinrich Bauer; Feb. 18, 1771.

MEINZER—Fronica, d. of Conrad Meinzer, decd., and Matthias Druckebrod, s. of Matthias Druckebrod, Nov. 25, 1783.

MEISTER—Johanes, s. of Johannes, Meister, and Maria, d. of Philip Kraffert; July 25, 1785.

MELLINGER—Magdalena, d. of Joseph Mellinger, and Adam Hissner, s. of Adam Hissner; Sept. 29, 1782.

MENNER—Gorg, widower, and Eva, d. of Gorg Meintzer; July 3, 1764.

MENZER—Elisabeth, w. of Conrad Menzer, and Peter Zeller, s. of Johann Nicolaus Zeller; Oct. 7, 1783.

MERCKEL—Barbara, d. of Jacob Merckel, decd., and Peter Bernhart, s. of Christian Bernhart, decd.; Apr. 17, 1775; on Easter Monday in Pastor's house.

MERCKEL—Barbara, and Nicolaus Heer, s. of Heinrich Heer; Aug. 11, 1779.

MERCKEL—Maria, d. of Johannes Merckel, and Phillipis Jacobus Meder, M. D., of the Court Town of Manheim, s. of Nicolaus Meder, decd.; Dec. 19, 1752, by Rev. J. W.

MERCKERT—Elisabeth, d. of Daniel Merckert, decd., and Johan Corner, s. of Justus Corner, decd.; Dec. 8, 1783.

MESSNER—Christian, s. of Christian Messner, and Catharina, d. of Jacob Schneder; Mch. 13, 1781.

MESSENER—Johannes, s. of Casper Messener, and Catharina, d. of Johannes Mosser; July 23, 1773.

METZGAR—Catharina, d. of Tobias Metzgar, and Thomas Butts, s. of Thomas Butts, decd.; Aug. 23, 1784.

METZGER—Elisabeth, w. of Tobias Metzger, and Casper Hemling, s. of Samuel Hemling, decd.; Aug. 9, 1785.

MEYER—Barbara, d. of Gorg Meyer, decd., and Johannes Gabel, s. of Wilhelm Gabel; Nov. 6, 1759.

MEYER—Catharina, d. of Elias Meyer, and Jacob Muller; June 5, 1759.

MEYER—Christophel, s. of Heinrich Meyer, and Magdalena, d. of the decd. Lehnhart Eckart; May 16, 1781.

MEYER—Gorg, s. Christophel Meyer, decd., and Catharina, d. of Heinrich Baumann; Apr. 15, 1760.

MEYER—Martin, s. of the decd. Gorg Meyer, and Catharine, d. of the decd. Jacob Neunzehnhalsser; Feb. 26, 1765; in Stophel Friedrich's house.

MEYER—Peter, s. Elias Meyer, and Elisabetha, d. of Gerhard Cafroth; Nov. 13, 1759.

MICHAEL—Christina, d. of Friedrich Michael, decd., and David Konner, s. of Reinhart Conner; Dec. 21, 1778.

MICHEL—Ludwig, s. of Joh. Eberhart Michel, and Anna Catharina, d. of Hanss Gorg Noll; July 8, 1757.

MILLER—Anna Maria, d. of Johann Adam Miller, and Johannes Krauss, s. of Johannes Heinrich Krauss; Dec. 11, 1753.

MILLINGER—Anthon, s. of Josef Millinger, and Elisabeth, d. of Peter Wittmer; Sept. 18, 1785.

MILLINGER—Joseph, s. of the decd. Christofel Millinger, and Dorrothea, d. of Anthony Dornbach; Apr. 6, 1762.

MITCHELL—Anna, and Joseph Blake; Mch. 28, 1759; in Thomas Knarry's house.

MISCHLER—Joseph, s. of Jacob Mischler, and Margaretha, d. of Michael Beer; Feb. 25, 1783.
MISS—Balsar, s. of the decd. Filip Miss, and Anna, d. of the decd. Christofel Becker; Apr. 1, 1783.
MOCHEL—Benjamin, s. of the decd. Jacob Mochel, and Sara, d. of Gorg Roth; Aug. 9, 1773.
MOHLER—Susanna, d. of Heinrich Mohler, decd., and Jacob Angwitch, s. of James Angwitch, decd., Dec. 2, 1783.
MOHLER—Susanna, d. of Heinrich Mohler, decd., and Benedict Bucher, s. of Benedict Bucher; Mch. 30, 1784; in Mohler's house.
MOHN—Margaretta, d. of Ludwig Mohn, and Jacob J. Griyer, s. of Gorg Grier; Jan. 1, 1771.
MOHR—Johann Freidrich, s. of the decd. Gorg Mohr, and Elisabeth, d. of Jacob Kinzer; July 2, 1765; in Millbach.
MOSSER—Anna Maria, d. of Johannes Mosser, decd., and Daniel Pannebecker, s. of Johannes Pannebecker; Mar. 2, 1784.
MOSSER—Catharina, d. of Johanes Mosser, and Johannes Messener, s. of Casper Messener; July 26, 1773.
MOSSER—Elisabeth, d. of Johannes Mosser, and Gorg Kuntz, s. of Johannes Kuntz, decd.; Dec. 29, 1785; in Riehm's Town.
MOSSER—Johan Nicolaus, s. of Johannes Mosser, and Anna Maria, d. of Christian Eschelmann, July 2, 1776.
MOSSER—Johanes, s. of the decd. Johannes Mosser, and Elisabeth, d. of the decd. Johannes Kleing; Apr. 12, 1784.
MUCKLERY (McCLEARY)—Margaretta, d. of Joseph Mucklery, and Abraham Law, decd.; Nov. 22, 1785.
MUHLEISEN—Elisabeth, d. of Johannes Muhleisen, and Lenhart Keller, widower (md. 2nd time); Nov. 9, 1779.
MUHLEISEN—Juliana, d. of Johannes Muhleisen, and Friedrich Schlott, s. of Johannes Schlott; Aug. 28, 1784.
MULLER—Abraham, s. of the decd. Andreas Muller, and Rebecca, d. of Philip Epprecht; Jan. 29, 1765.
MULLER—Anna Rosina, d. of Fredrich Muller, decd., and Samuel Sohl, s. of Dietrich Sohl; Sept. 26, 1765.
MULLER—Anna, d. of Johannes Muller, and Matthias Rieger, s. of Jacob Rieger, in Zuidobehil; July 28, 1760.
MULLER—David, s. of the decd. David Muller, and Elisabeth, d. of Gorg Trostel; Nov. 14, 1784.
MULLER—Elisabeth, d. of Christian Muller, decd,, and David Behringer, s. of Adam Behringer, decd.; June 9, 1783.
MULLER—Elisabeth, d. of Peter Muller, and Chilyan Kehll, widower; June 16, 1784.

MULLER—Eva, d. of Adam Muller, decd., and Johann Jacob Diefendorffer, s. of Johannes Diefendorfer; May 20, 1755.

MULLER—Christina, d. of Jacob Muller, decd., and 'Michael Katzemeyer, s. of Peter Katzemeyer; Oct. 5, 1779.

MULLER—Heinrich, s. of the decd. Heinrich Muller, and Catharina, widow of Johannes Tischhan (De Shon?); Apr. 1, 1783.

MULLER—Heinrich, s. of the decd. Matthias Muller, and Margaretha, d. of the decd. Nicolaus Franck; Feb. 8, 1784.

MULLER—Heinrich, s. of the decd. Tobias Muller, and Elisabeth, d. of Peter Reiger; May 10, 1780.

MULLER—Michael, s. of Hanss Ulrich Muller, and Christina, d. of Johannes Fiess; Dec. 3, 1759.

MULLER—Jacob, and Catherina, d. of Elias Meyer; June 5, 1759.

MULLER—Jacob, widower, second marriage, and Margaretha, d. of Adam Hissner; Jan. 7, 1782.

MULLER—Jeremiah, s. of the decd. Jacob Muller, and Angnes, d. of Heinrich Hoffman; July 20, 1779.

MULLER—Jeremias, widower, and Elisabeth, d. of Jacob Amweg; Oct. 14, 1782.

MULLER—Johannes, married for the third time, and Magdalena, widow of Martin Kirchstatter; May 19, 1760.

MULER—Jonas, ? s. of Michael Muller, and Anna, d. of the decd. Daniel Stubsch; Nov. 2, 1777.

MULLER—Martin, s. of Heinrich Muller, and Anna Maria, d. of the decd. Daniel Schmid; Dec. 14, 1784.

MULLER—Stephanus, and Salome Rosenbein; Feb. 24, 1761.

MULLER—Susanna, w. of Heinrich Muller, and Peter Leiss, widower; Apr. 21, 1781.

MULLER—Susanna, d. of Heinrich Muller, and Mr. John Jones; Apr. 9, 1776; in the evening.

MULLINGER—Susanna, w. of Jacob Mullinger, and Johannes Border, s. of Johannes Border, decd.; May 16, 1770.

MUMMA—Anna Christine, d. of Christian Mumma, decd., and Heinrich Herchelroth, s. of Johannes Herchelroth, decd.; Apr. 17, 1770.

MUMMA—David, s. of Lehnhart Mumma, and Elisabeth, d. of Jacob Frey; Dec. 26, 1785; Pastor's house.

MUMMA—Christian, m. 21st Nov., 1752, Anna Maria, (Born Dorr) widow of Heinrich Shorck; Rev. J. W.

MUMMA—Jacob, s. of Lehnard Mumma, and Juliana, d. of Jacob Frey; Feb. 28, 1786.

MYERS—Margaretha, d. of Elias Myers, and Wilhelm Schreiner; Jan. 28, 1754.

NAU—Peter, and Anna, widow of Zacharias Rast; Sept. 24, 1783.

NEIDIG—Catharine, d. of Johannes Adam Neidig, and Ludwig Leicht, s. of Johannes Martin Leicht, decd.; Oct. 15, 1771; at the Allegene Church.

NEIZER—Bernhardus, and Anna Maria, widow of David Albrecht; June 25, 1754.

NEUMANN—Johannes, widower & m. for the 3d time, and Barbara, widow of Daniel Frantz; Feb. 4, 1777.

NEUMANN—Peter, s. of Peter Neumann, and Maria Margaretha, d. of Matthias Achebach; Feb. 2, 1779.

NEUNZEHNHALSSER—Catharine, d. of Jacob Neunzenhalsser, and Martin Meyer, s. of Gorg Meyer, decd.; Feb. 26, 1765; in Stophel Friedrich's house.

NICODEMUS—Conrad, s. of Adam Nicodemus, and Anna Maria, d. of Bernhard Pfeifer; Apr. 15, 1760.

NOLL—Anna Catherina, d. of Hauss Gorg Noll, and Ludwig Michel, s. of John Everhardt Michel; July 8, 1757.

NOLL—Margaretta, d. of Michale Noll, decd., and Heinrich Walter; Apr. 17, 1758.

NOTT—Margaretta, d. of Jacob Nott, decd., and Heinrich Walter; Apr. 17, 1758.

NUEN—Heinrich, s. of the decd. Johan Heinrich Nuen, and Catherina, d. of the decd. Conrath Haass; Aug. 2, 1785.

NUN—Conrath, widower, and Maria, widow of Christofel Matthay; July 8, 1783.

NUSS—Elisabetha, d. of Jacob Nuss, decd., and Nicolaus Gottschall, s. of Christofel Gottschall; Sept. 12, 1758.

OBER—Anna Maria, d. of Johannes Ober, and Michael Schweickert, s. of Valentine Schweickert, decd.; June 22, 1784.

OBERHOLSS—Samuel, s. of the decd. Jacob Oberholss, and Maria Eva, d. of the decd. Hausswirth; Sept. 8, 1765.

OBERLY—Catharine, d. of Adam Oberly, decd., and Johannes Mayer, s. of Johannes Mayer, decd.; Jan. 23, 1781.

OBLINGER—Anna Maria, d. of Christian Oblinger, and Peter Feder, s. of Peter Feder; June 7, 1781.

OFFENBACH—Jacob, widower, and Magdalena, d. of Johannes Mayer; Mch. 7, 1786.

ORDER—Anna Maria, and Johanes Schmutz; Jan. 23, 1764.

OTT—Maria Fronica, w. of Jacob Ott, and Johannes Graff, widower; Nov. 27, 1770.

OTTENHEIM—Balsar, s. of Gorg Ottenheim, and Catherine, d. of Peter Holtzeder; Dec. 22, 1782.

OTTO—Anna Maria, d. of Heinrich Otto, and Anthonius Beltzer, s.of Christofel Belttzer; May 23, 1781.
OTTO—Gorg, s. of Heinrich Otto, and Anna Maria, d. of the decd. Christofel Horn; Dec. 21, 1784.
PALM—Catharine Elisabeth, d. of Johannes Palm, and Pann, and Catharina, d. of Christian Hirschberger; Oct. 25, PANN—Johann Adolph, s. of the decd. Casper Peter Davids Pann, and Catharina, d. of Christian Hirchberger; Oct. 25, 1785.
PANNEBECKER—Daniel, s. of Johannes Pannebecker, and Anna Maria, d. of the decd. Johannes Mosser; Mch. 2, 1784.
PANTZLER—Anna Eva, and Heinrich Weiss, s. of Jacob Weiss; Dec. 6, 1768.
PEHN—Hector, s. of Wilhelm Pehn, and Margaretha, d. of Conrath Hart; June 5, 1785.
PETRI—Hanns Adam, s. of Gorg Peter, m. Gorg. Roth's d.; July 1, 1766; in Moden Krick Church (Woman's name not given.)
PFEIFER—Anna Maria, d. of Bernhard Pfeifer, and Conrad Nicodemus, s. of Adam Nicodemus; Apr. 15, 1760.
PFEIFFER—Catharine Elisabeth, d. of Bernhart Pfeiffer, and Johann Adam Schally, s. of Carl Schally. "In Des Stenze Stad" (Lebanon). Not dated.
PFEIL—Catharina, d. of Peter Pfeil, and Ludwig Behl, s. of Ludwig Behl; Jan. 1, 1760.
PINNSSER—Christofel, s. of the decd. Christofel Pinnsser, and Anna Maria, d. of Paul Ehbrecht; July 28, 1782.
PRINTZ—Heinrich, s. of Michael Printz, and Phillipus, d. of Christian Wilks; May 28, 1765; in the Raeding Church.
PRY—Thomas, and Elisabeth, d. of the decd. Simon Weithaed; Aug. 26, 1782.
PURSOL—Zacharias, s. of the decd. Johannes Pursol, and Margretha, d. of Gabriel Davis; Aug. 17, 1779.

QUICKEL—Anna Catharina, d. of Johann George Quickel, decd., and Johann Gottlieb Engallend, s. of Johann Engallend; Aug. 21, 1753.
QUICKEL—Anna Catharina, d. of Philip Quickel, decd., and Lohrens Herchelroth, s. of Johannes Herchelroth, decd.; Aug. 2, 1763.

RANCK—Dorothea, d. of Phillip Ranck, and Johann Gorg Stahlin, s. of Johannes George Stahlin; Mar. 24, 1754.

RANCK—Valentin, s. of the decd. Michael Ranck, and Barbara, d. of Jacob Geyer; Apr. 9, 1780.

RANK—Michael, s. of Philip Rank, and Maria Margaretha, d. of the decd. Lehnhard Breitenstein. Date of m. not mentioned. The Record stands between one dated May 20, 1755, the other Oct. 21, 1755.

RAST—Anna, w. of Zacharias Rast, and Peter Nau; Sept. 24, 1783.

RAUB—Michael, s. of the decd. Michael Raub, and Elisabeth, d. of the decd. Andreas Zoller; Aug. 4, 1776.

RAUM—Anna Maria, d. of Friedrich Raum, and Rudolf Heberling, widower; Jan. 19, 1768; in the decd. Casper Hahn's house.

RAUSH—Juliana, d. of Casper Raush, and Gottfried Eichelbrenner, s. of Daniel Eichenbrenner. (Not dated, but between July 28, 1760, & Oct. 28, 1760—L. R. K.)

RAVENSBERGER—Juliana, d. of Peter Ravensberger, and Daniel Diest, s. of Johannes Diest, decd.; Nov. 9, 1762.

REDDY—Elias, and Rosina, widow of Adam Ziegler; Mch. 21, 1773.

REHEL—Anna Maria, widow of Jacob Rehel, and Bernhard Schneider; Dec. 24, 1753.

REICH—Dorrothea, d. of ―― Reich, decd., and Andreas Weih, s. of Andreas Weih, decd.; Feb. 4, 1755.

REICH—Margretta, and Phillip Roth; Jan. 9, 1759.

REICHMANN—Gorg, widower, and Christina, widow of Lorentz Keller; Sept. 9, 1776.

REICHWEIN—Maria, d. of Gorg Reichwein, and Jacob Roth, s. of Joseph Roth; May 31, 1784.

REIGER—Elisabeth, d. of Peter Reiger, and Heinrich Muller, s. of Tobias Muller, decd.; May 10, 1780.

REIGER—Samuel, and Eva Spiess; Apr. 1, 1760. This Eva was the widow of Jacob Lehnhard. Nun Johannes Unger weib.

REIGER—Sara, d. of Stofel Reiger, and Jacob Becker, s. of Peter Becker; Sept. 24, 1782.

REIGHT—Johannes, s. of Thomas Reight, and Elisabeth, d. of the decd. Jacob Beck; June 16, 1784.

REIN—Gorg, d. of Catharine Rein, and Daniel Gehr, s. of Andreas Gehr, decd.; Jan. 13, 1784; in Riehm's Town.

REINHOLD—Friedrich, s. of Christofel Reinhold, and Elisabeth, d. of Josef Wenger; July 31, 1785.

REINTREL—Maria Elisabeth, d. of Valentine Reintrel, and Johannes Mauntz, s. of Johannes Jacob Mauntz, decd.; Aug. 26, 1765; in Host Church.

REV. JOHN WALDSCHMIDT—1752-1786. 247

REISCH—Isaac, s. of the decd. Isaac Reisch, and Elisabeth, d. of the decd. Jost Schonnauer; Feb. 27, 1780.
REITEL—Juliana, d. of Jost Reitel, and Peter Fuhrmann, s. of Paul Fuhrmann; Apr. 19, 1783.
REITENBACH—Maria Elisabeth, d. of Nicolaus Reitenbach, and Matheus Schreiner, s. of Johan Jost Schreiner, decd.; Apr. 15, 1779.
REUTZ—Maria, and Conrad Kitzly; Jan. 30, 1759.
RESSLER—Peter, s. of the decd. Gorg Resler, and Fronica, d. of Rudolf Frey; Apr. 10, 1784.
RETTIG—Johannes, s. of the decd. Gorg Rettig, and Catharine, d. of Johannes Schilling; Apr. 25, 1786.
RETTIG—Lehnhard, s. of Gorg Rettig, and Anna, d. of Peter Zimmerman; Apr. 12, 1785.
RETTIG—Margaretta, d. of Gorg Rettig, decd., and Michael Bosshaar, s. of Gorg Bosshaar; Mch. 27, 1785.
RETTLOSS—Anna, d. of Gorg Rettloss, decd., and Jacob Zimmerman, s. of Peter Zimmerman; Apr. 3, 1785. "Ein kind von beides war schon gebohren."
REUEL—Anna Maria, w. of Jacob Reuel, and Bernhard Schneider; Dec. 24, 1753. She had an "Attestant" stating that I had married him to Anna Maria Reuel on above stated date, Rev. J. Waldschmidt, Recorder, July 3, 1772.
RHEIN—Susanna Margaretta, d. of Peter Rhein, and Michael Weinhold, s. of Nicolaus Weinhold; Apr. 4, 1780.
RIEGER—Matthias, s. of Jacob Rieger, and Anna, d. of Johannes Muller; Quidsbehil; July 28, 1760.
RIEHL—Anna Maria, d. of Jacob Riehl, and Casper Kabel, widower; Oct. 31, 1768.
RIEHM—Abraham, s. of Matthias Riehm, and Christina, d. of the decd. Samuel Bender; Dec. 9, 1783.
RIEHM—Elisabeth, d. of Abraham Riehm, and Johanes Adam Bohmer, s. of Adam Bohmer, decd; Apr. 18, 1786.
RIEHM—Johannes, s. of Andreas Riehm, and Rosina, d. of Friedrich Weitzel; Oct. 10, 1785.
RIEHM—Juliana, d. of Abraham Riehm, and Jacob Rub; Aug. 17, 1761.
RIEHM—Nicolaus, widower, and Anna Catharina, widow of Heinrich Hartmann; Aug. 15, 1769.
RIEHM—Tobias, s. of Johann Eberhart Riehm, and Juliana, d. of the decd. Johannes Keller; May 16, 1758.
RIETH—Elisabeth, d. of Michael Rieth, decd., and Andreas Gehr, s. of Paul Gehr, decd.; Jan. 16, 1781.
RIETHE—Henry, s. of Johannes Rieth, and Magdalena, d. of the decd. Gorg Haag; Dec. 31, 1778.

RIETH—Peter, s. of the decd. Peter Rieth, and Maria Elisabeth, d. of the decd. Nicolaus Bechtol; Feb. 15, 1780.

RIETSCHER— —— d. of Gabriel Rietscher, and Johann Jost, s. of Philip Filtsmeyer; Apr. 5, 1757. Christian name of daughter omitted.

RIHM—Heinrich, s. of Tobias Rihm, and Juliana, d. of the decd. Jacob Rupp; Nov. 30, 1783; in my house, J. W.

RIHM—Maria, w. of Johannes Rihm, and Heinrich Stephany, s. of Andreas Stephani, decd.; May 25, 1784.

RIPP—Heinrich, s. of Joh. Jacob Ripp, and Anna Catharina, d. of Heinrich Thost; Mch. 28, 1758.

ROHRER—Johannes, s. of the decd. Jacob Rohrer, and Susanna, d. of the decd. Engelhard Rother; June 19, 1781.

ROMMER—Anna Elisabeth, d. of Peter Rommer, and Ludwig Katzemeyer, s. of Peter Katzemeyer; Jan. 22, 1782.

ROSENBEIN—Salome, and Stephanus Muller; Feb. 24, 1761.

ROTH—Anna, d. of Jacob Roth, decd., and Johann Heinrich Lippel, s. of Andreas Lippel, decd.; July 25, 1785. "Er is ein Brannshweiger Soldat gewaren."

ROTH—Friedrich, s. of Gorg Roth, and Juliana, d. of the decd. Johannes Schweickert; Jan. 22, 1782.

ROTH—Jacob, s. of Joseph Roth, and Maria, d. of the decd. Gorg Reichwein; May 31, 1784.

ROTH—Jacob, s. of Philip Roth, and Christina, d. of Michael Haur; May 18, 1776; in the new congregation in Berne.

ROTH—Phillip, and Margretha Reich; Jan. 9, 1759.

ROTH—Sara, d. of Gorg Roth, and Benjamin, Mochel, s. of Jacob Mochel, decd.; Aug. 9, 1773.

ROTH— —— d. of Gorg Roth, and Hanns Adam Petri, s. of Gorg Petri; July 1, 1766; in Moden Creek Church. Woman's Christian name not given.

ROTHER—Susanna, d. of Engelhard Rother, decd., and Johannes Rohrer, s. of Jacob Rohrer, decd.; June 19, 1781.

RUB—Dorrothea, d. of Johannes Rub, and Johannes Keller, s. of Martin Keller, decd.; Oct. 4, 1772.

RUB—Jacob, and Juliana, d. of Abraham Riehm, Aug. 10, 1761.

RUBLET—Maria, d. of Ahraham Rublet, decd., and Peter Shaffner, s. of Casper Shaffner; Nov. 26, 1764; in Langester.

RUBLI—Margaretta, d. of Philip Rubli, decd., and Lorentz Schafer, s. of Peter Schaffer; May 13, 1771; Pastor's house.

RUDY—Andres, s. of Emmig Rudy, and Catharine, d. of Johannes Beer (Bare); July 3, 1785.

RUDY—Catharina, d. of Rudolf Rudy, decd., and Daniel Bosshar, s. of Johann Bosshar, decd.; Mch. 30, 1756.
RUDY—Daniel, s. of Daniel Rudy, and Barbara, d. of the decd. Christian Lang; Nov. 19, 1782.
RUDY—Elisabeth, d. of Danlei Rudy, and Nicolaus Huhn, s. of Valentine Huhn; Nov. 19, 1782.
RUHL—Anna Margaretta, d. of Jacob Kuhl, and Heinrich Schuckert, s. of Heinrich Schuckert; Apr. 23, 1767; in Kuhl's house.
RUHM—Andreas, s. of Ahraham Ruhm, and Barbara, d. of Christian Schwertztwaller.; May 31, 1782.
RUHM—Andreas, s. of Eberhard Riehm. and Susanna, d. of Nicholaus Fiesser; July 12, 1759.
RUHM—Barbara, d. of Tobias Ruhm, and Wilhelm Wuler; Apr. 8, 1781.
RUHM—Catharina, w. of Nicolaus Ruhm, and Jacob Dritsch, widower; Nov. 22, 1778.
RUHM—Elisabeth, d. of Gorg Ruhm, and Valentin Straub; Mar. 11, 1777; in my house (J. Waldschmidt).
RUNCKEL—Catharine, d. of Johannes Runckel, and Ernst Dietz, s. of Adam Dietz, decd.; June 17, 1771.
RUPP—Barbara, d. of Nicolaus Rupp, and Adam Lied, s. of Heinrich Lied; May 16, 1784.
RUPP—Juliana, d. of Jacob Rupp, decd., and Heinrich Rihm, s. of Tobias Rihm; Nov. 30, 1783; in my house (Rev. J. W.).
RUPP—Maria, d. of Nicolaus Rupp, and Johannes Bayer, s. of Adam Bayer; Aug. 16, 1785.
RUPPERT—Lehnhard, s. of Philip Ruppert, and Sara, d. of Michel Brecht; Mch. 24, 1786.
RUSSEL—Sara, d. of Joseph Russel, and Thomas Erwen, s. of John Erwen, decd.; Mch. 18, 1783.
RUTH—Gorg, s. of Peter Ruth, and Anna Maria, d. of Weyrich Benss; Jan. 21, 1766.
RUTH—Peter, s. of Peter Ruth, and Anna Margaretha, d. of the decd. Peter Hahn; Apr. 5, 1768.

SAGNER—Elizabeth, d. of Thomas Sagner, and Conrad Hertz, s. of Philip Hertz; Sept. 18, 1781.
SAUERBREY—Anna Maria, and Johannes Bayer; Nov. 29, 1768.
SCHAACK—Barbara, d. of Wilhelm Schaack, and Jacob Lein, s. of Jacob Lein, decd.; Feb. 26, 1782.
SCHAAR—Joseph, and Anna, d. of Matthias Schar; Sept. 1, 1757.

SCHAARMANN—Christina, d. of Peter Schaarmann, and Philip Hartmann, s. of Gorg Hartmann, decd.; June 10, 1777.

SCHACK—Wilhelm, s. of Michael Schack, and Maria Magdalena, d. of the decd. David Gunde; Apr. 21, 1755.

SCHAFER—Lorentz, s. of the decd. Peter Schaffer, and Margaretha, d. of the decd. Philip Rubli; May 13, 1771.

SCHALBT—Margaretta, d. of Frantz Schalbt, and Samuel Bernhard, s. of Adam Bernhard, decd.; July 4, 1785.

SCHALLY—Johann Adam, s. of Carl Schally, and Catharina Elisabeth, d. of Bernhard Pfeiffer. "In der stautze stad." In Steitztown, now Lebanon.

SCHANSCHACK—Rahel, d. of Jacob Schanschack, and Johannes Jund, widower (2 m.); Aug. 16, 1785.

SCHAR—Anna, d. of Matthias Schar, and Joseph Schaar; Sept. 1, 1757.

SCHARB—Gottfried, s. of the decd. Johannes Schard, and Anna Maria, d. of Johannes Carolas; Apr. 21, 1783.

SCHARB—Andreas, widower, and Dorrothea, widow of Jacob Jung; Jan. 4, 1769.

SCHAUB—Johann Peter, s. of Christofel Schaub, and Anna Maria, d. of Johannes Schwabt; Mch. 19, 1754.

SCHEIDER—Elisabeth, d. of Gorg Scheider, and Gorg Aache; Dec. 2, 1772.

SCHELL—Anna Catharina, d. of Peter Schell, and Johann Adam Schuts, s. of Johann Adam Schutz, decd.; Aug. 17, 1756.

SCHENCK—Magdalena, d. of Michael Schenck, decd., and Heinrich Hirschberger, s. of Johannes Hirschberger, decd.; May 15, 1781.

SCHERB—Christofel, widower, and Catharine, widow of Adam Beer (Bare); Aug. 16, 1785.

SCHERB—Christofel, s. of Christofel Scherb, and Catharina, d. of Jacob Beer (Bare); Apr. 8, 1783.

SCHERERTZWALLER—Barbara, d. of Christian Scherertzwaller, and Andreas Ruhm, s. of Abraham Ruhm; May 31, 1782.

SCHERRER—Barbara, d. of Christian Scheerrer, and Johannes Kolly, s. of Heinrich Kolly; May 13, 1754.

SCHILLING—Catharine, d. of Johannes Schilling, and Johannes Rettig, s. of Gorg Rettig, decd.; Apr. 25, 1786.

SCHLATTER—Anna Catherine, and Jost Heinrich Wehler, widower, m. for the 4th time; Feb. 16, 1763; in Abraham Farry's house.

SCHLAUCH—Margaretta, w. of Jacob Schlauch, and Christian Bixler, widower; Sept. 6, 1785.

SCHLEBACH—Phillipus, s. of Henrich Schlebach, and Elisabeth, d. of the decd. Adam Geeriss; Feb. 29, 1780.

SCHLECHLY—Christian, and Magdalena Dommain; July 4, 1764.

SCHLECHTY—Anna, d. of Christian Schlechty, decd., and Peter Zimmerman, s. of Adolph Zimmerman; Sept. 9, 1783.

SCHLECHTY—Barbara, d. of Christian Schlechty, and Heinrich Zimmerman, s. of Adolf Zimmerman; Jan. 9, 1785.

SCHLOTT—Friedrich, s. of Johannes Schlott, and Juliana, d. of Johannes Muhleisen; Aug. 28, 1784.

SCHMID—Anna Maria, d. of Daniel Schmid, decd., and Martin Muller, s. of Heinrich Muller; Dec. 14, 1784.

SCHMID—Peter, s. of the decd. Ludwig Schmid, and Susanna, d. of Peter Fusser; Mch. 21, 1780.

SCHMID—Philip, and Margaretha, d. of the decd. Peter Vornwaldt; Dec. 14, 1756.

SCHMIDT—Anna Maria, and Ernst Wilhelm Christ; Mch. 16, 1767.

SCHMIDT—Anna Margaretha, d. of Peter Schmidt, decd., and Carl Bingemann, s. of Peter Bingemann, decd.; Sept. 18, 1766.

SCHMIDT—Magdalena, d. of Jacob Schmidt, and Johannes Heberling, s. of Gorg Heberling; Feb. 1, 1757.

SCHMIED—Johann Peter, s. of Jacob Schmied, and Eva Maria, d. of Gorg Adam Wagner; May 14, 1770.

SCHMITT—Andreas, widower, and Catharina, widow of Heinrich Hart; Sept. 12, 1786.

SCHMUCK—Magdalena, d. of Jacob Schmuck, and Felix Schneider; Sept. 30, 1778.

SCHNEDER—Catharina, d. of Jacob Schneder, and Christian Messner, s. of Christian Messner; Mar. 13, 1781.

SCHNEDER—Jacob, s. of Jacob Schneder, and Anna Maria, d. of the decd. Heinrich Zimmerman; May 12, 1780.

SCHNEDER—Johannes, s. of Jacob Schneder, and Elisabeth, d. of Mr. Henry Hetzel; Aug. 6, 1782.

SCHNEIDER—Adam, s. of Daniel Schneider, and Catharina, d. of Ludwig Leib; Feb. 19, 1760.

SCHNEIDER—Bernhard, and Anna Maria, Jacob Rehel's (Reael?), s. widow; Dec. 24, 1753.

SCHNEIDER—Bernhard, had an "Attestat," stating that I had married him to Anna Maria, widow of Jacob Reuel on the 24th of Dec., 1753, Recorded July 3, 1772.

SCHNEIDER—Catharina, d. of Engelbert Schneider, and Michael Wittmann; Jan. 9, 1759.

SCHNEIDER—Catharina, w. of Jost Heinrich Schneider, and Heinrich Leide, widower; Oct. 11, 1785.

SCHNEIDER—Catharine, d. of Peter Schneider, and Johannes Conrad, s. of Lehnhard Conrad, decd.; Oct. 6, 1782.

SCHNEIDER—Christian, s. of Bernhard Schneider, and Margaretha, d. of the decd. Frantz Lambert; Nov. 7, 1775.

SCHNEIDER—Elisabeth, d. of Jost Schneider, decd., and Gorg Gehr, s. of Paul Gehr, decd.; Nov. 15, 1785.

SCHNEIDER—Eva, and Joh. Nicolaus Schub, s. of Gorg Schub; Feb. 22, 1763.

SCHNEIDER—Felix, and Magdalena, d. of Jacob Schmuck; Sept. 30, 1778.

SCHNEIDER—Heinrich, s. of the decd. Heinrich Schneider, and Anna Catharina, d. of Adam Krick; Jan. 21, 1783.

SCHNEIDER—Hermann, s. of Matthew Schneider, and Elisabeth, d. of Martin Baumann; Jan. 1, 1781.

SCHNEIDER—Johann Christophel, s. of Johann Wilhelm Schneider, and Rahel, d. of James Davis; July 11, 1786.

SCHNEIDER—Johannes, s. of Johannes Schneider, and Maria, d. of Peter Hildebrand; Oct. 31, 1782.

SCHNEIDER—Johannes, "Einem Hessen," from aus dem furstenthum, Ziegenheim, and Susanna Elisabeth, b. Apr. 26, 1757, d. of the Pastor (Rev. John Waldschmidt); Sept. 3, 1782; by Rev. Boos, in Reading.

SCHNEIDER—Margaretta, d. of Jostt Heinrich Schneider, decd., and Martin Kissing, s. of Philip Kissing, decd.; June 30, 1782.

SCHNEIDER—Peter, s. of the decd Jost Heinrich Schneider, and Catharina, d. of Johannes Kuntz; Apr. 5, 1785.

SCHNEIDER—Peter, s. of Valentin Schneider, and Anna Maria, d. of the decd. Conrath Zigler; May 26, 1782.

SCHNEIDER—Salome, w. of Valentine Schneider, and Johannes Baacken, s. of Jacob Baacken, decd.; Sept. 24, 1782.

SCHNEIDER—Sophia, d. of Gorg Schneider, and Joseph Leisig, s. of Gorg Leisig, decd.; Sept. 19, 1784.

SCHNEIDER—Peter, s. of Peter Schneider, and Anna Maria, d. of Heinrich Lied; Aug. 2, 1785.

SCHNUELER—Catharina, d. of Jacob Schnueler, and Martin Beer, s. of Ulrich Beer; May 6, 1781.

SCHNUTZ—Johannes, and Anna Maria Order; Jan. 23, 1764.

SCHONAUER—Anna, d. of Jost Schonauer, and Jacob Hoffer, s. of Johannes Hoffer; Dec. 8, 1782.

SCHONNAUER—Elisabeth, d. of Jost Schonnauer, decd., and Isaac Reisch, s. of Isaac Reisch, decd.; Feb. 27, 1780.

SCHOOWALTER—Valentin, s. of Christian Schoowalter, and Hanna, d. of Johannes Stellwager; Feb. 2, 1786.
SCHORCK—Sarah, d. of Ulrick Schorck, decd., and Adam Frantz, s. of Gorg Frantz; June 19, 1780.
SCHORCK—Maria, d. of Ulrick Schorck, decd., and Gorg Frantz, s. of Daniel Frantz, decd.; Jan. 20, 1780.
SCHOTTER—Johannes, married the 2nd time; Dec. 13, 1757, with ———. Name omitted,
SCHRACK—Johannes, s. of the decd. Adam Schrack, and Margaretha, d. of the decd. Heinrich Bosser; Feb. 11, 1777.
SCHRATER—Joh. Heinrich, s. of Heinrich Schrater, and Maria Elisabeth, d. of Ludwig Schweitzer; Mch. 27, 1764.
SCHRECK—Catharina, widow of Martin, and Jacob Arnold, widower; Aug. 23, 1785.
SCHREIBER—Johann Gorg, widower, and Maria Christina, d. of the decd. Peter Hab; July 23, 1774.
SCHREID—Susanna, d. of Casper Schreid, and Friedrick Lieder, s. of Heinrich Lieder; March 18, 1783.
SCHREINER—Mattheus, s. of the decd. Johan Jost Schreiner, and Maria Elisabeth, d. of Nicolaus Reitenbach; Apr. 15, 1779.
SCHREINER—Wilhelm, and Margaretha, d. of Elias Meyer; Jan. 28, 1754.
SCHREIT—Johannes, s. of Engelbert Schreib, and Barbara, d. of the decd. Johannes Hack; Nov. 20, 1756.
SCHREITEL—Michael, s. of Gorg Schreitel, and Magdalena, d. of Christian Weber; Nov. 30, 1756.
SCHROCK—Anna, w. Johann Adam Schrock, and Johann Christian Mann, now twice married; June 2, 1765; in Host Congregation.
SCHUB—Gorg Adam, s. of Gorg Schub, and Anna Maria, d. of Daniel Kiefer; Jan. 17, 1773.
SCHUB—Joh. Nicolaus, s. of Gorg Schub, and Eva Schneider; Feb. 22, 1763.
SCHUCKERT—Heinrich, s. of Heinrich Schuckert, and Anna Margaretha, d. of Jacob Kuhl; Apr. 23, 1767; in Kuhl's house.
SCHULTZ—Anna Maria, d. of Martin Schultz, decd., and Peter Beyer, s. of Adam Beyer, decd.; Apr. 20, 1762.
SCHUMACKER—Elisabeth, d. of Gorg Schumacker, and Isaac Feder, s. of Bernhard Feder, decd.; May 29, 1780.
SCHUTZ—Johann Adam, s. of the decd. Johann Adam Schutz, and Anna Catharina, d. of Peter Schell; Aug. 17, 1756.
SCHUTZ—Catharina, d. of Thileman Schutz, decd., and Simon Duy, s. of Conrad Duy; Apr. 23, 1754.

254 BAPTISMAL AND MARRIAGE RECORDS.

SCHUTZ—Johannes, s. Thilmann Schutz, and Catharina Elizabetha, d. of Adam Kuner; Nov. 27, 1759.

SCHUTZ—Margaretta, d. of Thilmann Schutz, and Wilhelm Klein, Oct. 30, 1759.

SCHUY—Catharina, d. of Daniel Schuy, and Jacob Griger, s. of Jacob Griger; Oct. 11, 1757.

SCHWABE—Anna Maria, d. of Johannes Schwabe, and Johann Peter Schaub, s. of Christophel Schaub; Mar 19, 1754.

SCHWARTZ—Christina, d. of Johann Gorg Schwartz, and Gorg Michael Wolff, s. of Gorg Michael Wolff, decd.; Jan. 10, 1757.

SCHWEICKERT—Juliana, d. of Johannes Schweickert, decd., and Frederick Roth, s. of Gorg Roth; Jan. 22, 1782.

SCHWEICKER—Catharina, d. of Jacob Schweicker, and Heinrich Trostel, s. of Gorg Trostel; Feb. 21, 1785.

SCHWEICKERT—Anna Maria, d. of Jacob Schweickert, and Jacob Heil, s. of Gorg Heil; Apr. 21, 1782.

SCHWEICKERT—Barbara, d. of Johannes Schweickert, decd., and Daniel Hahn, s. of Frantz Hahn; Mar. 4, 1781.

SCHWEICKERT—Jacob, s. of Gorg Schweickert, and Elizabeth, d. of Peter Benss; Dec. 7, 1784.

SCHWEICKERT—Michael, s. of the decd. Valentin Schweickert, and Anna Maria, d. of Johannes Ober; June 22, 1784.

SCHWEIGART—Barbara, w. of Valentine Schweigart, and Lorenz Duppel; June 5, 1781.

SCHWEIGER—Ludwig, s. of Heinrich Schweiger, and Anna, d. of the decd. Jacob Jung; Apr. 4, 1784.

He is a Braunschweiger Soldier.

SCHWEITZER—Barbara, d. of Casper Schweitzer, and Peter Kolb, s. of Krafft Kolb, decd.; Aug. 11, 1781.

SCHWEITZER—Maria Elizabeth, d. of Ludwig Schweitzer, and Joh. Heinrich Schrater, s. of Henrich Schrater; Mar. 27, 1764.

SEGNER—Melchoir, s. of the decd. Thomas Segner, and Catharina, d. of the decd. Gorg Funck; July 2, 1782.

SEIB—Catharina, d. of Ludwig Seib, and Adam Schneider, s. of Daniel Schneider, s. of Daniel Schneider; Feb. 19 1760.

SEIBERT—Heinrich s of the decd. Conrad Seibert, and Eva Catharina, d. of Johannes Hemmig; July 9, 1769.

SEIDENBANDER—Elizabeth, d. of Heinrich Seidenbander, and Johannes Adam, s. of Bernard Adam; June 13, 1779.

SEIDENBANDER—Gorg, s. of the decd. Heinrich Seidenbander, and Susanna, d. of Philip Brendel; Feb. 18, 1784.

SEILER—Jost, s. of Bastian Seiler, and Elizabeth, d. of Johannes Heckart; Mch. 10, 1777.

SEILER—Susanna, d. of Johannes Seiler, and Heinrich Hackman, s. of Heinrich Hackman; Aug. 8, 1785.

SERVIE, ZERBE?—Elizabeth, d. of Johannes Servie, and Adam Gramling, s. of Gorg Gramling; Mar. 28, 1780.

SHAFER—Anna Margaretta, d. of Johann Gerhart Shafer, and Nicolaus Dietrich, s. of Johann Jacob Dietrich, decd.; Oct. 31, 1752.

Rev. J. Waldschmidt.

SHAFFER—Catharine, d. of Michael Shaffer, and Johannes Zwally, widower; Oct. 20, 1765.

In Gorg Helle House.

SHAFFNER—Peter, s. of Casper Shaffner, and Maria, d. of the decd. Abraham Rublet; Nov. 26, 1764.

In Langeaster.

SHAW—Wilhelm, s. of the decd. Samuel Shaw, and Elizabeth, d. of Wilhelm Ferry; June 12, 1780.

SHIFFLER—Elizabeth, and Philip Hochwarter; Dec. 6, 1768, in Reading.

SHORCK—Anna Maria, (Born Dorr), w. of Heinrich Shorck, and Christian Mumma; Nov. 21, 1752. (Rev. J. W.)

SIEGETHALER—Barbara, d. of Gorg Siegethaler, and Johannes Forloh, s. of Ruppert Forlooh, decd.; Jan. 25, 1785.

SIEL—Elizabeth, s. of Etwart Siel, decd., and Michael Maurer, s. of Michael Maurer, decd.; July 24, 1785.

SODER—Johannes, s. of the decd. Nicolaus Soder, and Catharina, d. of Martin Allstadt; Nov. 8, 1764.

In the church at Reading.

SOHL—Anna Maria, d. of Detrich Sohl, and Johann Gorg Eurich; Dec. 20, 1769.

SOHL—Samuel, s. of Dietrich Sohl, and Anna Rosina, d. of the decd. Friedrich Muller; Sept. 26, 1765.

Sontag—Catharine, d. of Johann Adam Sontag, and Johannes Litzinger, s. of Conrad Litzinger; Aug. 9, 1768.

In Wilhelm Hedrich's House, Bern Township.

SPAHN—Anna Maria, d. of Adam Spahn, and Frantz Krick, s. of Franz Krick;. Apr. 4, 1758.

SPIESS—Eva, and Samuel Reiger; Apr. 1, 1760.

This Eva was the widow of Jacob Lehnhard.

Nun Johannes Unger's weib.

SPRENGER—Anna Maria, d. of Philip Sprenger, and Conrad Wolfskiehl, s. of Henry Wolfskiehl; Oct. 4, 1757.

SPRING—Margarettta, d. of Jacob Spring, and Tobias Horst, s. of Tobias Horst, decd.; Aug. 13, 1765.

In Pastor's House.

SPRINGER—Maria Magdalena, d. of Jacob Springer, and Johannes German; Apr. 27, 1760.

STAHLIN—Johannes Gorg, s. of Johannes George Stahlin and Dorothea, d. of Phillip Ranck; Mch. 24, 1754.

STAMM—Johan Jost, s. of Adam Stamm, and Elizabeth, d. of Anthon Faust; Nov. 2, 1768.

STARCK—Johannes, s. of the decd. Heinrich Starck, and Margaratha, d. of Conrad Van Almen; Mch. 1, 1781.

STAUFFER—Vicens (Vincent?), and Fronica, d. of Johannes Drachsel; June 15, 1762.

STEHL—Anna, d. of Christian Stehl, and Peter Wittmer; s. of Peter Wittmer; Aug. 10, 1784.

STELLWAGER—Hanna, d. of Johannes Stellwager, and Valetin Schoonwalter, s. of Christian Schoonwalter; Feb. 2, 1786.

STEPHANY—Heinrich, s. of the decd. Andreas Stephani, and Maria, widow of Johannes Rihm; May 25, 1784.

STIEHL—Maria Catharina, d. of Melchoir Stiehl, and Valentine Keyser, s. of Michael Keyser; June 11, 1782.

STIEHL—Maria Sybilla, d. of Melchior Stiehl and Gorg Andreas Gotz, decd.; June 11, 1782.

STIESS—Johannes, s. of Jacob Stiess, and Barbara, d. of Gorg Adam Frantz; Feb. 20, 1781.

STOBER—Gorg, s. of Gorg Stober, and Barbara, d. of Adam Beer (Bare); Feb. 17, 1784.

STOHLER—Sebastian, and Catharine, d. of Herman Limbert, decd.; Nov. 11, 1758.

STRAUB—Valentin, and Elizabeth, d. of Gorg Ruhm; Mch. 11, 1777. In my house.

STRAUBHAAR—Johannes, s. of Michael Straubhaas, and Agatha, d. of Joh. Wilhelm Vosag; Aug. 19, 1756.

STRICKHAUSER—Johannes, s. of Wilhelm Strickhauser, and Anna Elizabeth, d. of Heinrich Kunz; Oct. 19, 1762.

STRONCK—Jacob, and Margaretha Hausswirth; Mch. 7, 1765.
In Jacob Ruth's House.

STUBES—Barbara, d. of Jacob Stubes, decd., and Heinrich Zimmerman, decd.; Feb. 14, 1782.
By Heinrich Hetzel.

STUBSCHEN—Abraham, s. of Christian Stubschen, and Anna, d. of Jacob Kauffman; Dec. 14, 1783.
In Pastor's House.

STUDENROTH—Heinrich, s. of the decd. Heinrich Studenroth, and Susanna, d. of Jacob Zuger; Nov. 18, 1782.

SURRERUS—Andreas, s. of Andreas, Surrerus, and Maria Catharina, d. of Jacob Frey; Feb. 25, 1782.

THEEL—Christin, and Magdalena, d. of Peter Faust; Mch. 24, 1767.

THOST—Anna Catharina, d. of Heinrich Thost, and Heinrich Ripp, s. of Joh. Jacob Ripp, Mar. 28, 1758.

TISCHAN, DE SHON?—Catharina, w. of Johannes Tischan (De Shon)?, and Heinrich Muller, s. of Heinrich Muller, decd.; Apr. 1, 1783.

TOLL—Johannes, s. of Johannes Toll, and Elizabeth, d. of the decd. Michael Gessler; Nov. 24, 1763.

TRENTEL—Anna Sophia, and Wendel Fordine, s. of David Fordine; Nov. 14, 1784.

TROSTEL—Elizabeth, d. of Gorg Trostel, and David Muller, s. of David Muller; Nov. 14, 1784.

TROSTEL—Heinrich, s. of Gorg Trostel, and Catharine, d. of Jacob Schweiker; Feb. 21, 1785.

TWEED—John, s. of the decd. James Tweed, and Barbara, d. of the decd. John Law; Aug. 1, 1786.
In John Zuber's House.

ULRICH—Adam, s. of Gorg Ulrich, decd., and Margaretha, d. of Filipp Dock; Jan. 11, 1784.

ULRICH—Anna Maria, d. of Hans Jacob Ulrich, decd., and Jacob Bubykofer, s. of Franz Bubykofer; Aug. 1, 1756.

ULRICH—Anna Maria, d. of Hans Jacob Ulrich, decd.; Aug. 1, 1756.

UNGER—Jacob, s. of Johannes Unger, and Magdalena, d. of the decd. Conrath Engel; Feb. 19, 1785.

URICH—Anna Christina, d. of Frantz Urich, and Nicolaus Marhober; Aug. 26, 1753.

URICH—Christian, s. of the decd. Frantz Ury (sic), and Magdalena, Forsaken wife of Stphhel Frantz; Sept. 11, 1764.

VALENTINE—Johannes, s. of Heinrich Valentine, and Eva, d. of Peter Zeller; Mar. 4, 1783.

VOLLMER—Johann Adam, d. of Michael Vollmer, and Maria Rosina, d. of the decd. Johann Adam Bohn; Feb. 25, 1782.

VOLTZ—Gorg Michael, widower, and Anna Maria, d. of Peter Berthel; Apr. 20, 1773.

VAN ALMEN—Margaretta, d. of Conrad Van Almen, and Johannes Starck, s. of Heinrich Starck, decd.; Mch. 1, 1781.

VORNWALDT—Margaretta, d. of Peter Vornwaldt, decd., and Philip Schmid; Dec. 14, 1756.

VOSAG—Agatha, d. of Joh. Wilhelm Vosag, and Johannes Straubhaar, s. of Michael Straubhaar; Aug. 19, 1756.

VOSS—Johann Christofel, s. of the decd. Johan Adam Voss, ein Braunschweiger, and Juliana, d. of Adolf Zimmerman; Aug. 17, 1784.

WACKERMAN—Gorg, s. of the decd, Gorg Wackerman, and Catharina, d. of Nicolaus Hertzog; Apr. 25, 1786.

WAGNER—Johann Adam, widower, and School Master in Quidobehil, and Catharina Elisabeth, d. of the decd. Christian Heters; Apr. 28, 1760.

WAGMANN—Sarah, d. of Christian Martin Wagmann, and Christian Everhart, s. of Johan Everhart; July 3, 1753.

WAGNER—Eva Maria, d. of Gorg Adam Wagner, and Johann Peter Schmeid, s. of Jacob Schmeid; May 14, 1770.

WAGNER—John Jacob, s. of the decd. Gorg Wagner, and Anna Barbara, d. of the decd. Michael Hoffman, Oca 21, 1755.

WALDSCHMIDT—Anna Mary, d. of Rev. John Waldschmidt, and David Kring, s. of Gottfried Kring; Dec. 7, 1790.

WALDSCHMIDT—Catharina Margaretha, d. of Rev. John Waldschmidt, decd., and Abraham Hassler, s. of Abraham Hassler; Nov. 21, 1786. Recorded by a son of Rev. John Waldschmidt.

WALDSCHMIDT—Christina, d. of Rev. John Waldschmidt, and Heinrich Keller, s. of Martin Keller, decd.; Aug. 15, 1780; by Rev. Boos in Reading Town.

WALDSCHMIDT—Christian, s. of the Pastor (Rev. John Waldschmidt), and Catharina, d. of the decd. Peter Bollender; Aug. 15, 1780; by Rev. Boos in Reading Town.

WALDSCHMIDT—Wilhelm, widower, and Maria, d. of Casper Dill; Feb. 23, 1808; added by some other than Rev. J. W., who d. 1786.

WALDSCHMIDT—Wilhelm, s. of the decd. Rev. John Waldschmidt, and Barbara, d. of the decd. Abraham Hassler; Mch. 6, 1787.

WALDSCHMIDT—Johannes (Rev.), and Maria Elisabeth, d. of Christian Grube; May 14, 1754.

WALDSCHMIDT—Johannes, s. of the decd. Rev. John Waldschmidt, and Susanna, d. of the decd. Abraham Hassler; Dec. 19, 1786.

WALDSCHMIDT—Johannes, and Maria Kegereis; Mar. 8, 1835.

WALDSCHMIDT—Susanna Elisabeth, b. Apr. 26, 1757, d. of Rev. J. Waldschmidt, and Johannes Schneider "Einem Hessen," aus dem furstenthum, Ziegenheim; Sept. 3, 1782.

WALLEISEN—Michael, s. of the decd. Michael Walleisen, and Catharina, d. of Peter Haas; June 6, 1779.

WALLESS—Elisabetha, d. of Martin Walless, and John Gorg Albrecht; Mch. 27, 1759.

WALTER—Christian, s. of Jacob Walter, and Margaretha, d. of the decd. Fredrich Eschbach; Mch. 1, 1785.

WALTER—Eva, d. of Johann Jost Walter, and Johannes Hoschaar, s. of Heinrich Hoschaar; Apr. 17, 1781.

WALTER—Gerhard, s. of the decd. Johann Jost Walter, and Anna Maria, d. of Michael Huber; Aug. 28, 1780.

WALTER—Heinrich, and Margaretha, d. of the decd. Michael Noll; Apr. 17, 1758.

WALTER—Heinrich, and Margretha, d. of the decd. Jacob Nott; Apr. 17, 1758.

WALTER—Heinrich, s. of the decd. Johan Jost Walter, and Anna Eva, d. of Heinrich Hoffman; Oct. 22, 1776.

WALTER—Juliana, d. of Heinrich Walter, decd., and Ahraham Beer, s. of Michael Beer, decd.; Jan. 25, 1774.

WALTER—Margaretha, w. of Heinrich Walter, and Jacob Brucker, s. of Peter Brucker, decd.; Mch. 14, 1769.

WEBER—Anna Maria, d. of Christian Weber, and Peter Frey, s. of Jacob Frey; May 6, 1784.

WEBER—Catharine, d. of Matthias Weber, decd., and Daniel Gucker, s. of Henry Gucker; Apr. 2, 1782.

WEBER—Elisabeth, d. of Gorg Weber, and Johannes Gultin, s. of Etwert Gultin, decd; Apr. 15, 1783.

WEBER—Johan Christian, s. of Christian Weber, and Anna Maria, d. of Anthon Dornbach; Oct. 28, 1754.

WEBER—Johannes, and Elisabeth, d. of Filip Hautz; May 15, 1759.

WEBER—Magdalena, d. of Christian Weber, and Michael Schreitel, s. of Gorg Schreitel; Nov. 30, 1756.

WEBER—Magdalena, d. of Christian Weber, and Peter Fischer, s. of Heinrich Fischer; Oct. 8, 1783.

WEBER—Maria, d. of Christian Weber, and Heinrich Gut, s. of Christian Gut; Oct. 24, 1783.

WEBER—Maria Barbara, d. of Lorenz Weber, and Ludwig Peter Grub, s. of Christian Grub, in Christian Grube's house; May 6, 1755.

WEBER—Maria Elisabeth, d. of Gorg Weber, and Johannes Appel, s. of Heinrich Appel, decd.; Aug. 8, 1780; in Weber's house & in the presence of Mary Weber.

WEBER—Peter, s. of Gorg Weber, and Elisabetha, d. of Heinrich Hisband; Aug. 26, 1782.

WEHLER—Jost Heinrich, widower, m. for the 4th time, and Anna Catharina Schlatter; Feb. 16, 1763; in Abraham Farny's house.
WEHRHEIM—Philip, s. of Conrad Wehrheim, and Margaretha, d. of Gorg Hahn; Dec. 26, 1769.
WEICK—Magdalena, d. of Joseph Weick, and Johannes Diefendorfer, s. of Alexander Diefendorfer; Dec. 2, 1755.
WEIDMAN—Abraham, s. of Rudolf Weidman, and Anna Maria, d. of Joh. Engel Braun; June 5, 1764.
WEIH—Andreas, s. of the decd. Andreas Weih, and Dorrothea, d. of the decd. —— Reich; Feb. 4, 1755.
WEINHOLD—Barbara, d. of Nicholaus Weinhold, and Conrad Althaus, s. of Jacob Althaus; May 29, 1781.
WEINHOLD—Gorg Jacob, s. of the decd. Nicolaus Weinhold, and Margaretha, d. of Jacob Frey; July 27, 1773; in the Pastor's house & in the presence of 3 witnesses, viz. Jacob Frey, Nicolaus Weinhold & Conrad Hart.
WEINHOLD—Jacob, s. of the decd. Nicolai Weinhold, and Catharina, d. of the decd. Peter Buss; June 10, 1771.
WEINHOLD—Michael, s. of Nicolaus Weinhold, and Susanna Margaretha, d. of Peter Rhein; Apr. 4, 1780.
WEINHOLD—Nicolaus, widower,, and Barbara, d. of Jacob Brucker; Apr. 3, 1770.
WEITH—Jacob, s. of Heinrich Weith, and Margaretha, d. of Jacob Frey; Feb. 14, 1786.
WEITHAED—Elisabeth, d. of Simon Weithaed, decd., and Thomas Pry; Aug. 26, 1782.
WEIMER—Magdalena, d. of Nicolaus Weimer, and Heinrich Faust, s. of Peter Faust; June 12, 1769.
WEISS—Heinrich, s. of Jacob Weis, and Anna Eva Pantzler; Dec. 6, 1768.
WEISS—Johann Jacob, s. of Jacob Weiss, and Anna Maria, d. of Friedrich Haffner; July 8, 1770; at 6 o'clock at Jacob Weiss' House.
WEISS—Johannes, s. of Stophel, Weiss, and Elisabeth, d. of Adam Gerhart; June 11, 1776.
WEISS—Philip, widower, 2nd m., and Sabina, d. of the decd. Peter Bucher; Mch. 9, 1785.
WEISS—Friedrich, s. of the decd. Carl Weiss, and Catharina, d. of the decd. Johann Krieg; Aug. 22, 1786.
WEITZEL—Rosina, d. of Friedrich Weitzel, and Johannes Riehm, s. of Andreas Riehm; Oct. 10, 1785.
WELLER—Juliana, d. of Heinrich Weller, and Johann Siegfried Billing; Oct. 27, 1755.

WENGER—Elisabeth, d. of Josef Wenger, and Friedrich Reinhold, s. of Christofel Reinhold; July 31, 1785.
WENGERT—Maria Magdalena, d. of Johannes Wengert, and Killian Wolfkiehl, s. of Henry Wolfkiehl; June 30, 1754.
WENNERICK—Maria Catharina, d. of Balser Wennerick, and Christian Hillebrand, s. of Christian Hillebrand, decd.; Mch. 10, 1778.
WENSS—Johan Martin, s. of the decd. Gorg Wenss, and Catharina, d. of Johannes Bitzer; June 3, 1783.
WERNS—Johann Jacob, s. of Conrad Werns, and Magdalena, d. of Philip Hautz; Mch. 22, 1757.
WERNSS—Barbara, d. of Gorg Wernss, and David Bender, s. of Johannes Bender, decd.; June 26, 1770.
WERNER—Anna Maria, d. of Casper Werner, and Friedrich Betz; Dec. 27, 1763.
WESTHEBER—Johannes, s. of Gorg Westheber, and Elisabeth, d. of Martin Illess Ellis?); Dec. 23, 1782.
WHERNER—Isabella, d. of John Wherner, and David Kramer, s. of Carl Kramer; Apr. 23, 1782.
WICKS—Phillipine, d. of Christian Wicks, and Heinrich Printz, s. of Michael Printz; May 28, 1765; in the Reading Church.
WIDDER—Chrstofel, s. of Christofel Widder, and Anna Maria, d. of the decd. Gorg Ulrich; May 23, 1782.
WILBERT—Christhof, widower, and Dorrothea, widow of Peter Mayer; Oct. 28, 1783; in Riehms Town, in Lehnhard Keller's house.
WILHELM—Maria Barbara, d. of Jacob Wilhelm, and Philip Jacob Konig, s. of Nicolaus Konig; Apr. 12, 1763.
WILLAND—Christian, s. of Peter Willand, and Anna, d. of Philip Stertz; Sept. 6, 1775.
WINCKLER—Conrad, s. of Conrad Winckler, and Elisabeth, d. of Joseph Fischer; June 9, 1764; in Casper Strahole's house.
WINCKLER—Heinrich, and Agatha, d. of Christian Eberhart; Sept. 21, 1783.
WIRTZ—Friedrich, widower, and Margaretha, widow of Samuel Fix; May 27, 1784.
WITTMER—Peter, s. of Peter Wittmer, and Anna, d. of Christian Stehl; Aug. 10, 1784.
WITTMANN—Michael, and Catharina, d. of Engelbert Schneider, decd.; Jan. 9, 1759.
WITTMER—Elisabeth, d. of Peter Wittmer, and Anthon Millinger, s. of Josef Millinger; Sept. 18, 1785.

WITTNER—Rev. Johann Gorg, and Andreas Gehr's young d. who was called Salome until her baptism, Apr. 15, 1767, when she was baptized Johanna Christina, June 2, 1767.

WITZ—Sabina, and Peter Lehr, s. of Philip Lehr; Oct. 9, 1763; by Rev. Otterbein.

WOLFF—Gorg Michael, s. of the decd. Gorg Michael Wolff, and Christina, d. of Johann Gorg Schwartz; Jan. 10, 1757.

WOLFF—Johannes, s. of Bernhard Wolff, and Anna Maria, d. of the decd. Gorg Hingkell; Dec. 28, 1783.

WOLFSKIEHL—Conrad, s. of Henry Wolfskiehl, and Anna Maria, d. of Philip Sprenger; Oct. 4, 1757.

WOLFKIEHL—Killian, s. of Henry Wolfkiehl, and Maria Magdalena, d. of Johannes Wenhert; June 30, 1754.

WORSTEL—Marx, s. of the decd. Jacob Worstel, and Sara, d. of Dietrich Marshall; Nov. 24, 1771; in Pastor's house.

WULER—Wilhelm, and Barbara, d. of Tobias Ruhm; Apr. 8, 1781.

ZELLER—Eva, d. of Peter Zeller, and Johannes Valentine, s. of Heinrich Valentine; Mch. 4, 1783.

ZELLER—Johannes, s. of Nicolaus Zeller, and Rebecca, d. of Saul Gorg; June 15, 1786.

ZELLER—Peter, s. of Johannes Nicolaus Zeller, and Elisabeth, widow of Conrad Menzer; Oct. 7, 1783.

ZENT—Jacob, s. of Jacob Zent, and Susanna, d. of Isaac Hirschberger; May 3, 1785.

ZERFASS—Sabina, w. of Samuel Zerfass, and Adam Bauer, s. of Henry Bauer; Mch. 1, 1774; in Heinrich Muller's house, among many witnesses.

ZIEGLER—Anna, d. of Conrad Ziegler, decd., and Gottlieb Mack, s. of Gottlieb Mack; Nov. 22, 1778; in Ruhms Town.

ZEIGLER—Elisabeth, d. of Conrad Zeigler, decd., and Michael Chiljan (Killian?), s. of Matthias Chiljan, decd.; May 26, 1778.

ZIEGLER—Gorg, his father still in Germany, and Catharina, Casper Conrath's sister (Elisabeth's d.); June 13, 1780.

ZIEGLER—Rosina, w. of Afam Ziegler, and Elias Reddig; Mar. 21, 1773.

ZIGLER—Anna Maria, d. of Conrath Zigler, decd., and Peter Schneider, s. of Valentine Schneider; May 26, 1782.

ZIMMERMAN—Anna, d. of Peter Zimmerman, and Lehnhard Rettig, s. of Gorg Rettig; Apr. 12, 1785.

ZIMMERMAN—Anna Maria, d. of Heinrich Zimmerman, decd., and Jacob Schneder, s. of Jacob Schneder; May 12, 1780.

ZIMMERMAN—Heinrich, s. of the decd. Heinrich Zimmerman, and Barbara, d. of the decd. Jacob Stubes; Feb. 14, 1782; by Heinrich Hertzog.

ZIMMERMAN—Heinrich, s. of Adolf Zimmerman, and Barbara, d. of the decd. Christian Schlechty; Jan. 9, 1785.

ZIMMERMAN—Jacob, s. of Peter Zimmerman, and Anna, d. of the decd. Gorg Rettloss; Apr. 3, 1785. "Ein kind von beides war schon gebohren."

ZIMMERMAN—Juliana, d. of Adolf Zimmerman, and Johann Christofel Voss, s. of Johan Adam Voss, ein Brannschweiger; Aug. 17, 1784.

ZIMMERMAN—Maria Christine, d. of Adolph Zimmerman, and Johannes Aache, widower; July 21, 1767; in Heinrich Aache's house, Ille pater non aderat.

ZIMMERMAN—Peter, s. of Adolph Zimmerman, and Anna, d. of the decd. Christian Schlechty; Sept. 9, 1783.

ZOLLER—Elisabeth, d. of Andreas Zoller, decd., and Michael Raub, s. of Michael Raub, decd.; Aug. 4, 1776.

ZOLLER—Gorg, s. of Nicolaus Zoller, and Margaretha, d. of Johannes Bosshart; Aug. 2, 1781.

ZUBER—Catharine, and Stophel Albrecht; Sept. 22, 1761.

ZUBER—Johannes, s. of the decd. Daniel Zuber, and Juliana, d. of Martin Meichsel; Aug. 7, 1785.

ZUBER—Martin, and Catharina, d. of David Buchler, in Johannes Huber's Haus, in Ronnels Town; Nov. 10, 1760.

ZUCK—Johannes, s. of the decd. Rudy Zuck, and Susanna, d. of the decd. Martin Hoch; Nov. 20, 1780.

ZUGER—Susanna, d. of Jacob Zuger, and Heinrich Studenroth, s. of Heinrich Studenroth, decd.; Nov. 18, 1782.

ZWALLY—Johannes, widower, and Catharina, d. of Michael Shaffer; Oct. 20, 1765.

ZWERNSS—Magdalena, w. of Ludwig Zwernss, and Johannes Becker, s. of Michael Becker; Nov. 5, 1771.

———— —Catharine Elisabeth, d. of Georg ——, and Gorg Aache, s. of Johannes Aache; Dec. 17, 1754.

———— —name omitted, and Johannes Schotter, married 2nd time; Dec. 13, 1757.

———— —Catharina, Casper Conrath's sister's (Elisabeth) d., and Gorg Ziegler (his father is still in Germany); June 13, 1780.

Names omitted above in original.

COMMUNION SERVICES AND COMMUNICANTS.

COMMUNION SERVICES AND COMMUNICANTS.

1 Held on the Cocalico the Holy Communion, Nov. 19, 1752, after a Preparative Sermon on Nov. 18, and after creditable testimonials.
2 Apr. 15, 1753, Communion Service, 80 persons present, after a preparative Sermon Apr. 14, at which these communed for the first time:
Abraham Dorr, his youngest son, Abraham,
Heinrich Wolfskiel, his son, Conrad,
Weyericht Benss, his daughter, Catharina,
Johannes Herchelroth, his daughter, Elisabeth,
Martinus Walliser, his daughter, Elisabeth.
3 Holy Communion held July 8, 1753, 50 persons.
4 Holy Communion held September 28, 1753, 60 persons, Preparative Sermon September 27.
5 On the Holy Easter, Apr. 14, 1754, 60 persons.
1 Holy Communion first time, Nov. 26, 1752, at Sebastian Reyger's Church, 60 persons.
2 Communion Apr. 22, 1753, 60 persons.
3 Communion July 15, 1753, 45 persons.
4 Communion Nov. 4, 1753, 50 persons.
5 Communion Mch. 31, 1754, 50 persons.
Preparative Sermon Mch. 30,
6 Communion Aug. 25, 1754, 60 persons.
7 Communion Dec. 25, 1754, 50 persons.
8 Communion May 19, 1755, 60 persons.
It was Whit Monday.
Communion Sept. 14, 1755.
1 Holy Communion, Jan. 28, 1753, at Moden Krick, 80 persons.
2 Holy Communion May 6, 1753, 60 persons, of whom five, on Saturday were made members of the Refd. Church, viz:—
Peter Rup's son Jacob, and daug. Anna Maria,
Anna Margretha and her sister Maria,
Fronica, d. of the decd. Lehnhard Breitenstein, and Jacob Dautrick's d. Anna Barbara.
3 Holy Communion in the Congregation Aug. 26, 1753, with blessing and profit, 70 persons.
4 Holy Communion, Dec. 25, 1753, 50 persons.
5 Again on Whitsuntide, June 22, 1754, the last Holy Communion at Moden Krick.

COMMUNION SERVICES

6 Holy Communion at Michael Amwegs in the New Church, May 18, 1755, on Whitsuntide, 50 persons.
1 At Seltenrich Congregation Holy Communion was held, 70 persons, at which Adam Bender's son, Johannes, confessed his faith, Dec. 3, 1752.
2 Holy Communion June 10, 1753, 60 persons.
3 Holy Communion Sept. 2, 1753, 60 persons.
4 Holy Communion Jan. 1, 1754, 30 persons, after preparative, Dec. 30, 1756.

Johannes Boshaar's wife, and Abraham Rosenberger's wife confessed Dec. 31, 1753.

Jacob Joner presented to The Refd. Church at Seltenreich a beautiful linen table cloth, Dec. 27, 1753.

5 Holy Communion at Seltenreich Apr. 15, 1754, at which Philip Sprenger's s. & 2 drs. & J. Langen's 2 drs. were confirmed, altogether 60 persons.

Holy Communion at Cocalico, 14th. Apr. 1754, Preparative held Apr. 12th., or Good Friday, at which time the following were confirmed:—

1 Casper Egly, Mark Egly's son,
2 Heinrich Kaffroth, Gerhart Kaffroth's son, b. Dec. 1737.
3 Andreas Wolff, Gorg Wolff's son, b. Mch. 8, 1738.
4 Gorg Wolff, Gorg Wolff's son, b. Mch. 16, 1740.
5 Martin Weiss, Jacob Weiss' son, b. Oct. 30, 1737.
6 Joh. Lehhart, Jacob Weiss' son, b. Apr. 25, 1740.
7 Lorentz Herchelroth, Johannes' son, b. Jan. 18, 1739.
8 Wendel, Gerhart Hubschmann's son.
9 Maria Magdalena, Christian Bullinger's dr.
10 Maria Barbara, Wendel Laber's dr., b. May 8, 1740.
11 Elisabetha, Weyerick Benss' dr., b. Aug. 1, 1739.
12 Maria Catharina, Elias Meyer's dr.
13 Maria Elisabetha, Gerhart Kaffroth's dr., b. Oct. 24, 1739.
14 Anna Christina, Johannes Gutinger's dr.
15 Juliana, Lehnhart Keller's dr., b. Mch. 23, 1739.
16 Elisabeth, Balser Laber's wife, of Mennonite family, and not as yet baptized, confessed her faith, was baptized and confirmed on above date.

These 16 persons partook of the Sacrament, and with others numbered 60.

6 Holy Communion at Cocalico, Mch. 30, 1755, 70 persons.
Holy Communion at Cocalico Sept. 21, 1755.
Holy Communion, Apr. 27, 1755, Seltenreich, 50 persons.
Holy Communion, Oct. 14, 1755, Seltenreich.
Jacob and Christian Schneder, Apr. 18 (No other statement.)

Holy Communion at Michael Amwegs, Oct. 5, 1755.
Holy Communion at Seltenreich, Apr. 18, 1756.
Holy Communion at Seltenreich, Sept. 5, 1756.
Holy Communion at Cocalico, June 6, 1756.
Holy Communion at Reigers, May 16, 1756.
Holy Communion at Cocalico, Oct. 24, 1756.
Holy Communion at Seb. Reigers, Nov. 14, 1756.
Holy Communion at Reding thoun, Oct. 31, 1756.
Holy Communion at Lauer's Tolpenhacken, Nov. 7, 1756.
Holy Communion at Hoster Kirch, Nov. 28, 1756, 130 persons.
Holy Communion at Lauer's Tolpenhacken, Apr. 10, 1757, 80 persons.
Holy Communion at Hoster, May 1, 1757, 120 persons.
Holy Communion at Keyers, Apr. 17, 1757, 70 persons.
Holy Communion at Cocalico, May 8, 1757, 60 persons.
Holy Communion at Cacusy, May 15, 1757.
Holy Communion at Reding, May 29, 1757, 50 persons.
The Holy Communion was held Apr. 6, 1760, or Easter, in the Rohoher Congregation at Jer. Muller's, 54 persons, 3 confirmed,
Ulrich Sparr's son and Heinrich Meyer's two drs.
On 27th. Apr., 1760, at Weisseicken Congregation the Holy Communion was held, 60 persons, of which 15 informirte and confirmed,
Martin and Jacob Meyer.
Gorg Lang, DeWald Schneider,
Gorg Muller, Melchert Fordeni,
Conrath Blester, Johannes Stamm,
Jacob Schneider, Susanna Meyer,
Anna Barbara Blester,
Maria Rosina Fordini, Anna Maria Thehof (DeHoff),
Anna Maria Geiger,
On 4th. May, 1760, at Cacusy, the Holy Communion was held, 60 persons, and 7 informirte and confirmed, 4 boys and 3 girls,
Wilhelm Fischer's s. and d.,
Adam Span's s.,
Heckert baumgast Schmelin, Gorg Hain's dr.,
At Reyers Congregation, May 11, 1760, 60 persons, and 9— 3 boys and 6 girls came the first time to the Holy Communion, and were confirmed.
Christofel Gsell, Johannes Ernst,
Heinrich Hirchelroth, Cath. Elisabeth Hubsmann, Anna Margretha, Lorens Weber's dr., Anna Maria Hundsruck,

Anna Maria Prack, Susanna Margretha Laber, Maria Catharina Graf.

With the beginning of the year 1760 some of the Congregation in Quidopdehil where Mr. Templeman had heretofore served, but as he has lost his sight he cannot serve them, I began to serve in the work as I can.

In the Gruber Church on Ascension Day, May 15, 1760, held Holy Communion, 50 persons.

18th. May 1760, held Holy Communion at Quidopdehil, 105 persons, and 20 for the first time informirts and came to the Communion.

25th May, 1760, held Holy Communion at Cocalico, 52 persons and 2 informirte, David Schrecks' dr, and Johannes Meddauerr, these two were well taught and informed.

Aug. 31, 1760, Holy Communion at Cocalico, 52 persons.

Sept. 7, 1760, Holy Communion at Gruber's, 51 persons.

Nov. 30, 1760, Holy Communion at Cacusy at Hahn's, 50 persons.

Dec. 7, 1760, Holy Communion, Seb. Reigen, 36 persons.

Dec. 14, 1760, Holy Communion, Donnegahl at Jerom Mullers.

Dec. 21, 1760, Holy Communion, Quidopdehile.

Feb. 15, 1761, Holy Communion, Weisseichmland, 50 persons.

There were in the Cocalico Congregation, a number of persons in the year 1761 informirte and on 20 Mch. 1761, or Good Friday, were confirmed:—

Johannes Roth, Philip Roth's son,

Jacob and Johannes Meddauer, two sons of Johannes Meddauer,

Amelia and Susanna, drs. Heinrich Reiger.

Rebecca, dr. Philip Epprecht.

The Holy Communion was held Mch. 22, or Easter, 50 persons.

Holy Communion held at Donnegahl, Mch. 29, 1761, 40 persons.

Holy Communion held at Cacusy, Mch. 15, 1761, 48 persons.

Holy Communion held at Seb. Reigen, May 10, 1761, 60 persons.

5 ch. partook for the first time.

Holy Communion at Cacusy, Apr. 4, 1762, 65 persons.

Holy Communion, Cocalico, Apr. 11, 1762, 53 persons.

Holy Communion, Weissenthland, Apr. 18, 1762, 40 persons, and for the first time:—
Lehnhart Muller,
Melchoir and Jacob, Johann Meyer's sons,
Rudolp, son of Matthew Hoffer.
Peter Jung, the father is French and writes his name Peter Ac Min Jong.
Maria, d. of Casper Werner,
Maria Barbara, d. Matthias Hoffer,
Margretha Bohl,
Sophia Blester,
Fronica, d. of Gorg Ley.
Holy Communion at Reyer's "Platz", may 2, 1762, 64 persons.
Holy Communion at S. Reigen, Sept. 19, 1762, 35 persons, Isaac Barry's son and Capae's dr. for the first time.
Holy Communion at Weissenchland, Oct. 2, 1762, 36 persons.
Holy Communion at Cacusy, Oct. 17, 1760, 50 persons.
Holy Communion at Cocalico, Oct. 24, 1762, 39 persons.
Holy Communion at Reading, Sept. 5, 1762, 32 persons.
Holy Communion at Reading, Mch. 26, 1765, 70 persons.
Holy Communion at Cacusi, Apr. 3, 1763, 50 persons, the following communed for the first time,
Frantz, son of Wilhelm Fischer,
Wilhelm, son of Ulrich Michael,
Johannes, son of Adam Hain,
Peter, son of Nicolaus Zoller,
Anna Maria, dr. of Adam Hain.
Holy Communion at Cacusy, June 10, 1764, 60 persons.
Holy Communion at Cacusy, Apr. 7, or Easter, 1765, at which I preached and confirmed the following persons, viz:—
Peter Ruthe's son Heinrich,
Fried Hehn's 2 sons, Johan and Friedrich,
Heinrich Hehn's 2 sons, Johann and Friedrich,
Wilhelm Fischer's son, Friedrich,
Ludwig Mohn's son, Johann and dr. Margretha,
Adam Hehn's son, Elisabeth,
Anthon Faust's dr., Maria Elisabeth,
Susanna Margretha Hausswirth, 11 persons, In all 70 persons.
Holy Communion at Michael Amweg's, Apr. 14, 1765, 56 persons, at which the following children who were examined and confirmed for the first time, viz:—
Mr. Heinrich Walter's son Wilhelm,

COMMUNION SERVICES

Christian Schweitzer's son, Friedrich,
Johann Jost Walter's son, Ludwig,
Johannes Billman's son, Johannes & dr. Barbara,
Ludwig Schweitzer's dr., Anna,
Josef Neu's dr., Anna Maria, d. Jan. 17, 1769,
Gorg Schneider's two drs.,
Gorg Brunner's dr., Anna Maria,
Filip Kissinger's dr., Susanna,
Martin Brauninger's 2 drs.,
—— Shaarmann's dr.
Michael Muller's dr., who 5 yrs. ago had a child to Christian Lutz, having publicly repented, was made a member of the Congregation.
In Berne Township at Appler's I served a Congregation, Mch. 17, 1765, and held Holy Communion on 28 Apr. 1765, 60 persons, the following confirmed for the first time,
Gorg Germand's 2 sons,
Friedrich From's son,
Johannes Dauber, Michael Grauel's step son,
Absalom Willimson,
Michael Grauel's dr., Maria Sara,
Catharina, dr. of the decd. Johannes Hiester,
Maria Elisabeth, dr. Heinrich Gicker,
Maria Elisabeth, dr. Nicolaus Christ,
Anna Maria, dr. Valentin Eppler,
Maria Pauline, dr. Jacob Fessler, decd.,
Elisabeth, w. of Gottlied Groh, 12 persons.
Holy Communion at Tolpenhacken or Host Kirsh, Aug. 4, 1765, 200 persons.
Holy Communion, Cacusy's Ch., Sept. 8 1765, 90 persons,
Holy Communion, Muhlbach, June 23, 1765, 50 persons.
Holy Communion was held in the so called Stone Church in Berne Township, Sept. 23, 1765, 50 persons, on May 19, 1765, or 8 days before Whitsuntide 1 preached there.
On Whitsuntide, May 26, 1765, held Holy Communion at Reading, 50 persons.
Holy Communion at Cacusy, Mch. 30, 1766, 59 persons, and the following for the first time, viz:—
Johann Heinrich, Wilhelm Carl, and Tobias, all 3 sons of Heinrich Schucker,
Marx Hahn, son of Peter Hahn, decd.
Johann, son Michael Mell,
Frantz, son Peter Ruthe,
Anna Elisabeth, dr. Heinrich Schuckert,

Susanna, dr. Peter Klopp,
Magdalena, dr. Peter Ruth,
Maria Eva, dr. Martin Leyer,
Elisabeth, dr. Peter Braun,
Maria Barbara, dr. Adam Fellebaum,
Magdalena Barbara Weymert, then 13 and 57—70 persons.
Holy Communion, Muhlbach, Oct. 6, 1765, 50 persons, the following for the first time,
Frantz, son Peter Numan,
Walter Kinsser,
Johannes, s. Johann Null,
Magdalena Numann,
Susanna Hoffman, Catharine Hoffman, drs. Jost Hoffman.
Anna Maria Hartmann,
Anna Elisabeth and Elias, drs. Peter Naumann,
Anna Sabilla, dr. Jacob Kinsser, 10 persons.
Holy Communion, Berne Congregation, Sept. 28, 1766, 50 persons,
Holy Communion, Eppler's, Sept. 12, 1766, 30 persons,
Holy Communion Cacusy, Oct. 26, 1766, in the New Church, 75 persons.
Holy Communion, Michael Amweg's, Nov. 9, 1766, 40 persons.
New Year, 1767, Allegenc Ch. I began to serve.
Holy Communion, then, Apr. 5, 1767, 41 persons.
Holy Communion, Michael Amweg's, Apr. 19, 1767, 45 persons.
Holy Communion, Eppler's, May 3, 1767, 30 persons.
Holy Communion, Cocalico, or as called Michael Amweg's, Sept. 20, 1767, 45 persons, of which were the two drs. of Mr. Heinrich Walter.
On Whitsuntide, or June 7, 1767, held Holy Communion at Cacusy, 120 persons, of whom were 15 young persons.
In the following autumn, Oct. 18, 1767, Holy Communion held at Cacusy, 110 persons.
Holy Communion, Easter, Apr. 3, 1768, Cacusy, 100 persons.
Holy Communion, Allegence Congregation, Oct. 4, 1767.
Holy Communion, Eppler, Oct. 11, 1767, 35 persons.
Holy Communion, Eppler, Apr. 24, 1768, 40 persons.
The following partook for the first time, viz:—
Abraham, s. Jacob Rieser,
Nicolaus, s. Johannes Hacke, Decd.,
Johannes and Wilhelm, sons of Christian Albrecht,
Maria Margretha, dr. Gorg Neumann,

COMMUNION SERVICES

Anna Barbara, dr. Valentine Epler,
Catharina, dr. Heinrich Gicker,
Elisabeth, dr. Jacob Rieser.
Holy Communion, Michael Amwegs, on the Cocalico, May 22, 1768, 50 persons.
Holy Communion, Cacusy, Oct. 2, 1768, 52 persons.
Holy Communion, Cocalico, Oct. 9, 1768, 12 persons.
Holy Communion, Epler, Oct. 16, 1768, 40 persons.
Holy Communion, Allegenc, Oct. 28, 1768, 56 persons.
Cacusy, Mch. 26, 1768, 80, among them
Peter, s. Michael Lauer,
Johannes, s. Ulrich Ritscher,
Friedrich and Casper, s. Friedrich Hahn,
Casper, s. Jacob Kuhl, decd.,
Johann, s. Peter Braun,
Joh. Gorg, s. Wilhelm Fischer,
Christian, s. Nicolaus Schafer,
Sara, dr. Peter Rieth,
Juliana and Elisabeth, drs. Michael Lauer,
Anna Maria, dr. Johannes Eckert.
Holy Communion, Epler, Apr. 2, 1769, 45 persons.
Holy Communion, Cocalico, at Amwegs, May 4, 1769, 30 persons, of which there were 8 new ones, 6 boys and 2 girls.
Holy Communion, Allegenc Ch., May 14, 1769, 36 persons, confirmed 10.
Holy Communion, Epler, Benne Township, Sept. 24, 1769, 45.
Holy Communion, Allegenc Ch., Oct. 1, 1769, 53 persons.
Holy Communion, Cacusy, Oct. 8, 1769, 80 persons.
Cacusy, on Easter, or Apr. 15, 1770, 100 persons, at which the following 30 persons partook for the first time, viz:—
J. Adam, s. Michael Ruth,
Christian, s. Johannes Hacke, decd.,
Johannes & Filip, s. Heinrich Spohn,
Wilhelm, s. Peter Braun,
Peter, s. Frantz Krick,
Conrad, s. David Geissler,
Johannes, s. Peter Schaarmann,
Johannes, s. Michael Faust,
Gorg, s. Martin Leyer,
Gorg, s. Gorg Hahn,
Wilhelm, s. Henry Hettrich,
Catharina, d. Jacob Ruth,

Barbara, d. Adam Wagner,
Christina, d. Johannes Hack, decd.,
Magdalena, d. Frantz Grick,
Catharina Elisabeth, d. Jacob Schafer,
Catharina, d. Jacob Bullman,
Catharina, d. Michael Ruth,
Maria Elisabeth, d. Conrad Hart,
Maria Elisabeth, d. Abraham Kessler,
Elisabeth, d. Melchoir Mell,
Christina, d. Peter Shaarmann,
Maria Margaretha, d. Nicolaus Schafer,
Catharine, d. Ulrich Ritchart,
Maria Margretha, d. Anthon Faust,
Anna Maria, d. Anthon Faust,
Elisabeth, d. Nicolaus Weimert,
Catharina, d. David Giessler,
Rosina, d. Michael Muller.
Holy Communion, Allegenc Ch., May 6, 1770, 56 persons, at which were two girls of Johann Mosser.
Epler's, May 24, 1770, 68 persons, the following confirmed and partook for the first time,
Jacob Epler's son, Johannes,
Gorg & Catharina, ch. Johannes Schneider, decd.,
Jacob Maurer, Peter Epler's Man Servant,
Johannes Lowe,
Valentin & David Hufnagle,
Filip Shatz,
Johannes Aurand's dr. Catharina,
Johannes Haas's dr. Christina,
Heinrich Gicker's drs., Eva & Barbara,
David Wintermuth's drs. Elisabeth & Anna Elisabeth,
Catharina Barbara, d. Adam Wagner,
Adam Sontag's drs. Catharina & Anna Elisabeth,
Gorg Medler's dr., Catharina,
Filip Machmer's dr., Anna Maria,
Valentin Epler's dr., Margretha,
These and 20 persons, 7 men and 13 maidens.
Holy Communion, Allegene Ch., Sept. 30, 1770, 46 persons.
Holy Communion, Cacusy, Oct. 7, 1770, 100 persons.
Holy Communion, Michael Amweg's, Cocalico, Oct. 14, 1770, 15 persons.
Holy Communion, Eppler's, Oct. 21, 1775, 50 persons.
Holy Communion. Eppler's, May 9, 1771, 40 persons.
Holy Communion, Allegenc Ch., May 26, 1771, 32 persons.

Holy Communion, Cocalico, Michael Amweg's, May 19, 1771,
30 persons.
Holy Communion, Cocalico, Michael Amweg's, Easter, 1772,
35 persons.
Holy Communion, Eppler's, May 28, 1772, 50 persons.
Holy Communion, Allegenc, June 7, 1772, 55 persons.
Holy Communion, Cocalico, Oct. 4, 1772, 30 persons.
Holy Communion, Epler's, Oct. 18, 1772, 60 persons.
Holy Communion, Allegenc, Nov. 1, 1772, 50 persons.
(Location not stated) Apr. 11, 1773, 46 persons, of which
following 9 were confirmed, viz:—
Heinrich Walter,
Peter Schneider,
Stophel Burckholder,
My Daughter, Susanna Elisabeth (Rev. J. W.)
Johannes Keller's wife,
Johannes Rub's dr.
Martin Burckholder's dr.
Daughter of the decd. Jost Walter,
Elisabeth, dr. Martin Keller, decd.
Eppler's, May 30, 1773, 60 persons.
Allegenc, May 20, 1773, 50 persons.
Cocalico, at Michael Amweg's; Nahe gelegene Kirch, Nov.
7, 1773, 20 persons.
Eppler's Nov. 21, 1773, 20 persons.
Allegene Ch., Nov. 28, 1773, 40 persons.
The following were taken in the Ch., viz:—
Valentin Bohmer,
Barbara, wife of Conrad Dorr,
Regina, w. of Joh. Nicolaus Jost,
Anna Barbara, dr. Johannes Moser,
Anna Margretha, dr. Adam Bohmer, decd.,
Valentin Fehl,
Margretha Christine, dr. Arnold Schefer.
Holy Communion, Cocalico at Michael Amwegs, Apr. 3,
1774, 40 persons, of which were 3 sons of Bastain Hassler.
Allegene, May 8, 1774, 50 persons.
Eppler's, Berne Township, May 22, 1774, 45 persons, 14
confirmed and partook for the first time, viz:—
Daniel Albrecht,
Daniel Dippry,
Jacob & Adam, sons of Michael Wommers,
Valentin Moser,
Conrad Schmidt,
Catharine Albrecht,

Gerteraub Ditz,
Catharina Egle,
Catharina & Elisabeth Mayer, 2 sisters,
Margretha Wommers,
Christina Braun,
Gerteraub Kirschener.
Eppler's, Apr. 16, 1775, 45 persons, the following confirmed, viz.—
Heinrich, Johannes and Gorg, 3 sons Nicolaus Runckel, decd.
Daniel, s. Heinrich Gicker,
Nicolaus and Filip, s. Filip Machemer, decd.
Allegene, Apr. 9, 1775, 50 persons.
Cocalico, or Michael Amwegs, Apr. 23, 1775, 30 persons, of which for the first time were 2 sons of Abraham Hassler, decd.
Cocalico, Apr. 28, 1776, 35 persons, when my dr., Anna Christina, was instructed and confirmed.
Epler's, Apr. 7, 1776.
Allegene, May 16, 1776, wo neue gelassen worden als.
David & Heinrich, s. Marx Bohler,
Jacob Hoffer,
Johannes Dietrich,
Johannes Mosser,
Abraham Jost,
Adam Bohmer,
Elisabeth Jost,
Margretha Moser,
Filip & Wilhelm, sons Jacob Rempt.
At the New Church in Bernē Township, 2 miles from Philip Faust, May 26, 1776, 50 persons, the following were instructed and confirmed, viz:—
Jacob Burckerr, who was baptized 14 days before "Kam oon den Ammetisten her".
Jacob & Ludwig, s. Filip Faust,
Ludwig Lohr,
Gorg Muller,
Catharina, dr. Johannes Claus,
Margretha, dr. Heinrich Muller, decd.,
Catharina & Barbara, drs. Jacob Reichert.
Maria Margretha, dr. Nicolaus Muller,
Anna Maria, dr. Jost Schumacher.
Allegene, Dec. 14, 1777, 50 persons.
It was a dear time, a quart of wine cost 20 shillings.

COMMUNION SERVICES

Johann Moser died Dec. 7, 1777. He was a member of this Congregation, aged 65 yrs., 4 mos.
Cocalico, Michael Amwegs, May 10, 1778, 40 persons.
Aepler's, May 24, 1778, 35 persons.
Allegene, June 7, 1778, 46 persons.
Catharina & Maria Elisabeth, drs. of Peter Gruenewaldt, partook for the first time, and installed Heinrich Simmer and Nicolaus Jost, Vorstcher.
Cocalico, or Michael Amwegs, Apr. 4, 1779, 80 persons, of whom the following 26 were instructed and confirmed, viz:—
Ludwig Schweitzer's s. Ludwig,
Wilhelm, Conrath, Peter and Christina, ch. Jost Schneider, decd.,
Gorg Michael & Sophia, ch. Peter Brunner,
Gorg & Margretha, ch. Gorg Siegethaler,
Jacob, Elisabeth and Magdalena, ch. Sebastian Hassler,
Catharina Waldschmidt, my daughter,
Heinrich Hoffman's Phillipus,
Nicolaus Rup's dr. Margretha,
Jacob Amweg's dr., Elisabetha,
Henry Binckly's dr. Elisabetha,
Barbara & Magdalena, drs. of Peter Katzemeyer,
Barbara & Elisabeth, drs. Michael Walter,
Christina Muller,
Susanna & Barbara, drs. Abraham Hassler, decd.,
Barbara, dr. Christian Schlechly, decd.,
Sophie, dr. Gorg Schneider.
Holy Communion, Allegene, Apr. 11, 1779, 71 persons of whom the following 15 were instructed and confirmed:—
Abraham, s. Casper Eckert,
Abraham, s. Christian Eschelmann,
Heinrich, s. Johann Hoffer,
Gorg, s. Heinrich Trostel,
Philip, s. Adam Bohmer,
Daniel, s. Adam Lotz,
Catharina, d. Michael Stoltz,
Maria, s. Johannes Moser,
Catherina, d. Nicolaus Jost,
Maria Barbara, d. Heinrich Schlapbach,
Maria Margretha, d. Peter Hoschaar,
Maria Catharina, d. Gorg Gramler,
Magdalena, d. Michael Walliser,
Catharina, d. Heinrich Muller,
Magdalena Klingemann.

Holy Communion, Allegene, Refd. Ch., Apr. 30, 1780, 72
persons, of whom the following were on Apr. 29th. instructed and confirmed, viz:—
Marx & Peter, s. Bernhart Behler,
Jacob, s. Heinrich Worst,
Gorg, s. Filip Amme,
Bernhart & Johannes, s. Adam Bechter,
Phillipus, s. Gorg Funck, decd.,
Bernhart & Christian, s. Peter Zell,
Wilhelm, s. Peter Hoschaar,
Rosina Schlabach,
Elisabetha & Catharina, drs. Christian Eschelman,
Catharina, d. Peter Hoschaar,
Margretha, d. Heinrich Worst,
Dorothea & Elisabetha, d. Heinrich Menger,
Barbara, d. Bernhart Behler,
Barbara, d. Filip Amme,
Anna Maria, d. Philip Hertz,
Elisabeth, d. Gorg Trostel.
Holy Communion, Cocalico, May 7, 1780, 56 persons, the following for the first time:—
Gorg Michael Hell,
Anna Kummer (or Rummer, blotted),
Catharina Bullender,
Anna Maria Weinhold,
Johannes & Wilhelm, s. Gorg Hell,
Anna, wife Bastian Hassler.
Holy Communion, Epler, May 14, 1780, 40 persons, the following for the first time:—
Heinrich, s. Christian Albrecht,
Anna Maria & Maria Barbara, drs. Weyerich Moser.
Holy Communion, Epler, Apr. 15, 1781, 50 persons, the following for the first time:—
Filip, s. Johannes Ulrich,
Jost Heinrich, Johann Jost & Peter, sons of Heinrich Hedrich,
Magdalena, dr. Heinrich Gicker.
Holy Communion, Epler's, in their Church, Nov. 11, 1781, 50 persons, of whom the following 15 after instruction were admitted, viz:—
Adam, s. Peter Eppler,
Ludwig, s. Ludwig Tobias,
Filip & Heinrich, s. Johan Christian Berger, decd.,
Jacob, s. Johannes Klein,
Anna Elisabetha, dr. Jost Hister, decd.,

COMMUNION SERVICES

Anna Maria and Christine, drs. Gorg Medler,
Elisabeth, d. Ludwig Tobias,
Margretha & Rahel, dr. Michael Lauer,
Magdalena & Catharina, d. Heinrich Rath, decd.,
Elisabetha, dr. Johannes Gerner,
Barbara, dr. Johannes Klein.
Holy Communion, Cocalico, near Amwegs, Apr. 14, 1782,
  th) following 32 for the first time, viz, 50 persons.
Christian Harding, "Schon bein jahr ein Mann",
Peter, s. of Heinrich Wendel,
Johannes Waldschmidt (my son),
Johannes Ury, s. Gorg Urich (sic),
Heinrich, s. Heinrich Binckle,
Jacob, s. Gorg Michael Hell,
Johannes, s. Alstatt, decd., Jacob Meyer's, step-son.,
Johannes, s. Sebastian Hassler,
Gorg, s. Martin Burchholder,
Heinrich, s. Jacob Amweg,
Heinrich, s. Heinrich Gucker,
Heinrich, s. Heinrich Schlabach,
Anna Maria Waldschmidt, my daughter ,
Eva & Anna Maria, dr. Gorg Brunner,
Catharina, dr. Johannes Kuntz,
Anna, dr. Gorg Siegethaler,
Eva, dr. Nicolaus Bechtel, decd.,
Anna, dr. Christian Schlecti, decd.,
Rosina, dr. Gorg Michael Hell,
Christina, dr. Wendel Weynhold,
Anna Catharina, dr. Adam Krick,
Anna & Magdalena, dr. Jost Schonauer, decd., bapt. Apr.
  10, 1782,
Christina, Barbara & Anna Maria, 3 drs. Johannes Daut-
  rich,
Elisabeth & Margretha, dr. Jost Schneider, decd.,
Anna Maria, d. Gorg Ury,
Margretha, d. Heinrich Wendel,
Susanna, d. Johannes Hoffer.
Holy Communion, Eppler, May 9, 1782, 50 persons.
Holy Communion, Allegene, June 23, 1782, 40 persons.
Holy Communion, Cocalico, Apr. 20, 1783, about 50 persons.
Holy Communion, Allegny, May 25, 1783, 60 persons.
Holy Communion, Epler, June 8, 1783, 40 persons.

AND COMMUNICANTS. 281

Amwegs Ch. or Cocalico, May 9, 1784, 62 persons, 18 of
whom for the first time, viz:—
1 Michael Harting,
3 Johannes & Christian Harnisch,
5 Jacob & Heinrich Numann,
6 Wilhelm Waldschmidt (my son),
7 Peter Burckhold,
8 Johann Jacob Walter,
9 Heinrich, Adam Bohmer's son,
10 Anna Maria Dimmel, wife of Bastian D., a daughter of
Nicolaus Frantz,
11 Christina Numann,
14 Juliana, Magdalena and Barbara, drs. Christian Harting,
decd.,
15 Anna Maria, dr. Heinrich Binckli,
16 Elisabetha, dr. Gorg Siegethaler,
17 Catharina, dr. Michael Walter,
18 Anna Barbara, dr. Adam Bohmer, decd.
Holy Communion, Allegene, May 30, 1784, 40 persons.
Holy Communion, Cocalico, June 30, 1784, Jacob Amweg &
Gorg Brunner, Jr., Publicly installed a Deacon.
Holy Communion, Allegene, Oct. 24, 1784, 60 persons. The
Preparation, Oct. 23rd., on which day Heinrich Muller,
the Schoolmaster at Moden Krick died.
Holy Communion, Allegene, Apr. 17, 1785, 48—9 confirmed,
viz:—
Heinrich, s. Bernard Behler,
Heinrich, s. Andreas Burckert,
Johannes Kreih, Bauer's apprentice boy,
Elisabeth & Catharine, drs. Abraham Riehm,
Elisabeth, dr. Jacob Roth,
Anna Barbara, d. Andreas Burckert,
Elisabeth, dr. Heinrich Muller,
Elisabeth, dr. Bernhard Behler.
Holy Communion, Cocalico, Amwegs, Apr. 24, 1785, 45 persons for the first time,
Son & dr. Johannes Kuntz,
Conrad Schneider's wife and his sister Catharina,
Barbara, dr. Gorg Brunner.
Holy Communion, Allegene, Oct. 23, 1785, 45 persons, Multi
vocati, pauci Electi, Matt. 22.
Gorg Stephain, Nov. 6, 1785, installed Deacon, Allegene von
Peter Funck.
16 May, 1790, Johann Kuntz and Johann Waldschmidt were
publicly installed Deacon, Cocalico Ch.

COMMUNION SERVICES

June 1, 1794, Ludwig Schweitzer and Christian Harnisch, installed Deacon "in Schwamm".

Congregations served by Rev. John Waldschmidt, and no. of Communions, 1752-1786.

Cocalico, or Michael Amwegs,	41
Sebastian Reigen or Weisseichenland,	19
Moden Creek,	5
Seltenreich,	7
Reading,	4
Tulpehacken,	3
Host Krick,	2
Quiltapehill,	4
Cacusy,	20
Gruber's Ch.,	2
Donegal,	2
Aeppler's,	24
Muhlbach,	2
Stone Ch., Berne Twp.,	1
Bern Cong.,	1
Allegene,	24
New Ch., 2 m. from Philip Funck's,	1
	162

Gott des Almechtig hat unsern lieber Vater aus Dieser Zeit su sich in dis Seelige ewigkeit gerufften dn 14 Sept., 1786, zwischen 9 und 10 uhr vor mittage, und ist der erden uber liefret den 15 Sept. nach mittag um zwei uhr.

Herr Boos hat die leichte rete genomen aus dem 17 Psalm un daselbst den 3 und 24 sten vers. Gott wolle des wie alle zu ihm kommen Amen.

Die Graab gesteld 6 ten 8 bris 1787 Kost 7 pf. 12 schillings.

Maria, wife of Rev. John Waldschmidt, d. July 12, 1803.

Susanna Waldschmidt, born Hassler, d. Sept. 28, 1813.

Johannes Waldschmidt, d. 11 March 1829.

Anna Barbara Hassler, d. Apr. 22, 1791.

Johannes Waldschmidt, d. Oct. 16, 1851, aged 51 yrs., 11 mo & 7 days.

PENNSYLVANIA MARRIAGE LICENSES, 1784-86.

PENNSYLVANIA MARRIAGE LICENSES— 1784-86.

ABRAHAM, MARY, and WILLIAM FINN; August 17, 1785.

ADAMS, KATHERINE, and JOHN BECK; July 8, 1785.

ALDERSON, GEORGE, gentleman, and ANN ELLIS, adult and widow of Philadelpha County; October 1, 1786; Bond, 100£; Bondsmen, George Alderson, Charles Erdmann; Witness, Michael Schlatter.

ALLEN, JOSEPH, and MARY DELAPLINE, of the City of Philadelphia; November 17, 1785; Bond, 200£; Bondsmen, Joseph Allen, Jno. Claypoole; Witness, James Trimble.

ANDERSON, HETTY, and WILLIAM COOPER; June 82, 1785.

ARMSTRONG, JOHN, and EDITH SUTTON, of the County of Burlington, New Jersey; May 19, 1785; Bond, 200£; Bondsmen, John Armstrong, Isaac Smith; Witness, James Trimble.

ARN DANIEL, silversmith, and Dorothy Streeper, of the City of Philadelphia; November 16, 1785; Bond, 200£; Bondsmen, Daniel Arn, John Sweitzer; Witness, James Trimble.

ART, WILLIAM, and SARAH GARWOOD, of the City of Philadelphia; June 14, 1785; Bond, 200£; Bondsmen, James Alexander, William Art; Witness, James Trimble.

ASHBOURNE, MARTIN, tanner, and ELIZABETH THOMAS, of the City of Philadelphia; July 4, 1785; Bond, 200£; Bondsmen, Wm. Poultny, Martin Ashburn; Witness, James Trimble.

ASH, SAMUEL, single man, and ANNA KAISER, widow of Vincent Twp., Chester Co.; October 19,1784; Bond, 400£; Bondsmen, Samuel Ash, Edward Parker; Witness, Peter Defreiss, Edward Parker.

ASHTON, SARAH, and JACOB SHUBERT, November 17, 1785.

ATKINSON, SAMUEL, waterman, and RHODA OSBORNE, of the Northern Liberties; December 30th, 1784; Bond 200£; Bondsmen, Samuel Atkinson, Duncan Stewart; Witness, James Trimble.

BAKER, ELIZABETH, and JOHN CROSS; April 21, 1785.

BAKER, ESTHER, and JOHN BARTHOLOMEW DYCHE; October 12, 1786.

BAKER, SARAH, and THOMAS EGAN; August 17, 1785.

BAM, JACOB, and BARBARA CHARLES, of the City of Philadelphia; January 23, 1786; Bond, 200£; Bondsmen, Jacob Bam, Daniel Knodol; Witness, James Trimble.

BARKER, MARIA, and JOHN DENNIS; July 7, 1785.

BARNET, GEORGE, and SARAH FISHER, of New Jersey; July 18, 1785; Bond, 200£; Bondsmen, Carl Yost, George Barnet; Witness, James Trimble.

BARRON, JAMES, and MARY SINNERS, of the City of Philadelphia; June 14, 1786; Bond, 200£; Bondsmen, James Barron, Thos. Carroll; Witness, James Trimble.

BARRY, MARY, and JAMES BENNETT; May 29, 1786.

BARTLESON, BARTLE, gentleman, and ANN POWEL, adults, of Plimuth, Montgomery Co.; August 15, 1785; Bond, 100£; Bondsmen, Bartle Bartleson, Jonathan Colley; Witness, Michael Schlatter.

BARTHOLOMEW, ELIZABETH, and GREENBERRY DORSEY; October 4, 1786.

BARTON, WILLIAM, and HANNAH ROBERTS, of the County of Bucks; October 14, 1786; Bond, 200£; Bondsmen, Wm. Barton, Joseph Dungan; Witness, James Trimble.

BECK, JOHN, Blue Dyer, and KATHERINE ADAMS, of Germantown; July 8, 1785; Bond, 200£; Bondsmen, John Beck, Thos. Fisher; Witness, James Trimble.

BENINGHOVE, JACOB, tobacconist, and ELIZABETH KURTZ; February 8, 1786; Bond, 200£; Bondsmen, Jacob Beninghoff, Andrew Burkhard; Witness, James Trimble.

BENNET, JAMES, and MARY BARRY, of the City of Philadelphia; May 29, 1786; Bond, 200£; Bondsmen, James Bennett, J. Hamilton; Witness, James Trimble.

BENNET, MATTHEW, merchant, and MARY PARHAM, of the City of Philadelphia; March 9, 1786; Bond, 200£; Bondsmen, Matthew Bennett, Jacob Sommer; Witness, James Trimble.

BENNET, WILLIAM, yoeman, and KATHERINE CORNELL, of the County of Bucks; January 18, 1786; Bond 200£; Bondsmen, William Bennet, Abraham Cornell; Witness, James Trimble.

BENNEVILLE, DANIEL DE, practioner of physick, and ELIZABETH COATE, of New Jersey; April 13, 1785; Bond, 200£; Bondsman, Dan'l. De Benneville.

BENNINGTON, ELIZABETH, and GEORGE ELTON; March 30, 1785.

BERRETT, MARY, and ROBERT BROWN; December 22, 1785.

MARRIAGE LICENSES—1784-86.

BETTLE, LYDIA, and WILLIAM GARRICK; August 3, 1785.

BEWLEY, ISAAC, and HANNAH DAVIS, of the County of Chester; February 9, 1786; Bond, 200£; Bondsmen, Adam Siter, Isaac Bewley; Witness, James Trimble.

BICKERTON, ROBERT, cordwainer, and KATHERINE GAMBER, of the City of Philadelphia; June 16, 1785; Bond, 200£; Bondsmen, Robert Bickerton, Michael Gamber; Witness, James Trimble.

BICKLEY, SUSANNA, and JOHN STRICKERT, Jr.; June 1, 1786.

BOCKIUS, PETER, rope-maker, and ELIZABETH ETTER, of the County of Philadelphia; April 21, 1785; Bond, 200£; Bondsmen, Peter Bockius, Frederick Fifer; Witness, James Trimble.

BOWEN, JOHN, gentleman, and MARY SWOOPE, of the City of Philadelphia; January 25, 1786; Bond, 200£; Bondsmen, John Bowen, Thos. Tillyer; Witness, James Trimble.

BRADBERRY, MARY, and WILLIAM DAVENPORT, March 1, 1786.

BRADFORD, SARAH, and THOMAS CARSTAIRS, September 15, 1785.

BREWER, DANIEL, and ELIZABETH BROWN, of the City of Philadelphia; June 20, 1786; Bond 200£; Bondsmen, Evan Cook, Daniel Brewer; Witness, James Trimble.

BRIGHT, WILLIAM, gentleman, and MARY ROBERTS, of the City of Philadelphia; January 19, 1786; Bond, 200£; Bondsmen, Sam'l Tolbert, Wm, Bright; Witness, James Trimble.

BROCK, ANNE, and JOHN SPROSON; December 17, 1785.

BROCK, WILLIAM, and ANNE HACKET, late of Jamaica; July 15, 1785; Bond, 200£; Bondsmen, Will'm Brock, John Jameson; Witness, James Trimble.

BROWN, ABRA, gentleman, and MARAGARETH MONROW, adults of Philadelphia City; July 2, 1786; Bond, 100£; Bondsmen, Abra. Brown, Ahraham Coats; Witness, Mich'l Schlatter.

BROWN, ELIZABETH, and DANIEL BREWER; June 20, 1786.

BROWN, ROBERT, house carpenter, and MARY BERRETT, of the City of Philadelphia; December 22, 1785; Bond, 200£; Bondsmen, Robert Brown, John Brown; Witness, James Trimble.

BRYAN, GUY, merchant, and MARTHA MATLACK, of the City of Philadelphi; June 20, 1785; Bond, 200£; Bondsmen, Guy Bryan, Geo. Davis; Witness, James Trimble.

BURKE, SUSANNA, and CHRISTOPHER HARBERGER; June 9, 1786.

BURLEQUE, ANTHONY, yeoman, and POLLY DAWSON, of the City of Philadelphia, Pa.; May 28, 1785; Bond, 200£; Bondsmen, Antoine Bouleque, Tho's Fischer; Witness, John Lewis.

BURROWS, ELIZABETH, and ENOS GIBBS; December 17, 1785.

BURROWS, LOETITIA, and SAMUEL FRANKLIN, June 14, 1785.

BURTELOE, SUSANNA, and JESSE HOOD; January 24, 1785.

BUSBY, HANNAH, and WILLIAM WELLS, June 15, 1785.

BUTLER, JUDITH, and DENNIS CRONAN; February 14, 1786.

CAMERON, ANNE, and JEREMIAH FOX; August 26, 1785.

CAMPBELL, MARY, and BERNARD VANDEGRIFT, April 2, 1785.

CARSTAIRS, THOMAS, and SARAH BRADFORD, of the City of Philadelphia; September 15, 1785; Bond, 200£; Bondsmen, George Knox, Thomas Carstairs; Witness, James Trimble.

CARTER, MARY, and JOHN THOMPSON; June 1, 1785.

CASSEL, MARY, and JOSIAH PAUL; May 30, 1785.

CHAMBERLAINE, MARY, and CONRAD ROUW, July 12, 1785.

CHARLES, BARBARA, and JACOB BAM; January 23, 1786.

CHRISTIE, MARY, and PATRICK GLYN; April 7, 1785.

CLARK, JOSEPH, cabinet maker, and MARY MASTERS, of the City of Philadelphia; June 22, 1785; Bond, 200£; Bondsmen, Josiah Elfreth, Joseph Clark; Witness, James Trimble.

CLARKSON, CATHERIÑE, and BERNHART TWIEN, June 10, 1785.

CLAY, SUSANNA, and WILLIAM READ; December 15, 1785.

MARRIAGE LICENSES—1784-86.

CLEVER, PETER, and ELIZABETH EARNHART, of Bucks County; April 27, 1785; Bond, 200£; Bondsmen, Peter Clever, Wm. Banquett; Witness, James Trimble.

CLINE, JOHN, and HANNAH SHELLER, of the County of Philadelphia; July 21, 1785; Bond, 200£; Bondsmen, Jacob Salor, Thomas Hall, John Cline; Witness, James Trimble.

CLINGMAN, ANNE, and JOHN LEWIS; April 26, 1785.

COATE, ELIZABETH, and DANIEL DE BENNEVILLE; April 13, 1785.

COCHRAN, JOHN, mariner, and KITTY RUSH, of the City of Philadelphia; August 8, 1785; Bond, 200£; Bondsmen, Abraham Collings, John Cochran; Witness, James Trimble.

COGGLE, SARAH, and HENRY MILES, June 8, 1785.

COLEMAN, MARY, and WILLIAM DAVIS, March 28, 1785.

COLLINS, FRANCES, and MICHAEL MAHONY, June 20, 1786.

CONNAN, CHARLES, yeoman, and ELIZABETH GRISSLE, of Philadelphia City; January 26, 1786; Bond, 200£; Bondsmen, Charles Connan, Daniel McFaul; Witness, James Trimble.

COOPER, WILLIAM, and HETTY ANDERSON, June 28, 1785; Bond, 200£; Bondsmen, Jacob Stanton, Carl Yost; Witness, James Trimble.

CORNELL, CORNELIUS, yeoman, and PHEBE CORNELL, of the County of Bucks; March 1, 1785; Bond, £200; Bondsmen, William Bennet, Cornelius Cornell; Witness, James Trimble.

CORNELL, KATHERINE, and WILLIAM BENNET, January 18, 1786.

CORNELL, PHEBE, and CORNELIUS CORNELL; March 1, 1785.

COST, MARTIN, and CHRISTIANA LIMEBURNER, of the City of Philadelphia; May 31, 1786; Bond 200£; Bondsmen, Martin Cost, Philip Limeburner; Witness, James Trimble.

COUCH, CHARLES, trader, and ANNE WIGLEY, of the City of Philadelphia; July 28, 1785; Bond, 200£; Bondsmen, Charles Couch, Doct'r Michael Dietrick; Witness, James Trimble.

CRAIG, MARGARET, and WILLIAM MILLER; March 7, 1786.

CRAWFORD, ANNE, and THOMAS HILL; November 14, 1785.

CRAWFORD, ELIZABETH, and DAVID DOWLIN; August 10, 1785.

CREAN, JOHN, house carpenter, and MARY PRICHARD, of Philadelphia; June 23, 1785; Bond, 200£; Bondsmen, John Sellers, Jno. Crean; Witness, James Trimble.

CRONAN, DENNIS, gardener, and JUDITH BUTLER, of the City of Philadelphia; February 14, 1786; Bond, 200£; Bondsmen, Garret Barry, Dennis Cronen; Witness, James Trimble.

CROSS, HANNAH, and BENJAMIN HANCOCK; April 11, 1785.

CROSS, JOHN, tobacconist, and ELIZABETH BAKER, of the City of Philadelphia; April 21, 1785; Bond, 200£; Bondsmen, Joseph Baker, John Cross; Witness, James Trimble.

CROSSLEY, JOHN, yeoman, and TAMAR VICKERS, of Burlington County, New Jersey; June 14, 1785; Bond, 200£; Bondsmen, John Crossley, Samuel Franklin; Witness, James Trimble.

CRUGER, NICHOLAS, merchant, and MISS ANNE MARKOE, of NEW YORK; November 18, 1785; Bond, 200£; Bondsmen, Abra. Markoe N. Cruger; Witness, James Trimble.

CUMMINGS, PAUL, merchant, and CATHERINE ANNE WILLIAME, of the City of Philadelphia; February 6, 1786; Bond, 200£; Bondsmen, Philip Ryan, Pablo Commyns; Witness, James Trimble.

CURTAIN, ELIZABETH, and SAMUEL WAYNE, December 28th, 1784.

CUSTER, MARTHA, and DANIEL PAINTER; September 21, 1786.

DANNEKER, CHRISTIAN, Junr., and CATHERINE HAYNES, of the City of Philadelphia; July 12, 1785; Bond, 200£; Bondsmen, Christian Danneker, junr., George Strayley; Witness, James Trimble.

DANNEKER, JOHANNA, and GEORGE KIMBLE; June 5, 1786.

DAVENPORT, WILIAM, yeoman, and MARY BRADBERRY, of Bucks County; March 1, 1786; Bond, 200£; Bondsmen, William Davenport, Gilb't Rodman; Witness, James Trimble.

DAVIS, ANNE, and HENRY D. PURSELL; June 21, 1785.

DAVIS, ELIZABETH, and DAVID SHAKESPEAR; January 20, 1785.

DAVIS, HANNAH, and ISAAC BEWLEY; February 9, 1786.

DAVIS, MARTHA, and JAMES SNODGRASS; October 5, 1786.

MARRIAGE LICENSES—1784-86. 291

DAVIS, WILLIAM, and MARY COLEMAN, of Baltimore Town, Maryland; March 28, 1785; Bond, 200£; Bondsmen, William Davis, John Reed; Witness, James Trimble.

DAWSON, POLLY, and ANTHONY BURLEQUE; May 28, 1785.

DELAPLAINE, MARY, and JOSEPH ALLEN; November 17, 1785.

DELLWAY, CATHERINE, and HENRY HARRIS; June 22, 1785.

DENNIS, EDWARD, and ANNE TOOMEY, of the City of Philadelphia; January 5, 1786; Bond, 200£; Bondsmen, John Farran, Edward Dennis; Witness, James Trimble.

DENNIS, JOHN, cordwainer, and MARIA BARKER, of the City of Philadelphia; July 7, 1785; Bond, 220£; Bondsmen, John Morton, John Dennis; Witness, James Trimble.

DEVAN, MARY, and WILLIAM DONOVAN; November 11, 1785.

DEWEES, JOHN, paper maker, and SARAH DILWORTH, adults of Springfield, Montgomery Co.; October 15, 1786; Bond, 100£; Bondsmen, John Dewees, George Hitner; Witness, Michael Schlatter.

DIETRICK, SUSANNA, and NICHOLAS WYRICK; June 12, 1786.

DILL, NICHOLAS, and CHRISTIANA GOOSMAN, of the City of Philadelphia; June 1, 1786; Bond, 200£; Bondsmen, Nickolaus Dill, Merten Haas; Witness, James Trimble.

DILWORTH, SARAH, and JOHN DEWEES; October 15, 1786.

DONOVAN, WILLIAM, and MARY DEVAN, of the City of Philadelphia; November 11, 1785; Bond, 200£; Bondsmen, Wm. Donovan, John Rice; Witness, James Trimble.

DORSEY, GREENBERRY, merchant, and ELIZABETH BARTHOLOMEW, of the City of Philadelphia; October 4, 1786; Bond, Geo. Fox, Green Dorsey; Witness, James Trimble.

DOWLIN, DAVID, yeoman, and ELIZABETH CRAWFORD, of Montgomery Co.; August 10, 1785; Bond, 200£; Bondsmen, David Dowlin, Baker Barns; Witness, James Trimble.

DRAYS, MARY, and WILLIAM LAWRENCE; June 10, 1785.

DUBLIN, CATHERINE, and JOSEPH MILEHAM; July 18, 1785.

DUCOMB, VINCENT, hair dresser, and ROSE RIBAND, of the City of Philadelphia; November 12, 1785; Bond, 200£; Bondsmen, Vincent Ducomb, Francois Serre; Witness, James Trimble.

DUEY, ELIZABETH, and PATRICK THOMAS; June 15, 1786.

DUFFIN, MARY, and JOHN JOHNSTON; February 8, 1785.

DUGNID, MARY, and JAMES KENNEDY; June 18, 1785.

DUNGAN, MARY, and ABEL MORRIS; October 9, 1786.

DYCHE, JOHN BARTHOLOMEW, and ESTHER BAKER, of the County of Philadelphia; October 12, 1786; Bond, 200£; Bondsmen, Joseph Page, J. B. Dyche; Witness, James Trimble.

EAGER, ELIZABETH, and GEORGE WATT; November 11, 1785.

EARNHART, ELIZABETH, and PETER CLEVER; April 27, 1785.

ECKHART, MARY, and GEORGE OZEAS; February 13, 1786.

EDGE, ANNE, and JOSEPH TOMKINS; February 3, 1786.

EGAN, THOMAS, and SARAH BAKER, of the City of Philadelphia; August 17, 1785; Bond, 200£; Bondsmen, Thomas Egan, Richard Cole; Witness, James Trimble.

ELLIS, ANN, and GEORGE ALDERSON; October 1, 1786.

ELTON, GEORGE, cabinet maker, and ELIZABETH BENNIGTON, of the City of Philadelphia; March 30, 1785; Bond, 200£; Bondsmen, George Elton, Eberhard Longcope; Witness, James Trimble.

ENGLE, JAMES, chair maker, and MARGARET MARSHALL, of the City of Philadelphia; May 4, 1785; Bond, 200£; Bondsmen, James Engle, Arch'd Engle; Witness, James Trimble.

ETTER, ELIZABETH, and PETER BOCKIUS; April 21, 1785.

EVANS, AMOS, and MARY EVANS, both free and single persons of Lemerick Twp., Montgomery Co.; October 17, 1786; Bond, 300£; Bondsmen, Amos Evans, W'm Evans; Witnesses, Matthew Brooke, Owen Evans.

EVANS, MARY, and AMOS EVANS; October 17, 1786.

FALCONER, WILLIAM, and MARY McCULLOUGH, of the City of Philadelphia; June 15, 1785; Bond, 200£; Bondsmen, W'm Falconer, Robert Cather; Witness, James Trimble.

FARMER, LEWIS, Esquire, and ELIZABETH FOHRER, of the City of Philadelphia; February 2, 1786; Bond, 200£; Bondsmen, Lewis Farmer, Dean Timmons; Witness, James Trimble.

FARRELL, JOSHUA, mariner, and MARY ANNE McCARTNEY, of the City of Philadelphia; May 5, 1785; Bond, 200£; Bondsmen, Thomas Harrison, Joshua Farrell; Witness, James Trimble.

FEAIRBAN, JOHN, and MARIA HUSTON, of the City of Philadelphia; March 1, 1785; Bond, 200£; Bondsmen, Will'm Stiles, Robert McClintuck; Witness, James Trimble.

FERGUSON, ARCHIBALD, and MARY WHITTE, of the City of Philadelphia; June 3, 1786; Bond, 200£; Bondsmen, Archibald Ferguson, Joseph Wirt; Witness, James Trimble.

FETTERS, WILLIAM, and ANNE MADERA, of the State of New Jersey; October 17, 1786; Bond, 200£; Bondsmen, Will'm Fetters, Phillip Brady; Witness, James Trimble.

FIELD, CHRISTINA, and SAMUEL McMINN; March 29, 1785.

FINN, WILLIAM, and MARY ABRAHAM, of the City of Philadelphia; August 17, 1785; Bond, 200£; Bondsmen, David Abraham, William Abraham; Witness, James Trimble.

FIPS, SUSANNA, and ALEXANDER THOMPSON; May 25, 1785.

FISHER, ELIZABETH, and WILLIAM KAHMER; June 2, 1785.

FISHER, REBECCA, and JONATHAN ZANE; March 6, 1786.

FISHER, SARAH, and GEORGE BARNET; July 18, 1785.

FLECK, WILLIAM, biscuit baker, and MARY SHEAF, of the City of Philadelphia; February 11, 1786; Bond, 220£; Bondsmen, Wm. Flack, Merten Haas; Witness, James Trimble.

FOGERTY, MARY, and JACKSON MACKEYSEY; June 10, 1785.

FOHRER, ELIZABETH, and LEWIS FARMER; February 2, 1786.

FOX, ELIZABETH, and CHRISTOPHER SPITTER; September 7, 1785.

FOX, JEREMIAH, and ANNE CAMERON, of the City of Philadelphia; August 26, 1785; Bond, 200£; Bondsmen, W'm Watkins, Jeremiah Fox; Witness, James Trimble.

FRANCIS, ELIZABETH, and ELISHA GORDON; December 29th, 1784.

FRANKLIN, SAMUEL, yeoman, and LOETITIA BURROWS, of the County of Burlington, New Jersey; June 14, 1785; Bond, 200£; Bondsmen, Samuel Franklin, John Crossley; Witness, James Trimble.

FRECOURT, LOUISA MARY, and LOUIS POTTER LEFE BURE; December 31, 1784.

FRENCH, NANCY, and DAVID RICHEY; May 20, 1785.

GAMBER, KATHERINE, and ROBERT BICKERTON; June 16, 1785.

GAMBLE, OLIVE, and ABRAHAM GARDNER; August 31, 1785.

GARDNER, ABRAHAM, potter, and OLIVE GAMBLE, of the City of Philadelphia; August 31, 1785; Bond, 200£; Bondsmen, Abraham Gardiner, John Barker; Witness, James Trimble.

GARLINGER, MICHAEL, labourer, and MARY GROVE, of the Northern Liberties, of the City of Philadelphia; January 26, 1785; Bond, 200£; Bondsmen, George Garlinger, Michael Garlinger; Witness, James Trimble.

GARRICK, WILLIAM, mariner, and LYDIA BETTLE, of the City of Philadelphia; August 3, 1785; Bond, 200£; Bondsmen, Philip Redmond, Wm. Garrick; Witness, James Trimble.

GARWOOD, SARAH, and WILLIAM ART; June 14, 1785.

GEORGE, DAVID, and MARY GODFREY, of Montgomery Co.; March 10, 1786; Bond, 200£; Bondsmen, Thos.. Fitzgerald, David George; Witness, James Trimble.

GIBBS, ENOS, yeoman, and ELIZABETH BURROWS, of Gloucester Co., New Jersey; December 17, 1785; Bond, 200£; Bondsmen, John Blackwood, Enos Gibbs; Witness, James .Trimble.

GLYN, PATRICK, taylor, and MARY CHRISTIE, of the City of Philadelphia; April 7, 1785; Bond, 200£; Bondsmen, James Linville, Pat'k Glyn; Witness, James Trimble.

GODFREY, MARY, and DAVID GEORGE; March 10, 1786.

GOOSMAN, CHRISTIAN, and NICHOLAS DILL ;June 1, 1786.

GORDON, ELISHA, and ELIZABETH FRANCIS, of the City of Philadelphia; December 29th, 1784; Bond, 200£; Bondsmen, Thos Fitzgerald, Elisha Gordon; Witness, James Trimble.

GREAVES, MARGARET, and JOHN REYNOLDS; February 28, 1785.

GREBLE, CURTIS, sadler, and MARY WEST, of the City of Philadelphia; April 6, 1785; Bond, 200£; Bondsmen, Curtis Grebble, Jacob Kuefer; Witness, James Trimble.

GREEN, ANNE, and TIMOTHY RYAN; July 11, 1785.

GRIFFITH, ANNE, and JOSEPH LUNN; September 20, 1785.

MARRIAGE LICENSES—1784-86.

GRISCOM, GEORGE, and KITTY SCHREINER, of the State of New Jersey; July 28, 1785, Bond, 200£; Bondsmen, Jacob Carver, George Griscom; Witness, James Trimble.

GRISSLE, ELIZABETH, and CHARLES CONNAN; January 26, 1786.

GROVE, MARY, and MICHAEL GARLINGER; January 26, 1785.

GRUBB, GRACE, and BENJAMIN HARPER, May 29, 1786.

HACKET, ANNE, and WILLIAM BROCK, July 15, 1785.

HAIR, WILLIAM, and REBECCA WATSON, of the County of Bucks; October, 1786; Bond, 200£; Bondsmen, William Hair, Benj'n Watson; Witness, James Trimble.

HANCE, ANN, and BENJAMIN MORTON; January 31, 1786.

HANCOCK, BENJAMIN, and HANNAH CROSS, of New Jersey; April 11, 1785; Bond, 200£; Bondsmen, Benjamin Hancock, Lewis Burn; Witness, James Trimble.

HANLON, MARMADUKE, storekeeper, and MARY LONG, of the City of Philadelphia; February 2, 1785; Bond, 200£; Bondsmen, Joseph Johnston, Marmaduke Hanlon; Witness, James Trimble.

HARBERGER, CHRISTOPHER, and SUSANNA BURKE, of the City of Philadelphia; June 9, 1786; Bond, 200£; Bondsmen, Christopher Harberger, Henry Harberger; Witness, James Trimble.

HARPER, BENJAMIN, and GRACE GRUBB, of Blackford; May 29, 1786; Bond, 200£; Bondsmen, Benjamin Harper, Robert Davidson; Witness, James Trimble.

HARRIS, HENRY, and CATHERINE DELLWAY, of the City of Philadelphia; June 22, 1785; Bond, 200£; Bondsmen, Wm. Hodgson, Christian Kauch; Witness, James Trimble.

HASTINGS, ELIZABETH, and JOHN HARPER; July 15, 1785.

HASTINGS, JAMES, taylor, and MARY HIGGINS, of the City of Philadelphia; July 18, 1785; Bond 200£; Bondsmen, James Hastings, John Carroll; Witness, James Trimble.

HAYES, MICHAEL, and SARAH McNAIR, of the City of Philadelphia; June 14, 1786; Bond, 200£; Bondsmen, Mich'l Hayes, John Connor; Witness, James Trimble.

HAYNES, CATHARINE, and CHRISTIAN DANNEKER, junr.; July 12, 1785.

HEISER, MARY, and PHILLIP KOHL; September 26, 1786.

PENNSYLVANIA

HEISER, WILLIAM, painter, and MARGARET McDANIEL, of the City of Philadelphia; June 2, 1785; Bond, 200£; Bondsmen, William Heiser, Cosmas Smith; Witness, James Trimble.

HEISS, CHRISTIAN, cordwainer, and SARAH NANSANT, of the City of Philadelphia; December 16, 1785; Bond, 200£; Bondsmen, Christian Heiss, Jacob Sheble; Witness, James Trimble.

HENDERSON, ELEANOR, and JAMES POALK; March 15, 1786.

HENRY ANNE, and AUGUSTUS MORRIS; April 28, 1785.

HIGGINS, MARY, and JAMES HASTINGS; July 18, 1785.

HILL, THOMAS, labourer, and ANNE CRAWFORD, of the City of Philadelphia; November 14, 1785; Bond, 200£; Bondsmen, William Collings, Thomas Hill; Witness, James Trimble.

HINTON, JOHN, and ELIZABETH PIDGEON, of the State of New York; February 14th, 1786; Bond, 200£; Bondsmen, John Hinton, Conrad Pidgeon; Witness, James Trimble.

HOOD, JESSE, cordwainer, and SUSANNA BURTELOE, of the City of Philadelphia; January 24, 1785; Bond, 200£; Bondsmen, Morris Dickinson, Jesse Hood; Witness, James Trimble.

HUGHES, JOHN, and ELIZABETH HASTINGS, of the City of Philadelphia; July 15, 1785; Bond, 200£; Bondsmen, William Cummings, John Hughes; Witness, James Trimble.

HUNTER, JAMES, mariner, and SARAH SHUTE, of the City of Philadelphia; August 9, 1785; Bond, 200£; Bondsmen, Sam Jervis, James Hunter; Witness, James Trimble.

HUSTON, HANNAH, and PATRICK MOORE; August 18, 1785.

HUSTON, MARIA, and JOHN FEAIRBAN; March 1, 1785.

HYDE, ANDREW, blacksmith, and MARY KAMMER, of the City of Philadelphia; September 12, 1785; Bond, 200£; Bondsmen, Andrew Hyde, Frederick Rethier; Witness, James Trimble.

INGELS, THOMAS, cooper, and MARY VANNOSTEN, of Lower Dublin Twp., Phila. Co.; January 24, 1785; Bond, 200£; Bondsmen, Thomas Ingels, John Hall; Witness, James Trimble.

JEWSON, MARY, and WILLIAM TRAUTWINE, jr.; July 14, 1785.

JOHNSTON, ELIZABETH, and JOHN SCANLAN; February 5, 1785.

MARRIAGE LICENSES—1784-86.   297

JOHNSTON, JOHN, mariner, and MARTHA THOMPSON, of the City of Philadelphia; July 14, 1785; Bond, 200£; Bondsmen, John Johnston, Robert Johnson; Witness, James Trimble.

JOHNSTON, JOHN, storekeeper, and MARY DUFFIN, of the City of Philadelphia; February 8, 1785; Bond, 200£; Bondsmen, Barnabas Duffin, John Johnson; Witness, James Trimble.

JOHNSTON, SAMUEL, carrier, and MARY KINSLEY, of the Northern Liberties; February 17, 1786; Bond, 200£; Bondsmen, Michael Streckler, Samuel Jobson; Witness, James Trimble.

JOLLY, RACHEL, and WILLIAM JONES; December 27, 1785.

JONES, DAVID, sail maker, and ROSANNA REEDLE, of the City of Philadelphia; May 31, 1786; Bond, 200£; Bondsmen, Abraham Collings, David Jones; Witness, James Trimble.

JONES, JOHN M., and MARY WALKER, of the City of Philadelphia; December 22, 1785; Bond, 200£; Bondsmen, John M. Jones, Isaac Coats, Junr.; Witness, James Trimble.

JONES, REBECCA, and GEORGE SHEED; September 3, 1785.

JONES, WILLIAM, and RACHEL JOLLY, of the City of Philadelphia; December 27, 1784; Bond, 200£; Bondsmen, Evan Cook, Wm. Jones; Witness, James Trimble.

JUSTICE, LAWRENCE, house carpenter, and ELIZABETH SMITH, of the City of Philadelphia; January 3, 1785; Bond, 200£; Bondsmen, Lawrence Justice, Robert Towers, Jun.; Witness, James Trimble.

KAHMER, WILLIAM, and ELIZABETH FISHER, of the City of Philadelphia; June 2, 1785; Bond, 200£; Bondsmen, W'm Collady, William Kahmar; Witness, James Trimble.

KAIN, JOHN, labourer, and MARY KALEY, of the City of Phiadelphia; February 1, 1786; Bond, 200£; Bondsmen, John Kain, Hugh Mooney; Witness, James Trimble.

KAISER, ANNA, and SAMUEL ASH; October 19, 1784.

KALEY, MARY, and JOHN KAIN; February 1, 1786.

KAMMER, MARY, and ANDREW HYDE; September 12, 1785.

KEEL, BALTUS, painter, and CHRISTIANA SHIEVELL, of the City of Philadelphia; February 18, 1786; Bond, 200£; Bondsmen, Boltos Keel, Phillip Burkhard; Witness, James Trimble.

KEN, PETER, joiner and cabinet maker, and REBECCA WESSEL, of the City of Philadelphia; April 22, 1785; Bond, 200£; Bondsmen, Peter Keen, Christian Keen; Witness, James Trimble.

KEILER, BARBARA, and FREDERICK MILEY; September 22, 1785.

KEMBLE, JOSEPH, and HANNAH REYNOLDS, of the City of Philadelphia; January 27, 1785; Bond, 200£; Bondsmen, Stephen Page, Joseph Kimble; Witness, James Trimble.

KENNARD, ELIZABETH, and MARTIN WHITE; August 18, 1785.

KENNEDY, ELIZABETH, and JOHN McGINNIS; July 28, 1785.

KENNEDY, JAMES, storekeeper, and MARY DUGUID, of Maryland; June 18, 1785; Bond, 200£; Bondsmen, James Kennedy, Joseph Slay; Witness, James Trimble.

KIMBLE, GEORGE, cordwainer, and JOHANNA DANNEKER, of the City of Philadelphia; June 5, 1786; Bond, 200£; Bondsmen, Michael Breish, George Kemble; Witness, James Trimble.

KINSLEY, MARY, and SAMUEL JOHNSTON; February 17, 1786.

KLINE, JOHN, and ELIZABETH KRUG, of the City of Philadelphia; March 26, 1785; Bond, 200£; Bondsmen, John Kline, George Reinhart; Witness, James Trimble.

KNOX, WILLIAM, and HANNAH NASH, of the City of Philadelphia; June 13, 1786; Bond, 200£; Bondsmen, Wm. Knox, Alex. Bensted; Witness, James Trimble.

KOHL, PHILIP, single person, and MARY HEISER, widow, both of Frederick Twp., Montgomery Co.; September 26, 1786; Bond, 200£; Bondsmen, Phillip Kohl, Math. Grist; Witnesses, Henry Muhlenberg, Samuel Bradford.

KRUG, ELIZABETH, and JOHN KLINE; March 26, 1785.

KURTZ, ELIZABETH, and JACOB BENINGHORE; February 8, 1786.

LAND, HENRY, druggist, and CATHERINE OTTO, of the City of Philadelphia; May 19, 1785; Bond, 200£; Bondsmen, Henry Land, John Reed; Witness, James Trimble.

LAND, JOHN, yeoman, and PHOEBE NOBLE, of Philadelphia County; March 7, 1786; Bond, 200£; Bondsmen, John Land, James Smith; Witness, James Trimble.

LAUKE, JOHN, cooper, and HANNAH YEAKER, of the City of Philadelphia; August 9, 1785; Bond, 200£; Bondsmen, Mark Yuenger, John Lauck; Witness, James Trimble.

LAWRENCE, WILLIAM, gentleman, and MARY DRAYS, widowers (?), of the City of Philadelphia; June 10, 1785; Bond 100£; Bondsmen, Wm. Lawrence, David Taggart; Witness, Michael Schlatter.

LEFEBURE, POTTER LOUIS, merchant, and MARY LOUISA FRECOURT, of the City of Philadelphia; December 31, 1784; Bond, 200£; Bondsmen, Joseph Donath, Pottin Lefebure; Witness, James Trimble.

LEIDIG, LEONHARD, and CATHARINE NEISS, of Frederich Twp., Phila. Co.; July 16, 1784; Bond, 300£; Bondsmen, Leonard Leidig, Franz Leidig; Witnesses, Nicholas Gilbert, Henry Muhlenberg.

LETELLIER, PETER, and SARAH WHITPAINE, of the City of Philadelphia; May 29, 1786; Bond, 200£; Bondsmen, John Wattson, Peter Letellier; Witness, James Trimble.

LEWIS, JOHN, scrivener, and ANNE CLINGMAN, of the City of Philadelphia; April 26, 1785; Bond, 200£; Bondsmen, John Lewis, William Hartung; Witness, James Trimble.

LEWIS, RUTH, and JOHNSTON VAUGHAN; June 16, 1785.

LIEB, SARAH, and JOHN REILY, December 30, 1784.

LIEBRICH, HANNAH, and CHARLES WILSTACH; June 8, 1785.

LIMEBURNER, CHRISTIANA, and MARTIN COST; May 31, 1786.

LOGAN, ALEXANDER, and ELIZABETH WATT; March 3, 1786; Bond, 200£; Bondsmen, David Correy, William Graham; Witness, James Trimble.

LONG, MARY, and MARMADUKE HANLON; February 2, 1785.

LORD, MARY, and REUBEN MUNYAN; July 12, 1785.

LOWRY, PETER, butcher, and JANE WILLIAMS, of the City of Philadelphia; June 20, 1786; Bond, 200£; Bondsmen, Peter Lowry, George Savell; Witness, James Trimble.

LOWMAN, ELIZABETH, and CHRISTOPHER SCHREINER, June 14, 1785.

LUNN, JOSEPH, yeoman, and ANNE GRIFFITH, of the County of Bucks; September 20, 1785; Bond, 200£; Bondsmen, Joseph Lunn, Benjamin Griffith; Witness, James Trimble.

LYNCH, MICHAEL, of Providence Twp., Montg. Co., and REBECCA PAWLING, daughter of Jno. Pawling, of Sckippack & Perkiomen Township & County aforesaid; April 13, 1786; Bond, 200£; Bondsmen, Michael Lynch, Francis Swaine; Witnesses, H. Muhlenberg, Christian Breymann.

LYNK, REBECCA, and FRANCIS TAYLOR; September 15, 1785.

McCARTNEY, MARY ANNE, and JOSHUA FARRELL; May 5, 1785.

McCAUL, JAMES, mariner, and MARGARET McCLOSKEY, of the Citty of Philadelphia; November 15, 1785; Bond, 200£; Bondsmen, George Watt, Jas. McCaul; Witness, James Trimble.

McCAULEY, JANE, and MICHAEL WELSH; June 5, 1786.

McCLOSKEY, MARGARET, and JAMES McCAUL; November 15, 1785.

McCULLOUGH, MARY, and WILLIAM FALCONER; June 15, 1785.

McDANIEL, MARGARET, and WILIAM HEISER; June 2, 1785.

McDONALD, ALEXANDER, and ELIZABETH SMITH, of the City of Philadelphia; June 5, 1786; Bond, 200£; Bondsmen, Alex'r McDonald, John Service; Witness, James Trimble.

McDONALD, WILLIAM, house carpenter, and MARY MARTIN, of the City of Philadelphia; December 30, 1784; Bond, 200£; Bondsmen, John King, William McDonnald; Witness, James Trimble.

McDOUGALL, STEWART, and MALCOLM McNERAN; November 17, 1785.

McGINNIS, JOHN, labourer, and ELIZABETH KENNEDY, of the City of Philadelphia; July 28, 1785; Bond, 200£; Bondsmen, Joseph Thornhill, John McGinnis; Witness, James Trimble.

McGOWAN, MARY, and HUGH SWEENY; June 6, 1785.

MACKEYSEY, JACKSON, merchant, and MARY FOGERTY, of the City of Philadelphia; June 10, 1785; Bond, 200£; Bondsmen, Thos. Hurly, Jackson McKenzie; Witness, James Trimble.

McMINN, SAMUEL, yeoman, and CHRISTINA FIELD, of the County of Chester; March 29, 1785; Bond, 200£; Bondsmen, Aaron Johnson, Samuel McMinn; Witness, James Trimble.

McNAIR, SARAH, and MICHAEL HAYES; June 14, 1786.

McNERAN, MALCOLM, cooper, and STEWART McDOUGALL, of the City of Philadelphia; November 17, 1785; Bond, 200£; Bondsmen, Alexr. Steel, Malcom McNeran; Witness, James Trimble.

MARRIAGE LICENSES—1784-86. 301

MADERA, ANNE, and WILLIAM FETTERS; October 17, 1786.

MAHONY, MICHAEL, and FRANCES COLLINS, of the City of Philadelphia; June 20, 1786; Bond, 200£; Bondsmen, Jeremiah Sullivan, Michael Mahony; Witness, James Trimble.

MANNY, MARY, and JOHN MARKLAND; September 12, 1785.

MARKLAND, JOHN, and MARY MANNY, of the City of Philadelphia; September 12, 1785; Bond 200£; Bondsmen, Richd. Fullerton, Jno. Markland; Witness, James Trimble.

MARKOE, ANNE, and NICHOLAS CRUGER; November 18, 1785.

MARPLE, DOROTHY, and ISAAC VANHORNE; March 26, 1785.

MARSHALL, MARGARET, and JAMES ENGLE; May 4, 1785.

MARTIN, MARY, and WILLIAM McDONALD; December 30, 1784.

MARTIN, SUSANNA, and LAWRENCE HAYES; September 12, 1785.

MASTERS, MARY, and JOSEPH CLARK, June 22, 1785.

MATLACK, MARTHA, and GUY BRYAN, June 20, 1785.

MATTHEW, MARY and THOMAS MILLARD; November 17. 1785.

MATTHEWS, ANNE and JOHN VICAR; September 16, 1785.

MEANS, ELIZABETH and JONATHAN PAUL; August 30, 1786.

MILEHAM, JOSEPH, Anchor Smith, and CATHERINE DUBLIN, of the County of Philadelphia; July 18, 1785; Bond, 200£; Bondsmen, Joseph Mileham, John Sulliver; Witness, James Trimble.

MILES, HENRY and SARAH COGGLE, of the City of Philadelphia; June 8, 1785; Bond, 200£; Bondsmen, Alexander Gowns, Henry Miles; Witness, James Trimble.

MILEY, FREDERICK. and BARBARA KEILER, of the City of Philadelphia; September 22, 1785; Bond, 200£; Bondsmen, Jacob Myers, Frederick Miley; Witness, James Trimble.

MILLARD, THOMAS, and MARY MATTHEW, of the County of Philadelphia; November 17, 1785; Bond, 200£; Bondsmen, John Thomas, Thomas Millard; Witness, James Trimble.

MILLER, CHRISTINA, and JOHN YELLES; December 23, 1784.

MILER, HUGH, and REBECCA POUGE, of Cumbd. County; October 11, 1786; Bond, 200£; Bondsmen, Hugh Miller, Joseph Hart; Witness, James Trimble.

MILLER, WILLIAM, and MARGARET CRAIG, of York County; March 7, 1786; Bond, 200£; Bondsmen, William Miller, William Bailey; Witness, Jas. Trimble.

MILNOR, MARTHA, and TOBIAS RUDOLPH; February 13, 1786.

MILNOR, RACHEL, and ABRAHAM ROBERTS; December 22, 1785.

MISTAR, ELIZABETH, and DENNIS MORIARTY; January 4, 1784.

MONROW, MARGARETH, and ABRA BROWN; July 2, 1786.

MOORE, PATRICK, merchant, and HANNAH HUSTON, of the City of Philadelphia; August 18, 1785; Bond, 200£ Bondsmen, Patk. Moore, John Taylor; Witness, James Trimble.

MORIARTY, DENNIS, Bricklayer, and ELIZABETH MISTAR, of Philadelphia; January 4, 1784; Bond, 200£; Bondsmen, Christian Kirkhoff, Dennis Moriarty; Witness, James Trimble.

MORRIS, ABEL, and MARY DUNGAN, of Bucks Co.; October 9, 1786; Bond, 200£; Bondsmen, Isaac Williams, Abel Mearis; Witness, James Trimble.

MORRIS, AUGUSTUS, and ANNE HENRY, of the City of Philadelphia; April 28, 1785; Bond, 200£; Bondsmen, Augustus Maurice, John Stauch; Witness, James Trimble.

MORRIS, LUKE, merchant, and ANN WILLING, of the City of Philadelphia; March 7, 1786; Bond, 200£; Bondsmen, Luke Morris, Junr., Jas. Willing; Witness, James Trimble.

MORTON, BENJAMIN, of Wilmington, Del., and ANN HANCE, of East Bradford, Chester Co.; January 31, 1786; Bond, 100£; Bondsmen, Benjamin Morton, James Hance; Witness, Abel Griffith.

MULFORD, MARTHA, and NATHAN SHEPPARD; October 4, 1786.

MUNYAN, REUBEN, taylor, and MARY LORD, of the City of Philadelphia; July 12, 1785; Bond, 200£; Bondsmen, Jonathan Edwards, Reuben Munyan; Witness James Trimble.

NANSANT, SARAH, and CHRISTIAN HEISS; December 16, 1785.

NASH, HANNAH, and WILLIAM KNOX; June 13, 1786.

NEISS, CATHARINE, and LEONHARD LEIDIG; July 16, 1784.

MARRIAGE LICENSES—1784-86. 303

NOBLE, PHOEBE, and JOHN LAND, March 7, 1786.

OSBORNE, RHODA, and SAMUEL ATKINSON; December 30, 1784.

OTTO, CATHARINE, and HENRY LAND; May 19, 1785.

OZEAS, GEORGE, grocer, and MARY ECKHART, of the City of Philadelphia; February 13, 1786; Bond, 200£; Bondsmen, George Ozeas, Peter Ozeas; Witness, James Trimble.

PAGE, STEPHEN, gentleman, and ELIZABETH SPONG, of the City of Philadelphia; August 1, 1785; Bond, 200£; Bondsmen, Stephen Page, John Smith; Witness, James Trimble.

PAINTER, DANIEL, and MARTHA CUSTER, both free and single persons, of Skippack Twp., Montgomery Co.; September 21, 1786; Bond, 200£; Bondsmen, Daniel Painter, Nicholas Custer; Witnesses, Jacob Pannapacker, Henry Muhlenberg.

PARHAM, MARY, and MATTHEW BENNET; March 9, 1786.

PARRY, JOHN, cordwainer, and ANNE WEAVER, of Lancaster County; June 2, 1786; Bond, 200£; Bondsmen, Adam Siter, John Parry; Witness, James Trimble.

PAUL, JONATHAN, yeoman, and ELIZABETH MEANS, of Whitemarsh, Montgomery Co.; August 30, 1786; Bond, 100£; Bondsmen, Jonathan Paul, Joseph Fairby; Witness, Michael Schlatter.

PAUL, JOSIAH, and MARY CASSEL, of the City of Philadelphia; May 30, 1785; Bond, 200£; Bondsmen, Sam Hodgson, Josiah Paul; Witness, James Trimble.

PAULING, REBECCA, and MICHAEL LYNCH; April 13, 1786.

PIDGEON, ELIZABETH, and JOHN HINTON, February 14, 1786.

POALK, JAMES, and ELEANOR HENDERSON, of Bucks County; March 15, 1786; Bond, 200£; Bondsmen, Wm. Shannon, Jas. Poalk; Witness, James Trimble.

POLLARD, PETER, mariner, and HANNA STITES, of the City of Philadelphia; August 24, 1785; Bond, 200£; Bondsmen, Peter Pollard, Nathan Church; Witness, James Trimble.

POTTER, MARGARET, and LEONARD SAYRE; April 1, 1785.

POUGE, REBECCA, and HUGH MILLER; October 11, 1786.

POULTNEY, WILLIAM, hatter, and CATHERINE RICHEY, of the City of Philadelphia; December 16, 1785;

Bond, 200£; Bondsmen, James Smith, William Poultney; Witness, James Trimble.

POWEL, ANN, and BARTLE BARTLESON; August 15, 1785.

PRICHARD, MARY, and JOHN CREAN, June 23, 1785.

PURSELL, HENRY D., engraver, and ANNE DAVIS, of the City of Philadelphia; June 21, 1785; Bond, 200£; Bondsmen, Hen'y D. Pursell, Wm. Watkins; Witness, James Trimble.

READ, WILLIAM, and SUSANNA CLAY, of the County of Chester; December 15, 1785; Bond, 200£; Bondsmen, Willm. Read, Joshua Lawrence; Witness James Trimble.

REEDLE, ROSANNA, and DAVID JONES; May 31, 1786.

REILY, JOHN, watchmaker, and SARAH LIEB, of the City of Philadelphia; December 30, 1784; Bond, 200£; Bondsmen, John Riley, John Carrell; Witness, James Trimble.

REINHARD, PETER, wheelwright, and SARAH TAYLOR, of the City of Philadelphia, Pa.; May 27, 1785; Bond, 200£; Bondsmen, Peter Raenhart, John Lowdon; Witness, John Davis.

REYNOLDS, HANNAH, and JOSEPH KEMBLE, January 27, 1785.

REYNOLDS, JOHN, and MARGARET GREAVES, of the City of Philadelphia; February 28, 1795; Bond, 200£; Bondsmen, John Reynolds, Thomas Proctor; Witness, James Trimble.

RIBAUD, ROSE, and VINCENT DUCOMB, November 12, 1785.

RICHEY, CATHERINE, and WILLIAM POULTNEY; December 16, 1785.

RICHEY, DAVID, and NANCY FRENCH, of the County of Philadelphia; May 20, 1785; Bond, 200£; Bondsmen, David Ritchee, Andrew French; Witness, James Trimble.

ROBERTS, ABRAHAM, merchant, and RACHEL MILNOR, of the City of Philadelphia; December 22, 1785; Bond, 200£; Bondsmen, Abraham Roberts, William Milnor; Witness, James Trimble.

ROBERTS, HANNAH, and WILLIAM BARTON; October 14, 1786.

ROBERTS, MARY, and WILLIAM BRIGHT; January 19, 1786.

ROEHR, MARTIN, cordwainer, and CATHERINE SWEERY, of the City of Philadelphia; February 9, 1786; Bond, 200£; Bondsmen, Charles Rupert, Martin Roehr; Witness, James Trimble.

MARRIAGE LICENSES—1784-86. 305

ROSS, THOMAS, yeoman, and JANE VANHORNE, of Bucks Co.; July 7, 1785; Bond, 200£; Bondsmen, Thomas Ross, Matthew Bennet; Witness, James Trimble.

ROUW, CONRAD, biscuit baker, and MARY CHAMBERLAINE, of the City of Philadelphia; July 12, 1785; Bond, 200£; Bondsmen, Gabriel Kern, Conrad Rouw; Witness, James Trimble.

RUDOLPH, TOBIAS, and MARTHA MILNOR, of the State of Maryland; February 13, 1786; Bond, 200£; Bondsmen, Tobias Rudulph, Jr., Sam Nicholas; Witness James Trimble.

RUSH, KITTY, and JOHN COCHRAN; August 8, 1785.

RYAN, TIMOTHY, and ANNE GREEN, of the City of Philadelphia; July 11, 1785; Bond, 200£; Bondsmen, Michael Dowling, Timothy Ryan; Witness James Trimble.

SAYRE, LEONARD, tailor, and MARGARET POTTER, of the City of Philadelphia; April 1, 1786; Bond, 200£; Bondsmen, Leonard Sayre, Uriah Mills; Witness, James Trimble.

SCANLON, JOHN, porter, and ELIZABETH JOHNSTON, of the City of Philadelphia; February 5, 1785; Bond, 200£; Bondsmen, John Scanlon, Lewis Connor; Witness, James Trimble.

SCHREINER, CHRISTOPHER, schoolmaster, and ELIZABETH LOWMAN, of Philadelphia; June 14, 1785; Bond, 200£; Bondsmen, John Alburger, Christopher Schreiner, Senr.; Witness, James Trimble.

SCHREINER, KITTY, and GEORGE GRISCOM; July 28, 1785.

SHAKESPEAR, DAVID, merchant, and ELIZABETH DAVIS, of the City of Philadelphia; January 20, 1785; Bond, 200£; Bondsmen, Thomas Cumpston, David Shakespear; Witness, James Trimble.

SHALCROSS, WILLIAM, yoeman, and ELIZABETH WALTON, of Philadelphia; March 9, 1786; Bond, 200£; Bondsmen, James Dungan, William Shallcross; Witness, James Trimble.

SHEAF, MARY, and WILLIAM FLECK; February 11, 1786.

SHEED, GEORGE, plaisterer, and REBECCA JONES, of the City of Philadelphia; September 3, 1785; Bond, 200£; Bondsmen, George Sheed, Jno. Douglasse; Witness, James Trimble.

SHELLER, HANNAH, and JOHN CLINE; July 21, 1785.

SHEPPARD, NATHAN, and MARTHA MULFORD; October 4, 1786; Bond, 200£; Bondsmen, Wm. Rogers, Nathan Sheppard; Witness, James Trimble.

20—Vol. VI—6th Ser.

SHERCOTT, JOHN, music-master, and PRISCILLA SWAINE, of Philadelphia County; January 4, 1784; Bond, 200£; Bondsmen, Samuel Wallees, Johannes Kuntzer; Witness, James Trimble.

SHIEVELL, CHRISTIAN, and BALTUS KEEL, February 18, 1786.

SHUBERT, JACOB, blacksmith, and SARAH ASHTON, of the City of Philadelphia; November 17, 1785; Bond, 200£; Bondsmen, Adam Keller, Jacob Shubert; Witness, James Trimble.

SHUTE, SARAH, and JAMES HUNTER; August 9, 1785.

SINNERS, MARY, and JAMES BARRON, June 14, 1786.

SMITH, ELIZABETH, and ALEXANDER, McDONALD; June 5, 1786.

SMITH, ELIZABETH, and LAWRENCE JUSTICE; January 3, 1785.

SMITH, ELIZABETH, and WILLIAM WHITE; February 10, 1786.

SNITZER, REGINA, and JACOB TRESSLEY; September 20, 1785.

SNODGRASS, JAMES, and MARTHA DAVIS, of Bucks County; October 5, 1786; Bond, 200£; Bondsmen, Wm. Oliphant, James Snodgrass.

SOUDER, JOHN, baker, and MARGARET SWEM, of the City of Philadelphia; July 22, 1785; Bond, 200£; Bondsmen, John Sowthern, Georg Herr; Witness, James Trimble.

SPITTER, CHRISTOPHER, labourer, and ELIZABETH FOX, of the City of Philadelphia; September 7, 1785; Bond, 200£; Bondsmen, Paul Schuck, Chrytoph Spitter; Witness, James Trimble.

SPONG, ELIZABETH, and STEPHEN PAGE; August 1, 1785.

SPROSON, JOHN, chair-maker, and ANNE BROCK, of the City of Philadelphia; December 17, 1785; Bond, 200£; Bondsmen, John Sproson, Bernhard Bruchhold; Witness, James Trimble.

STAYGOE, HANNAH, and JOHN DAVIS WOELPPER; December 24, 1785.

STITES, HANNAH, and PETER POLLARD; August 24, 1785.

STOWMETZ, JOHN, cooper, and GRACE WATT, of the City of Philadelphia; January 4, 1785; Bond, 200£; Bondsmen, Matthias Gravel, John Stowmetz; Witness, James Trimble.

STREEPER, DOROTHY, and DANIEL ARN; November 16, 1786.

STUCKERT, JOHN, jr., and SUSANNA BICKLEY, of the City of Philadelphia; June 1, 1786; Bond, 200£; Bondsmen, Thos. Wildbahn, John Stuckert, Junr.; Witness, James Trimble.
SUTTON, EDITH, and JOHN ARMSTRONG; May 19, 1785.
SWAINE, PRISCILLA, and JOHN SHERCOTT, January 4, 1784.
SWEM, MARGARET, and JOHN SOUDER; July 22, 1785.
SWEENY, HUGH, and MARY McGOWAN, of the City of Philadelphia; June 6, 1785; Bond, 200£; Bondsmen, Hu. Sweeney, John Johnson; Witness, James Trimble.
SWEERY, CATHERINE, and MARTIN ROEHR; February 9, 1786.
SWOOPE, MARY, and JOHN BOWEN; January 25, 1786.

TAYLOR, FRANCIS, scrievener, and REBECCA LYNK, of the City of Philadelphia; September 15, 1785; Bond, 200£; Bondsmen, James Frazer, Francis Taylor; Witness James Trimble.
TAYLOR, SARAH, and PETER REINHARD; May 27, 1785.
THOMAS ELIZABETH, and MARTIN ASHBOURNE, July 4, 1785.
THOMAS, ESTHER, and SAMUEL THOMAS, November 16, 1785.
THOMAS, PATRICK, and ELIZABETH DUEY, of the City of Philadelphia; June 15, 1786; Bond, 200£; Bondsmen, Edward Keran, Frederick Thomas; Witness, James Trimble.
THOMAS, SAMUEL, yeoman, and ESTHER THOMAS, of the County of Chester; November 16, 1785; Bond, 200£; Bondsmen, John Teaney, Samuel Thomas; Witness, James Trimble.
THOMPSON, ALEXANDER, yeoman, and SUSANNA FIPS, of Cheltenham Twp., Montgomery Co., Pa.; May 25, 1785; Bond, 200£; Bondsmen, Alexander Thompson, Dennis Dermatt; Witness, John Lewis.
THOMPSON, JOHN, blacksmith, and MARY CARTER, of Philadelphia; June 1, 1785; Bond, 200£; Bondsmen, John Thompson, Conrad Hanse; Witness James Trimble.
THOMPSON, MARTHA, and JOHN JOHNSTON; July 14, 1785.
TOMKINS, JOSEPH, yeoman, and ANNE EDGE, of the City of Philadelphia; February 3, 1786; Bond, 200£; Bondsmen, Joseph Tomkins, George Bewley; Witness, James Trimble.

TOOMY, ANNE, and EDWARD DENNIS; January 5, 1786.
TRAUTWINE, WILLIAM, jr., and MARY JEWSON, of the Northern Liberties; July 14, 1785; Bond, 200£; Bondsmen, Wm. Trautwine, Wm. Trautwine, Junior; Witness, James Trimble.
TRESSLEY, JACOB, and REGINA SNITZER, of the City of Philadelphia; September 20, 1785; Bond, 200£; Bondsmen, David Ott, Jacob Tresley; Witness, James Trimble.
TURIN, BERNHART, storekeeper, and CATHERINE CLARKSON, of the City of Philadelphia; June 10, 1785; Bond. 200£; Bondsmen, Bernhart Turin, John Albert; Witness, James Trimble.

VANDEGRIFT, BERNARD, tanner, and MARY CAMPBELL, of the County of Bucks; April 2, 1785; Bond, 200£; Bondsmen, Bernard Vandegrift, Christian Hess; Witness James Trimble.
VANHORNE, ISAAC, and DOROTHY MARPLE, of the County of Bucks; March 26, 1785; Bonds, 200£; Bondsmen, Isaac Vanhorne, G. Evans; Witness James Trimble.
VANHORNE, JANE, and THOMAS ROSS, July 7, 1785.
VANNOSTEN, MARY, and THOMAS INGELS, January 24, 1785.
VAUGHN, JOHNSTON, weaver, and RUTH LEWIS, of the County of Chester; June 16, 1785; Bond, 200£; Bondsmen, Johnson Vaughan, Wm. Lewis; Witness, James Trimble.
VICAR, JOHN, and ANN MATTHEWS, of the City of Philadelphia; September 16, 1785; Bond, 200£; Bondsmen, Vicard, Johan Bowrschetz; Witness, James Trimble.
VICKERS, TAMAR, and JOHN CROSSLEY; June 14, 1785.

WALKER, MARY, and JOHN M. JONES; December 22, 1785.
WALTON, ELIZABETH, and WILLIAM SHALLCROSS; March 9, 1786.
WATSON, REBECCA, and WILLIAM HAIR; October, 1786.
WATT, ELIZABETH, and ALEXANDER LOGAN; March 3, 1786.
WATT, GEORGE, mariner, and ELIZABETH EAGER, of the City of Philadelphia; November 11, 1785; Bond, 200£; Bondsmen, Alexander Phillips, George Watt; Witness, James Trimble.
WATT, GRACE, and JOHN STOWMETZ; January 4, 1785.
WAYNE, SAMUEL, house carpenter, and ELIZABETH CURTAIN, of the City of Philadelphia; December 28, 1784;

MARRIAGE LICENSES—1784-86. 309

Bond, 200£; Bondsmen, Samuel Wayne, Richard Guy; Witness, James Trimble.

WEAVER, ANNE, and JOHN PARRY; June 2, 1786.

WELLS, WILLIAM, yeoman, and HANNAH BUSBY, of Philadelphia County; June 15, 1785; Bond, 200£; Bondsmen, William Wells, Harry Rice; Witness James Trimble.

WELSH, MICHAEL, and JANE McCAULEY, of the City of Philadelphia; June 5, 1786; Bond, 200£; Bondsmen, Michal Welsh, John Lane; Witness, James Trimble.

WESSEL, REBECCA, and PETER KEEN; April 22, 1785.

WEST, MARY, and CURTIS GREBLE; April 6, 1785.

WEYLAND, CONRAD, brickmaker, and MARY YOUNG, of the County of Philadelphia; June 30, 1785; Bond, 200£; Bondsmen, Conrad Wilen, Wolfgang Hoffman; Witness, James Trimble.

WHITE, MARTIN, and ELIZABETH KENNARD, of the City of Philadelphia; August 18, 1785; Bond, 200£; Bondsmen, Martin White, Thomas Simmons; Witness, James Trimble.

WHITE, WILLIAM, butcher, and ELIZABETH SMITH, of the City of Philadelphia; February 10, 1786; Bond, 200£; Bondsmen, Wm. White, Wm. Heard; Witness, James Trimble.

WHITPAINE, SARAH, and PETER LETELLIER, May 29, 1786.

WHITTE, MARY, and ARCHIBALD FERGUSON, June 3, 1786.

WIGLEY, ANNE, and CHARLES COUCH; July 28, 1785.

WILLIAMS, CATHERINE ANNE, and PABLO COMMYNS; February 6, 1786.

WILLIAMS, JANE, and PETER LOWEY; June 20, 1786.

WILLING, ANN, and LUKE MORRIS; March 7, 1786.

WILSTACH, CHARLES, inn-keeper, and HANNAH LIEBRICH, of the City of Philadelphia; June 8, 1785; Bond, 200£; Bondsmen, Charles Wilstach, Daniel Braeutigan; Witness, James Trimble.

WOELPPER, JOHN DAVID, late Captain in the Penna. Line, and HANNAH STAYGOE; December 24, 1785; Bond, 200£; Bondsmen, D. Woelpper, Henry Sherer; Witness, James Trimble.

WOOD, WILLIAM, mariner, and ELIZABETH YOUNG, of the City of Philadelphia; September 13, 1785; Bond, 200£; Bondsmen, William Wood, Mark Junger; Witness, James Trimble.

WYRICK, NICHOLAS, and SUSANNA DIETRICK, of the City of Philadelphia; June 12, 1786; Bond, 200£; Bondsmen, Andrew Boshart, Nicholas Wyrick; Witness James Trimble.

YEAKER, HANNAH, and JOHN LAUKE, August 9, 1785.
YELLES, JOHN, and CHRISTINA MILLER, of Toyamensin Twp., Montgomery Co.; December 23, 1784; Bond, 400£; Bondsmen, John Yelles, Paul Kugler; Witnesses, John Holman, Henry Muhlenberg, Abraham Seipfer.
YOUNG, ELIZABETH, and WILLIAM WOOD, September 13, 1785.
YOUNG, MARY, and CONRAD WEYLAND; June 30, 1785.

ZANE, JONATHAN, tanner and currier, and REBECCA FISHER, of the City of Philadelphia; March 6, 1786; Bond, 200£; Bondsmen, Samuel Bonsoll, Jonathan Zane; Witness, James Trimble.

www.ingramcontent.com/pod-product-compliance
Lightning Source LLC
Chambersburg PA
CBHW060820190426
43197CB00038B/2168